Don't Feed
the
Narcissists!

*The Mythology and Science
of Mental Health*

ALSO BY
LAURIE ENDICOTT THOMAS

Not Trivial:
How Studying the Traditional Liberal Arts Can Set You Free
(www.nottrivialbook.com)

Thin Diabetes Fat Diabetes:
Prevent Type 1, Cure Type 2
(www.thindiabetes.com)

No More Measles!
The Truth About Vaccines and Your Health
(www.nomeasles.com)

Don't Feed *the* Narcissists!

The Mythology and Science of Mental Health

LAURIE ENDICOTT THOMAS

KERMIT PRESS
Veritas Vos Liberabit

Kermit Press
PO Box 425
Chatham, NJ 07928

Cover and interior design, David Moratto

The cover image is from John William Waterhouse's 1903 oil painting,
Echo and Narcissus. The painting illustrates a scene from
the Ovid's Metamorphoses.

ISBN: 978-0-9968818-3-8

You're so vain.
You probably think this song is about you.

—CARLY SIMON

Contents

~

Chapter 1

The Greatest Love of All?

For centuries, storytellers, theologians, and philosophers have warned us of the dangers of pride. Ancient Greek dramatists wrote comedies that poked fun at the vanity of powerful men. They wrote tragedies that warned of the dangers of a form of contemptuous behavior called *hubris*. In the Middle Ages, Roman Catholic theologians considered *superbia* (pride) to be one of the seven deadly sins. They thought that *humilitas* (humility) is one of the seven heavenly virtues. Hindu, Buddhist, and Muslim theologians and philosophers teach surprisingly similar lessons. But in the 1960s, some prominent psychologists and educators in the United States started arguing that low self-esteem, or lack of pride, lay at the root of most of our social problems.

Some of the members of the self-esteem movement claimed that if we simply boosted children's self-esteem, we could solve many of our pressing social problems, such as poor school performance, teen pregnancy, and crime. In 1985, Whitney Houston topped the charts with a song that summed up this idea: "Learning to love yourself is the greatest love of all." However, since the rise of social media and the selfie stick, many people are starting to wonder whether too many people admire themselves too much. This problem of excessive self-love is called narcissism.

The word *narcissism* comes from the ancient Greek myth of Echo and Narcissus. Narcissus was a young man who was so handsome that many people fell in love with him. However, Narcissus cared nothing for them. One of his admirers was a nymph named Echo. She was so hurt by his callous rejection that she wasted away until there was nothing left but her voice. She could not even speak for herself. All she could do was repeat what someone else had just said.

Nemesis, who was the spirit of divine vengeance, was angered by how badly Narcissus treated others. As a punishment, Nemesis lured Narcissus to a pool. There, Narcissus developed a fatal attraction to his own reflection. According to some versions of the story, Narcissus drowned while trying to embrace his reflection. According to other versions, he starved to death because he could not stop gazing at his reflection. After he died, he became the flower that bears his name. Thus, people started to use the term *narcissist* to describe people who love themselves too much and other people too little.

Most fables teach a simple lesson about good sense or good morals. The fable of Narcissus and Echo teaches us two lessons. First, don't be Echo. If you dedicate yourself to someone who does not love you back, you end up losing yourself. Second, don't be Narcissus. If you care only for yourself, you deserve to come to a bad end.

In the 19th century, French people started using the word *mégalomanie* to refer to overly high self-esteem. The word was applied to people who thought that they were greater, more powerful, and more important than they really were. The word was derived from the Greek roots *megalo-*, which meant large or great, and *-mania*, which meant madness. *Mégalomanie* entered the English language as *megalomania*. However, psychiatrists in the United States now use the term *narcissistic personality disorder* to describe this mental problem.

As I will explain in more detail in later chapters, narcissism is a character flaw. If a case of narcissism is persistent and is serious enough to cause suffering or disability, it can be considered a mental illness. If your case of narcissism is worse than your psychiatrist would expect from someone of your social background, you would get a diagnosis of a mental disorder called narcissistic personality disorder.

Mental health professionals may be startled to hear me describe narcissism as a character flaw. In general, mental health professionals are encouraged to view mental problems as illnesses, as opposed to moral failings. To their ears, the term *character flaw* sounds like a moral judgment, as opposed to a medical diagnosis. It sounds pejorative. The English word *pejorative* implies criticism, hostility, disregard, or disrespect. In contrast, mental health professionals are supposed to be welcoming, compassionate, and respectful. However, the English word *pejorative* comes from a Latin adjective *pejoratus*, which in turn comes from the Latin verb *pejorare*, which means to make things worse. The important question is whether the label makes people seem worse than they really are. Of course, a label can be accurate but not tactful. The word *tact* came from the Latin word for touch. In English, *tact* means the ability to do or say things without offending or upsetting other people. Unfortunately, some truths are bound to be offensive or upsetting, regardless of how they are phrased.

I am not sure that the term *personality disorder* is any more tactful than *character flaw*. Each of us has character flaws. Even famous diamonds like the Koh-I-Noor (one of the British Crown Jewels) have flaws. But to qualify for a diagnosis of a personality disorder, your character flaws must be serious enough to cause suffering (for yourself or for other people) or disability. In other words, your behavior could be causing other people to suffer. Some people with personality disorders actually enjoy making other people suffer. Others are simply indifferent to other people's suffering: they do not care one way or the other.

I suspect that much of the caseload for mental health professionals consists of decent people who have been emotionally wounded, often by people with personality disorders. Meanwhile, the people with the personality disorders either would shun therapy or would seek out the kinds of therapy that would make them worse, not better. Thus, I would expect a narcissist to seek out therapy designed to boost his or her self-esteem, while shunning constructive criticism. In contrast, someone who seeks out or at least accepts constructive criticism from wise people would outgrow their narcissism.

With the rise of social media and the invention of the selfie stick, there has been increasing concern that we might be in the midst of an epidemic of narcissism. Even so, many people might be surprised to hear that abnormally high self-esteem could be a mental illness. For decades, we have been told to worry about low self-esteem.

In the mid-20th century, psychologists started to pay a lot of attention to self-esteem. In particular, they developed simple paper-and-pencil tests to measure it. However, self-esteem involves a complicated mixture of ideas and feelings. How can you collapse all of that information into a test score? What does the score of a self-esteem test really mean? How would those test scores relate to the things we really care about, such as whether a person is honest, kind, generous, productive, and happy?

Self-esteem is an idea that can include many different ideas and feelings. Some of these ideas and feelings might be helpful in some situations but harmful in others. This principle was dramatized in the television series *The Sopranos*. The attitudes and behaviors that helped Tony Soprano claw his way to the top of a criminal organization caused problems for him in his family life.

Starting in the 1960s, psychologists and educators in the United States started to pay a lot of attention to the concept of self-esteem. This concern arose in the context of social reform movements, especially the Civil Rights Movement and the Women's Liberation Movement and the Gay Rights Movement. These movements promoted social equality for black people, women of any color, and gay people, respectively. Activists in these movements wanted black people, women, and gays to view themselves as worthy of the same civil rights as straight white men. These social reformers also wanted whites to accept blacks as equals and men to accept women as equals. For these changes to come about, the humble and meek would have to be exalted, while the mighty are put down from their seat. Yet because of the current emphasis on self-esteem, people are being encouraged to exalt themselves, even when they need to learn humility.

In the 1980s, a California state assemblyman named John Vasconcellos argued that low self-esteem was an important underlying cause of social problems such as poor school performance, teenage pregnancy, and crime. He believed that boosting children's self-esteem could make the children immune to such problems, just as a vaccine would make them immune to an infectious disease. But like the early 20th-century advocates of Prohibition, some of the members of the self-esteem movement were offering an overly simplistic solution to a large and complex set of problems. Predictably, the results of the programs they promoted were often disappointing.

Even within the self-esteem movement, there has been little agreement on what self-esteem is or how it should be promoted. Nathaniel Branden, who has been called the father of the self-esteem movement, advocated a tough regimen of training to boost skills. Branden's goal was to enable and encourage his students to take responsibility for themselves and their lives. In contrast, many public schoolteachers are being told to shield children from even constructive criticism. Instead, children are often being encouraged to brag about themselves. However, some critics fear that the techniques used in these programs might actually promote narcissism, anxiety, and even depression. Thus, there is clearly a need to think carefully about the concept of self-esteem, as well as to cast a critical eye on any program designed to promote self-esteem. Some of these programs may offer something useful, at least for some individuals. However, each program must be evaluated on its own merits.

By the 1990s, it was clear that low self-esteem, as measured by standard psychological tests, did not always go hand-in-hand with social problems. Even when the low self-esteem seemed to occur alongside some other problem, you could not always tell whether the low self-esteem was the *cause* of the other problem. Sometimes, low self-esteem could be an effect, as opposed to a cause. Sometimes, low self-esteem and some other problem, such as teenage pregnancy, could both be the results of some other cause, such as the humiliating experience of being sexually abused. Some results can have a feedback effect, which means that the result goes on to become a cause. As George Orwell noted in his essay Politics and the English Language, "A man may take to drink because he feels himself to be a failure, and then fail all the more completely because he drinks." Thus, it can be hard to figure out the role that self-esteem plays in other psychological or social problems.

Nevertheless, many psychologists are still quick to use low self-esteem as a catchall explanation. Many psychologists even insist that narcissists are suffering from low self-esteem. How could that be? The word *narcissism* means that a person has abnormally high self-esteem, just as the word *fever* means that a person has an abnormally high body temperature. You cannot have a fever (abnormally high body temperature) and hypothermia (abnormally low body temperature) at the same time. However, many psychologists think that the narcissist's apparently high self-esteem is just a façade. They believe that the narcissist's apparent insecurity springs from low self-esteem that is carefully hidden. Narcissists often seem to be addicted to even meaningless praise, which psychologists call narcissistic supply. Narcissists may also seem to take offense (narcissistic injury) in response to any kind of criticism or even to imagined slights. Psychoanalyst Heinz Kohut called the resulting anger narcissistic rage.

Why might a person with overly high self-esteem come across as insecure and touchy? One simple explanation springs from a concept that is taboo for many people in the United States: the concept of social rank. Like many other social animals, from chickens to chimpanzees, human beings tend to organize themselves into dominance hierarchies. People who wish to rise within their social hierarchy are called ambitious. When people try to occupy a higher position than they can defend, their critics call them narcissistic.

Narcissists have an odd mixture of personal security and social insecurity. They are secure in their belief that they deserve a high social rank. Yet they find it hard to get other people to grant them the social position that they want to occupy. In other words, narcissists seldom get all of the admiration and special privileges that they feel that they deserve. As a result, narcissists continually feel that they are being unfairly disrespected and shortchanged.

Narcissists want other people to submit to them. The narcissistic supply that narcissists crave actually consists of signs of submission. If you express anything less than perfect submission, as judged by the narcissist, the narcissist may feel narcissistic injury, which is actually the narcissist's perception that you are posing a challenge to his or her social rank. The narcissist may then go on the offensive, to try to bully you into submission. These aggressive outbursts are called narcissistic rage.

The narcissist's rages can set off a vicious circle. The narcissist feels that other people do not respect him or her. In response, the narcissist throws tantrums, to try to bully the other people into submission. Yet such behavior does not inspire the admiration that the narcissist craves. Instead, it damages the narcissist's reputation. As a result, other people lose respect for the narcissist. Their disrespect causes more narcissistic injury and triggers further narcissistic rages. Only the narcissist can break this vicious circle. The hard way would be for the narcissist to find some way to earn other people's admiration. The easy way would be to accept a realistic, lower social rank.

Narcissists cannot achieve the social rank that they think they deserve, and they are unwilling to accept anything less. Of course, the question of what someone deserves implies a personal, social judgment. Thus, narcissism, like beauty, is in the eye of the beholder. How you make that judgment may say more about your own biases than it says about the person you are judging. A bigot would assign some people to a low rank simply because of their sex or ethnic background. Anyone who tries to rise above that assigned station may be punished for being "uppity." Thus, the conclusion that another person is narcissistic is a subjective, social judgment with political implications. To understand narcissism, you must confront the question of how people are ranked within society.

By calling someone narcissistic, you express a harsh moral judgment. In contrast, you may use kinder words for people who are simply unskilled and unaware of their lack of skill. If someone attempts to do something that is impossible, you may call him or her a fool. If the person attempts something that is needlessly risky, you may call him foolhardy. However, you probably would not judge that person harshly unless he or she is taking the kind of damned fool chances that will get us all killed. When the person is simply wasting his or her own time and risking his or her own skin, you may feel pity or concern. When the person poses a threat to others, especially to you or your loved ones, you may start to get angry.

When low-ranking people are arrogant, we see them as narcissistic. Meanwhile, many high-ranking people often seem humble, usually because they have nothing to prove. Great people seldom have to boast;

other people sing their praises! For example, when Albert Einstein was a minor civil servant (a patent clerk) in Switzerland, he solved some of the biggest riddles in the history of science. As a result, Einstein quickly became a worldwide celebrity. His name became a metaphor for genius. Nobody would have considered Einstein to be arrogant or narcissistic if he thought that he was smarter than most other people. In contrast, narcissists want to be admired like Einstein even when they don't know what they are talking about. In other words, narcissists want to be recognized as "the one who knows." As a result, they tend to heap scorn on anyone who knows more than they do. For that reason, narcissists often appear to be shallow and anti-intellectual. By trying to look smarter than they are, they end up looking stupid.

After Einstein became famous as a scientific genius, he did not have to struggle to get his opinions taken seriously, even by the President of the United States. Once Einstein's reputation as a genius was established, he had no further need to struggle to be taken seriously. That is why truly great people often seem humble. Unfortunately, many brilliant people are ignored, often because they are trying to convey messages that are unwelcome. Thus, they may be dismissed as narcissistic or as just plain crazy. For that reason, I try to judge people according to what they say and do, not according to what other people say about them.

Narcissists want other people to admire them for their brilliance, their beauty, and their possessions. Narcissists want to call the shots. They feel that they should be entitled to special privileges. However, not everyone is willing to give the narcissist the admiration and special privileges that the narcissist expects. As a result, narcissists may feel that they are continually being unfairly challenged, disrespected, and disobeyed. Thus, narcissists may feel that they have the right and even the obligation to discipline the lesser beings.

Narcissists are annoying because they think that they are smarter than they really are, better informed than they really are, and entitled to more special privileges than other people think they deserve. Thus, the diagnosis of narcissism is a social judgment that is based on personal opinion. Moreover, it is a judgment that is made from a particular point of view, often from a social rank that is roughly equal to that of the narcissist.

Narcissists are typically most obnoxious to people whom they view as potential rivals. In contrast, the narcissist may show fawning submission to his or her superiors. The narcissist may also be kind and generous to submissive underlings who provide narcissistic supply and never cause narcissistic injury. The narcissist may simply ignore insults from the people who pose no threat to the narcissist's standing. In a business, a narcissist may try to curry favor with upper management, in the hopes of winning promotions. A narcissistic middle manager may be warmly supportive to his or her least capable subordinates, who reliably provide narcissistic supply and never cause narcissistic injury. As a result, the narcissist may enjoy some degree of popularity. Unfortunately, the narcissistic manager may ignore important input from brighter people on the lower rungs of the organization. Worst of all, narcissists may use dirty tricks to derail the careers of anyone they view as a potential critic or rival—usually their most capable peers and subordinates. Thus, narcissistic middle managers often make bad decisions and can cause a company to lose its most capable and most productive employees. Like termites, narcissistic middle managers can destroy a company from within.

Animals also struggle with each other for social rank. Animals fight over territory and food resources and mating opportunities. However, human beings have a lot more to fight about. Thus, narcissism is more than just a problem with social dominance. It has something to do with self-concept. At about the age of 6 months, human babies develop the ability to understand that their reflection in a mirror is a moving picture of themselves in real time, rather than being another baby behind a window. Only a few other species of animal, including chimpanzees and dolphins, seem to be able to recognize themselves in a mirror. Chickens can struggle ruthlessly with other chickens for dominance, but they lack the brainpower to recognize themselves in a mirror. Many behaviorists have concluded that chickens therefore lack self-awareness. Thus, many of a narcissistic human being's dominance games might be propelled by primitive drives. However, the fact that human beings have self-awareness gives them more to fight about. Human beings may fight to defend their dignity.

I think of dignity as the set of concerns that would matter to a human being but would not matter to a dog. A dog may want to control territory and resources, but it does not care if you think it is stupid or ugly. Dogs do not mind running around naked, but human beings often have nightmares in which they find that they are naked in public. Dogs often make a point of defecating in front of other dogs; but when human beings have no choice but to defecate in public, it is considered an affront to their dignity.

In the Greek myth, Narcissus fell in love with his reflection. In contrast, the evil stepmother in the fairy tale Snow White and the Seven Dwarves regarded her mirror as a servant. She would consult her mirror every day: "Mirror, mirror, on the wall. Who is the fairest one of all?" For many years, the mirror would tell her that she was. Eventually, the mirror told her that Snow White had become prettier than she was. The evil stepmother flew into a rage and ordered Snow White to be killed. Like many victims of raging narcissists, Snow White had no idea that she was in danger.

To a narcissist, social life is an unending game of king of the hill. Snow White's stepmother wanted to be considered the most beautiful. By simply existing, Snow White posed a threat to her stepmother's role as the most beautiful. Thus, the stepmother perceived Snow White as a challenger, even though Snow White herself would have been unaware that there was any sort of competition.

Narcissists often view their peers as enemies. However, they may view their underlings as pawns or even tools. Dr. Seuss expressed this idea in his book *Yertle the Turtle*. "I'm Yertle the turtle, oh marvelous me! For I am the king of all I can see!" Unfortunately, Yertle was not satisfied with being the king of the turtles in his pond. He decided that he would have a larger kingdom if he could see farther. So he decided that he needed a higher throne. To that end, he ordered some other turtles to stack themselves up so that he could sit on top of the stack. Yertle was not satisfied with a nine-turtle stack, so he commanded ever more turtles to add themselves to the stack.

Dr. Seuss's *Yertle the Turtle* teaches children important lessons about narcissism. No matter how high Yertle rose, he was still unhappy. The moon was always higher than he was! Eventually, the bottom-most turtle started to complain. His back hurt and he was hungry. He started to argue that even the turtles at the bottom should have rights. Eventually, the bottom-most turtle burped, which toppled the stack. Yertle then fell back into the pond. Now Yertle is the king of the mud, which is all that he can see. And the other turtles are free, "as turtles and all other creatures should be." Yertle the turtle had some thrilling short-term victories because he was able to persuade many other turtles to do his bidding. But he was never satisfied; and in the end, he was humiliated and the other turtles lived happily ever after.

Narcissists love to win and hate to lose, even in meaningless games. Thus, they are willing to pick fights that they think they can win, but they may avoid fights that they are certain that they will lose. For that reason, they often surround themselves with fawning admirers who pose no threat to them but rather follow their bidding and give them endless praise. Thus, the narcissist may lure other people into an unhealthy relationship that can be described as a co-dependency. In a co-dependency, one person supports another's addiction, poor mental health, immaturity, irresponsibility, or underachievement. Yertle the turtle lured many other turtles into a co-dependent relationship with him, at least for a while. Among human beings, co-dependent relationships can last a lifetime.

Narcissists are continually searching for co-dependent admirers to supply the praise that the narcissist desires but does not deserve. In the end, co-dependency is bad for both parties. Praising a narcissist is a lot like feeding a wild bear. In 1902, the officials at Yellowstone National Park in the United States started forbidding people to feed the wild bears. The bears were becoming dependent on handouts, and the young bears were failing to learn how to forage for themselves in the wild. Also, the bears were losing their natural fear of human beings. As a result, they were becoming dangerous.

Like bears, narcissists can become unpredictably dangerous if they do not get what they want. Narcissists can respond with seemingly irrational rage to an imagined slight. Thus, you should avoid giving narcissists the unearned praise that they seek. It is bad for them. In fact, it is best to keep away from narcissists as much as possible. Narcissists, like bears, should be observed only from afar.

I wish that I could call this book *Overcoming Narcissism*. Unfortunately, narcissism is not easily overcome. Actually, it would be easy to overcome it if you are the narcissist. To overcome narcissism, you need to get down off your high horse. You need to learn how to see yourself from other people's perspective. You need to learn how to use feedback from other people constructively. You need to base your social relationships on mutual respect, as opposed to dominance and submission. In other words, you need to practice humility as opposed to indulging in pride. It is easy if you try, and the results are gratifying. Yet narcissists will not bother to try because they do not know what they are missing.

Narcissists may feel some satisfaction from the tiny victories that they win, often in pointless games that other people do not want to play. However, narcissists are often unhappy people, largely because their emotional lives are so empty. They want things they cannot have, and they do not appreciate what they can have. They are so preoccupied with the desire for social climbing that they cannot relate to other people as equals. As a result, they cannot experience true love and friendship.

Narcissists may realize that they are arrogant. However, they may be proud of their arrogance. They may realize that their arrogance causes problems for other people, but they do not care about that. They simply feel some sort of desire or even compulsion to play pointless dominance games. The excitement generated by their tiny victories helps to fill in some of the emptiness of their emotional life. Narcissists want you to worship them, but they should actually be objects of pity. Of course, if they sense that you pity them, they may react with rage. By pitying them, you put yourself in the one-up position and them in the one-down position.

There is another, more serious reason for not calling this book *Overcoming Narcissism*. I do not want to give people the idea that they can overpower a narcissist. Never try to play any sort of game against someone who has an unhealthy need to win. If you play, you will probably lose. Narcissists think that winning is everything. They do not care about rules. They often rewrite the rules in the middle of the game. Unlike the narcissist, you will be held back by common decency and even basic sanity. At best, you will simply lose the game. At worst, you will become as emotionally unbalanced as the narcissist. As a result, you could lose your dignity or even your job. In short, you have nothing to gain and everything to lose when you tangle with a narcissist.

In many social settings, someone has the power to get the narcissist to behave. For example, upper-level managers could discipline or even fire a narcissistic middle manager. Unfortunately, the upper-level managers seldom see that the narcissistic middle manager is causing problems. Upper-level managers typically have an unrealistically rosy view of the narcissist. Narcissists are often good at self-promotion. They can also be ruthless in suppressing any information that would make them look less than perfect. This can be a serious problem in settings where upper management ignores all information that does not flow through "proper channels" (i.e., through the narcissist). The process of 360-degree assessment, or multi-rater feedback, was developed to get around this problem. In that process, an individual is reviewed by peers and subordinates, as well as by his or her supervisor. On the plus side, this process provides a way for people to alert upper management to the bad behavior of a narcissist. On the other hand, it gives the narcissist a chance to attack his or her peers and supervisor. Thus, the reports that come in through this process should be evaluated cautiously.

Whether or not you are in a position to discipline narcissists, you need to understand them. Narcissists can be dangerous, for two basic reasons. One reason is their overconfidence. They are the sort of fool who rushes in where angels fear to tread. The other reason is the pointless conflict they create. Narcissists seldom work or play well with others. A sane person would not want to hire a narcissist or work for one. If you want to have a happy marriage, you would certainly want to avoid marrying a narcissist. If you cannot avoid narcissists, you may need to tiptoe around them. Thus, narcissists can waste your time or sap your energy, even if they do not directly attack you.

An understanding of narcissism can help you recognize and avoid narcissists, at work and in your personal life. It can help you avoid promoting narcissism in your children. It can even help you recognize and correct your own narcissistic tendencies. As parents and as citizens, we must all think about how the schools are shaping young people's character. We do want our schools to teach young people how to earn a living. However, we also want young people to become wise and good —to become happy and healthy members of a just society. Before we can achieve those goals, we must think about what good character is.

Chapter 2

Personality Traits and Character Flaws

~

Narcissism is a disorder of the personality. Psychologists have come up with many different definitions for the word *personality.* Each of these definitions reflects the psychologist's school of thought and the particular scientific puzzles that he or she is trying to solve. In general, however, we can think of a person's personality as that the long-lasting patterns in how that person thinks, feels, and behaves.

At least since the days of ancient Greece, physicians and philosophers have wondered about the causes of bad behavior. Is it due to a moral problem or a medical problem? Is it due to some defect in education, or perhaps to some supernatural problem? Theophrastus, who was a student of the ancient Greek philosopher Aristotle, wrote, "Often before now have I applied my thoughts to the puzzling question—one, probably, which will puzzle me forever—why it is that, while all Greece lies under the same sky and all the Greeks are educated alike, it has befallen us to have characters so variously constituted."

Theophrastus wrote a set of 29 character sketches. Each of them described a way in which an ordinary man could be unpleasant. For example, there was the surly man ("Surliness is discourtesy in words") and the superstitious man ("Superstition would seem to be simply cowardice in regard to the supernatural"). There is also the arrogant man ("Arrogance is a certain scorn for all the world beside oneself.") Theophrastus gives us a set of descriptions of how some men misbehave, but he did not claim to have any idea of why they misbehave in those ways. He mentioned some of the bad things that a bad man might do to a "freeborn woman." Yet Theophrastus did not talk about how women might misbehave. Even aristocratic Greek women were not expected to play a role in public life. Nor did Theophrastus seem to worry about how female slaves were treated.

Ancient Greek physicians thought that differences in personality reflected differences in the physical makeup of the body. They believed that all matter was made up of a mixture of four elements: air, fire, earth, and water. They believed that a person's emotional balance depended on the balance (temperament) of those elements within the body (Table 1). We no longer think that personality is due to the balance of the atoms of earth, water, fire, and air in the body. However, we still use the word *temperament* to mean personality. We even still use the four basic temperaments (sanguine, choleric, melancholic, and phlegmatic) to describe individuals.

Table 1. The ancient Greeks believed that personality depended on the mixture (temperament) of four elements in the body.

Humor	Season	Element	Organ	Qualities	Ancient name	Tempera-ment	Traits
Blood	Spring	Air	Heart	Warm and wet	*Sanguis*	Sanguine	Cheerful, playful, brave
Yellow bile	Summer	Fire	Liver	Warm and dry	Kholé	Choleric	Ambitious, domineering, restless, quick to anger
Black bile	Autumn	Earth	Spleen	Cold and dry	Melaina kholé	Melancholic	Sad, quiet, analytical, serious
Phlegm	Winter	Water	Brain	Cold and wet	Phlégma	Phlegmatic	Calm, patient thoughtful, peaceful

To understand the concept of personality, it may help to think about some familiar characters from popular fiction. For example, Winnie-the-Pooh is a humble stuffed bear of very little brain. He is naïve and slow-witted, yet he is thoughtful and sometimes insightful. He is always willing to try his very best to help his friends, but his love for honey sometimes leads him into trouble. Piglet is a tiny young pig who is often fearful. Yet with the proper encouragement from his friends, Piglet can be brave in a crisis. Eeyore is a donkey who shows signs of chronic depression. He is pessimistic and sarcastic. He is also cautious and slow in moving, often to the point of total passivity. In contrast, Tigger is a tiger who is energetic (bouncing all over the place), exuberantly cheerful, and often irresponsible. Owl is a stuffy and talkative character who takes on the role of teacher. Rabbit is energetic and can be bossy, and he sometimes gets angry. These characters are satisfying as literary characters because each has a clear set of character traits that make sense and that stay consistent from one story to the next. Likewise, many real human beings have character traits that stay remarkably consistent over time.

As the Winnie-the-Pooh stories illustrate, a person's character traits can cause trouble for him- or herself or for other people. For example, Eeyore lacks the energy to build himself a proper house. He even finds it hard to keep his tail attached to his body. In contrast, Tigger is filled with such boundless energy that he annoys other people. Likewise, a real person's enduring character traits can cause problems for him- or herself or for other people. When someone's character traits are causing serious problems for that person or for others, the person may qualify for a diagnosis of a personality disorder.

The characters in the Winnie-the-Pooh stories have character traits that stay the same from one story to the next. To qualify as a character trait, the trait must be expressed in many different situations. For example, Pooh is always phlegmatic, Eeyore is always melancholic, Tigger is always sanguine, and Rabbit tends to be choleric. Also, Piglet is always timid and Owl is always pedantic. But like real people, these characters sometimes have thoughts, feelings, or behaviors that deviate from their normal pattern. These deviations are often important to the story. Most children seem to understand that when Piglet is brave, his bravery is meaningful because Piglet is normally fearful. They seem to understand that when something makes Eeyore happy, this happiness is meaningful because Eeyore is normally sad.

Winnie-the-Pooh and his friends were featured in two books of short stories by A. A. Milne, as well as in various other books, plays, movies, films, and television programs. In a short story, the characters respond to a particular situation or conflict. However, the short story itself does not have a long enough timeframe for characters to grow and develop. Nor do they grow and develop much between stories. The Winnie-the-Pooh stories can be read or watched in nearly any order because the characters change remarkably little from one story to another. Similarly, a classic television situation comedy (sitcom) is like a series of short stories. In each episode, the characters react to a new situation; however, the characters change remarkably little from one episode to the next. As a result, the installments of the sitcom can be watched in nearly any order.

In contrast, a serial is an ongoing story that allows the characters to have a story arc, which means that the main character or characters undergo important transformations during the course of the story. The episodes often begin with a narrator intoning "previously on (show name)," followed by clips from the previous episodes. Because of the serial format, you may need to watch the episodes in the proper order for them to make sense.

Characters in a television serial can make use of lessons that they learned in previous episodes. Similarly, a novel allows a sufficient timeframe for a character arc. During the course of a novel, a character may learn important lessons or overcome important obstacles. As a result, the character's personality is significantly different at the end of the story than it was at the beginning. For example, in a coming-of-age story, the character makes a transition from youth to adulthood. In a redemption story, the character attempts to atone for his or her past wrongdoings.

These concepts of characterization and character arc can help you appreciate works of fiction. These concepts can help you learn to use literary models for understanding and solving problems, such as those related to personality disorders. A person with a personality disorder is like a fictional character with serious, persistent character flaws. To qualify for a diagnosis of a personality disorder, the person's character flaws must create problems for him- or herself or for other people. Also, the flaws must be persistent. There does not seem to be a character arc. The biography of someone with a personality disorder generally lacks a coming-of-age story arc. People with personality disorders often behave in ways that would be normal and acceptable for a small child or perhaps for an adolescent but are inappropriate for a grownup. Thus, the diagnosis of a personality disorder is a judgment based on social expectations for that individual. This judgment is a social phenomenon that takes place within a social context. It is not always fair.

Chapter 3

Setting and Conflict

～

Narcissism is a character flaw that tends to generate conflict. To understand narcissism, we can use some of the tools of literary criticism. Characterization and conflict are two of the five elements of fiction. The others are setting, plot, and theme. In a work of fiction, characters exist within a setting and deal with conflicts. The setting is the time, place, and conditions in which the story takes place. A conflict is some sort of disagreement or struggle. The plot is the sequence of events that take make up the story. The plot includes what happens to the characters, and how they respond to those events and attempt to resolve the conflicts. A theme is an idea that the writer wants to convey to the audience, such as "crime does not pay," or "war is hell." The oldest surviving Greek comedies are satires that deal with the themes of the foolishness and vanity of powerful men. Ancient Greek tragedies dealt with somber themes, such as the dangers of pride, the abuse of power, and the relationships between human beings and the gods.

The setting of a work of fiction can be based on some real time and place, or it can be entirely a product of the writer's fantasies. Sometimes, a single work can include realistic as well as fantastical settings. For example, L. Frank Baum's *The Wonderful Wizard of Oz* begins in Kansas. From there, Dorothy and Toto are transported to the fantastical world of Oz. The contrast between the two settings—Kansas and Oz—allows the author to explore the themes of wanderlust and homesickness. Dorothy was unhappy with her bleak, hardscrabble life in Kansas. But as soon as she arrives in Oz, she sets out on a quest to find her way home to her family. During that quest, she meets three other characters, each of whom is on his own quest. The Scarecrow is searching for a brain (wisdom), the Tin Woodman for a heart (compassion), and the Cowardly Lion for courage. Dorothy and her new friends find themselves in conflict with a wizard (who turns out to be an ordinary man with serious character flaws) and a wicked witch (whom Dorothy unwittingly kills while trying to put out a fire). At the end of the story, Dorothy and Toto are magically transported back to the loving arms of Auntie Em in Kansas.

In some works of fiction, the setting is an imaginary place that was inspired by a real place. For example, the Winnie-the-Pooh stories take place mainly in the Hundred Acre Wood, which is sometimes spelled Hundred Aker Wood. It is a fantastical setting that was inspired by the Five Hundred Acre Wood in Ashdown Forest in East Sussex, England. However, the Hundred Acre Wood in the stories represents the woods as imagined by a child who is playing with his toys. Christopher Robin's stuffed animals and the wild animals in the woods (such as a rabbit and an owl) are like people. They usually live in proper houses, with doors. (Eeyore's pitiful house made of sticks is an exception.) The animals talk to each other and often visit each other's houses. Some of the animals wear clothes.

The Pooh stories have a fantastical setting. So do works of science fiction and fantasy. In contrast, many other kinds of fiction have a highly realistic setting, where the usual laws of nature apply and the characters think and behave more or less like real people. Often, the setting of a work of fiction is not just temporal (time) and geographic (place) but also social. Thus, there can be two social settings within the same house. The British television series *Upstairs, Downstairs* and *Downton Abbey* depicted the lives of a wealthy family (who lived "upstairs") and their servants (who lived "downstairs" or "below stairs"). The boundary between these parallel universes is often called the green baize door. Baize is a coarse woolen or cotton cloth that was tacked to the back of the door to the servants' quarters and the work areas to deaden the noise from the kitchen and other work areas.

The conflict in a work of fiction can be external or internal. In an external conflict, a character contends with nature or with other characters. In an internal conflict, the character is struggling against him- or herself. For example, Shakespeare's Hamlet struggles with the question of whether to kill himself: "to be, or not to be. That is the question." External struggles are easier to write about and easier to depict on film. That is why so many novels and movies are set in wartime.

War is a conflict on an international scale. In war movies, the war creates many conflicts for the characters. Thus, the conflicts in a work of fiction may arise from some aspect of the setting or the characterization. During wartime, people think and feel and do things that would be unthinkable or inexcusable during peacetime. As the French philosopher Voltaire wrote, "It is forbidden to kill; therefore, all murderers are punished unless they kill in large numbers and to the sound of trumpets." Thus, when we judge someone's character or behavior, we generally take the context of the behavior into account. In law, the facts or events that make an offense seem less blameworthy are called extenuating circumstances. For example, in Victor Hugo's novel *Les Misérables*, Jean Valjean steals bread to feed his sister's starving children. It is a crime to steal bread; but unlike Police Inspector Javert, most readers would find Valjean's crime to be excusable.

Even in peacetime, an institutional setting can cause people to do unthinkable things. The classic illustration of this principle was the Stanford Prison Experiment, which was conducted at Stanford University in California from August 14 to 20, 1971. The goal of the experiment was to show whether the abusive conditions in prisons were due to the pre-existing personalities of the guards and prisoners or to the prison environment itself. The researchers recruited 24 mentally healthy young men and randomly assigned them to be either "prisoners" or "guards" in a makeshift prison in the basement of the psychology building. The experiment was supposed to last for two weeks, but it was stopped after six days because a graduate student named Christina Maslach, who was dating the lead investigator Philip Zimbardo, was horrified by the conditions in the "prison." Zimbardo noted that of more than 50 people who observed the experiment, only Maslach objected to it on moral grounds. (Zimbardo and Maslach eventually married.)

Upstairs, Downstairs and *Downton Abbey* deal with conflicts that arise from differences in wealth and social rank, as do the works of Jane Austen. In the opening line of *Pride and Prejudice,* Austen wrote, "It is a truth universally acknowledged, that a single man in possession of a good fortune, must be in want of a wife." This opening line is bitterly ironic. A wealthy man could get along quite well without a wife, but the daughters of even wealthy families had to marry well if they wanted to maintain their social standing.

In Jane Austen's world, everybody knew his or her place within a highly stratified social hierarchy. The details of this hierarchy were set forth in the Order of Precedence. At the top was the sovereign (the king or ruling queen). The other members of the royal family were then ranked according to sex and birth order. Underneath the royalty were the nobility or peers (in order of precedence: dukes, marquises, earls, viscounts, barons). Originally, the bearers of these titles had landed estates, which were the primary source of wealth in the feudal system. Beneath the nobility were the gentry (baronets, knights, and untitled gentlemen). Many of the gentry also owned land. Holding an important office in the government or the church or being an officer in the military could also raise a man's social standing. A woman's social standing was derived from that of her father and her husband.

The Order of Precedence was only part of a larger hierarchy called the Scala Naturae or ladder of life. In English, it is sometimes called the Great Chain of Being. God is at the top. Underneath Him are the angelic beings, then humanity, then animals, then plants, and then minerals. Within each of these major divisions were subdivisions. For example, royalty were superior to the nobility, just as gold is superior to silver. Philosophers worked out rules for how to draw the boundaries between these divisions. One interesting line is the one between human beings and other animals. Human beings like to treat their pets as if they were people and their slaves as if they were animals. Mark Twain illustrated this concept in a footnote to *The Adventures of Tom Sawyer*: "If Mr. Harbison had owned a slave named Bull, Tom would have spoken of him as 'Harbison's Bull,' but a son or a dog of that name was 'Bull Harbison.'"

According to Max Weber, a German political economist who is one of the founders of the field of sociology, social stratification is based primarily on the "three p's": property, prestige, and power. Property refers to material possessions, including real estate. Prestige is respect or admiration from other people. Power is the ability to get what you want, regardless of what other people want. The three p's are not independent of each other. People use power to get property, and owning property gives them power. Likewise, prestige can help you gain power and property, while having power and property can help you gain prestige.

Weber also explained how three sources of power (class power, social status, and political power) can be used to stratify society. Class power refers to unequal access to resources. It gives you bargaining power over other people. Social status can confer power if lower-status people defer to higher-status people. Political power refers to the ability to influence other people's behaviors and to make and enforce society's rules.

During the feudal era, wealth was based on land ownership. Land was either inherited or granted by the sovereign. For example, after King Henry VIII of England broke with the Roman Catholic Church, he sold or gave much church-owned land to his supporters. However, the Industrial Revolution made it possible for businessmen who came from the lower classes to become richer than many aristocrats. Thus, a man who had made a fortune in business could have more wealth and power than someone who outranked him socially. As a result, there was rivalry between people who had status derived from the old system and people who had power and influence because of their newfound wealth. One way to solve this problem was for titled European aristocrats to marry an American heiress.

In a small-scale society, everyone knows everyone else personally. As a result, there is no need for symbols of rank. But as the scale of a society increases, the need for symbols of rank also grows. If you lived in ancient Rome, you could tell a man's rank at a glance, just from what he was wearing. Slaves generally wore a simple tunic but no hat or shoes. When a man was freed from slavery, he would start wearing a soft felt cap called a pileus. Only adult male Roman citizens could wear a toga, and they generally wore an iron ring. Public officials generally wore a gold ring, which they could use for making an impression on the wax seal on documents. The toga of a Senator would bear a Tyrian purple stripe. Only the emperor was allowed to wear a Tyrian purple cape trimmed in gold thread.

The laws that prevented people from dressing like a higher-ranking person are often called sumptuary laws. Sometimes, these laws were intended to prevent an imbalance of trade, such as to keep Roman silver reserves from being drained by the silk trade. Yet sumptuary laws were often intended to ensure that clothing could serve as a uniform that indicated social rank. In the United States during the days of slavery, there was no need for special clothing to indicate who was a slave. Skin color served that purpose.

The United States does not have a royal family or any titled nobility. The framers of the U.S. Constitution decided that the United States should not have a king. They also forbade the federal and state governments from granting titles of nobility. The framers felt that such titles had no place in a free and equal society. Yet the framers did not forbid slavery, which also has no place in a free and equal society. Some historians believe that many of the Founding Fathers of the United States were motivated by fear that the British Empire would abolish slavery. In 1772, the English Court of King's Bench had decided (in the case of *Somerset v Stewart*) that chattel slavery was unsupported by common law in England and Wales. Some of the Founding Fathers (including Presidents George Washington, Thomas Jefferson, and James Madison) owned slaves. However, a few of the important figures in the American Revolution, such as Thomas Paine and the Marquis de Lafayette, advocated the abolition of slavery.

To understand a fictional character, you may need to understand that character's backstory. A backstory consists of events that happened before the action of the story begins. Likewise, to understand a fictional tale or even current events, you may need to understand historical events that happened generations ago. As novelist William Faulkner put it, "The past is never dead. It's not even past."

Europeans generally grow up with an awareness of social rank. They may regard the hereditary aristocracy with either nostalgia or distaste, but at least they know that it exists. British people tend to be acutely aware of class distinctions. Even today, it would be difficult for anyone in Britain to hide his or her social class background. One television character who tries valiantly to hide her working-class background is Hyacinth Bucket (she pronounces it "boo-kay") from the British sitcom *Keeping Up Appearances*, which ran from 1990 to 1995. Hyacinth's primary aim in life is to impress the people of the upper classes, and to give the impression that she herself has high social standing. Yet despite her vanity, she is a warm-hearted person and will rush to her family's aid at a moment's notice.

In contrast, many white Americans grow up without an understanding of the history of class distinctions, inherited privilege, and racial privilege. Although the United States has no royalty or titled aristocracy, it has prominent families that have been wealthy and powerful for many generations. During the colonial era, New York and the South even had a system that was a lot like the European feudal system.

In 1629, the Dutch West India Company created a system called patroonship in the Hudson River Valley. The company would grant the title to a huge tract of land to an individual called a patroon, who would then rent the land to tenants. (Some of the land was then worked by slaves.) The patroon was a lot like a feudal lord. He could create civil and criminal courts and appoint local officials. At his death, he would pass the patroonship to his eldest son. This system persisted until 1775, when the British redefined the patroonships as estates and took away the patroon's judicial powers. This action angered many ethnic Dutchmen, many of whom then supported the American cause in the Revolutionary War.

In Britain, many of the landed estates were entailed. When the owner of an entailed estate died, the entire estate had to be passed down to his eldest son (or to his nearest male relative, if he had no son). A younger son would inherit practically nothing unless all of his older brothers died. Traditionally, the younger sons of the nobility went into the church or the military. But during the colonial era, the younger sons of many English noblemen received large land grants in Virginia. There, they established plantations, which were large estates dedicated to the production of some cash crop, such as tobacco. During the English Civil War and the Restoration, these well-born planters tended to support the king, rather than Parliament. For that reason, they were called Cavaliers.

The founders of the Commonwealth of Virginia wanted to re-create something like the feudal system. Initially, the plantations were worked by indentured servants: poor English or Scottish immigrants who agreed to work without pay for a set period to pay for their passage. After their term of indenture, they could become tenant farmers. However, the plantation owners turned increasingly to enslaved Africans as laborers. The slaves were treated more as livestock than as human beings. Thus, the plantation system in the New World was worse in many respects than the traditional feudal system.

From the beginning, the Massachusetts Bay Colony had a social structure that was different from that of the Hudson Valley or Virginia. The main purpose of the Massachusetts Bay Colony was to create a refuge for Puritans. The Puritans were English Reformed Protestants who wanted to purify the Church of England by removing all Roman Catholic practices. The Puritans drew their numbers and their strength from the merchant class, rather than from the nobility. Thus, they saw no need to spread the feudal system to a new continent. To ensure the survival and prosperity of their new colony, they decided to establish a social system in which property and political power were distributed far more widely. As a result, Massachusetts developed a mixed merchant economy. Many of the merchants in Boston enriched themselves through the slave trade or trade in products produced by slaves. However, there were relatively few slaves in Massachusetts itself. (Slaves accounted for roughly 2.2% of the total population of Massachusetts in 1760.) The wealthy, educated elite of Boston came to be called Brahmins, after the priest caste in Hinduism.

Hindu philosophers teach us that any society tends to divide naturally into four varnas, which means types or classes: Brahmins, Kshatriyas, Vaishyas, and Shudras. Each of these varnas corresponds to a type of political power. In India, the Brahmins were the priests, scholars, and teachers. They represent the power of knowledge. The Kshatriyas were the rulers, warriors, and administrators. They represent the power of military force and temporal authority. The Vaishyas were farmers, artisans, and merchants. They represent economic power. The Shudras were laborers. They represent the power of sheer numbers.

This concept of varna overlapped with the Hindu concept of jati or caste. A varna is a concept related to social class, whereas a jati is a form of extended family. In traditional societies, occupations were passed down from father to son. That is why so many English people have surnames like Baker, Brewer, Carpenter, Miller, Smith, or Taylor. Likewise, many Indians have surnames like Gandhi (perfume seller), Patel (landowner or village chief), or Srivastava (military scribe). In medieval Europe, people who had a particular occupation often joined an organization called a guild. However, a young person could easily join a particular occupation through apprenticeship. In India, however, the families who had some hereditary occupation tended to form a self-governing social group or tribe, called a jati. The word *jati* came from the Sanskrit word *jāta*, which literally means born. People are born into a particular jati, and they would eventually marry someone from within their jati. The jati served as a community that provided mutual support, and it had a system of governance for resolving disputes. Although an individual could not move from one jati to another, a jati could rise socially or even merge with another jati.

By the beginning of the 20th century, there were thousands of jatis within India. At that point, the British started assigning each jati to a particular varna, for census purposes. Nevertheless, many of the jatis had occupations that had features of more than one varna. For example, if the members of a particular jati served both as soldiers and as saddle makers, would they belong to the Kshatriya or Vaishya varna?

There were also many jatis that did "unclean" jobs, such as cleaning latrines or dealing with animal carcasses. These jatis were considered to be below the traditional varnas. The members of those jatis were therefore considered "untouchable." They were subjected to forms of segregation and discrimination that were similar to what happened to black Americans before the Civil Rights Act. Gandhi called them harijans, which means the people of the Lord Vishnu. However, that term came to be viewed as an insult. Today, the members of these groups call themselves Dalits, which means divided.

Of course, even people who were not born into one of the four varnas can acquire and use the kind of power associated with those varnas. One prominent example is Dr. Bhimrao Ramji Ambedkar, also known as Babasaheb. Although he was a Dalit, he was a dedicated scholar (traditionally a Brahmin pursuit). He earned doctorates in economics from Columbia University and the London School of Economics. He became active in the India's independence movement. Later, he became the principal architect of the Indian constitution, which abolished untouchability. Ambedkar also served as independent India's first law minister. (Politics and public administration were traditionally a Kshatriya pursuit.) He also published journals and led campaigns advocating political rights and social freedom for Dalits. In 1956, he converted to Buddhism. He saw Buddhism as a way to end the caste system in India and thus to promote equality and democracy in India. Yet Buddhism also includes the idea that social status in this life depends on one's behavior in past lives.

The word *varna* came from the Sanskrit word for color. Until the mid-20th century, many anthropologists believed that the concept of varna was originally based on skin color. However, the Vedic literature often used color-coding as a metaphor for classification. Nevertheless, skin color became an important indicator of social caste in the Americas because of the African slave trade. In 1990, the First Pan-African Conference, which was held in London, England, adopted an Address to the Nations of the World that stated, "The problem of the Twentieth Century is the problem of the colour-line." Largely because of the British influence, skin color also became a political issue in India.

Although Americans were never expected to observe an official Order of Precedence, there have been important differences in social rank. Social rank has been based partly on wealth but also partly on ancestry. New Englanders could gain prestige for being able to trace their ancestry to someone who came to Massachusetts on the *Mayflower* in 1620. New Yorkers who could trace their ancestry to the Dutch settlers of New Amsterdam were called Knickerbockers. The First Families of Virginia were people who could trace their ancestry to Englishmen who had settled in the James River area in the 17th century. In the late 19th century, lineage-based organizations such as the Sons of the American Revolution, the Daughters of the American Revolution, and the Colonial Dames were founded.

By the late 19th century, the white Anglo-Saxon Protestants (WASPs) who could trace their ancestry to the early colonial period often felt superior to recent immigrants, especially immigrants from Ireland or Southern or Eastern Europe. Thus, it was considered normal and natural for Protestants of Northern European ancestry to have certain privileges, even if they were relatively recent immigrants. Eventually, the "white ethnics," such as people of Irish, Italian, or Polish ancestry, became more integrated into the larger "white" community. Asian immigrants were initially subjected to harsh discrimination and brutal suppression. Today, Asian Americans are the highest-income, best-educated, and fastest growing ethnic group in the United States, yet they are still often subjected to discrimination.

Unfortunately, blacks have always been pushed to the bottom of the social hierarchy, whereas the indigenous peoples were nearly wiped out. In fact, Adolf Hitler consciously modeled his "final solution to the Jewish problem" on the way that the United States had treated the indigenous peoples of North America.

The people who benefit from a hierarchical social structure often feel that the system was ordained by God. To reinforce this social structure, they often support policies that are not only unfair but also stupid—policies that harm the people on the lower rungs of the society without benefiting anyone else. You can see this kind of dynamic play out in everyday experiences. In a badly run school, the teachers and administrators may allow an unpopular child to be verbally and even physically abused. If that unpopular child should try to defend him- or herself, even nonviolently, the administration may then punish the unpopular child for the "crime" of self-defense. This crime is punished severely because it poses a threat to the existing social order. That is exactly what happened at a public school in Pennsylvania.

Christian Stanfield, a 15-year-old boy in South Fayette High School in South Fayette, Pennsylvania, had grown tired of being verbally and physically attacked by other students. Some of these attacks were occurring during his math class. The teacher failed to protect him, and even his mother did not take his complaints seriously. So he used his iPad (which he was allowed to bring to class) to make an audio recording of his torment. His mother was shocked by what she heard in the recording. She was even more shocked by the school principal's reaction. The principal could have simply sent Christian to a better math class. He could have taken some sort of action to stop the bullying in the hallways of the school. Instead, he called the police and tried to have federal wiretapping charges brought against Christian. However, those charges did not stick because the principal had deleted the evidence from Christian's iPad. Instead, Christian was charged with disorderly conduct, a charge that was eventually dropped because of public outrage.

Bullying is all about power and social rank. Bullies use their power to humiliate their targets, thus establishing the bully's superiority to that target. Often, schoolyard bullying is tolerated because the bullies attack the sort of children whom the adults in charge also despise: poor children, members of ethnic or religious minorities, children with disabilities such as autism, unusually bright children, and children who do not conform to gender norms. Sometimes, the adults in charge ignore the bullying because they do not know what to do about it. However, adults often condone the bullying because the bullying serves to enforce social norms. When adults allow the bullying to go on, the bullies conclude that the adults approve of their behavior. Thus, the bullies start to view themselves as a police force. Of course, a society that is policed by emotionally disturbed children is likely to be nasty and brutish.

Bullying is permitted because the bullies serve to maintain the social hierarchy. Likewise, rapists go unpunished because the fear of rape serves the social purpose of keeping girls and women in line. The fear of rape causes girls and women to restrict their scope of activity and become dependent on male protectors. Female victims of sexual assault have been criticized for wearing the wrong clothes or drinking too much or even for just leaving their homes. Meanwhile, untested rape evidence kits sit on shelves, while the rapists go on to attack more victims. However, not everyone believes that the victims should be blamed. When Golda Meir was Prime Minister of Israel, someone suggested a curfew for women, to prevent women from being raped. In response, Meir suggested that the curfew should be for men because men were committing the rapes.

Any social structure is narrow at the top. No society has enough room at the top for all of the ambitious people. As a result, the people who are already at the top of the society do things to protect their own position and to save places for their children. To achieve that goal, they have to thwart the ambitions of the people beneath them. Often, they can do this simply by making it hard to get the kind of education or other opportunities one would need in order to advance.

Societies differ in terms of how much upward mobility is permitted. A class-based society allows a few ambitious individuals to rise beyond the station to which they were born. In contrast, a caste-based society makes it hard or impossible for people to cross social barriers. For example, in the United States during segregation, there were strict color lines that could not be crossed. To escape from the oppression of Jim Crow segregation, an individual had to pass for white. Many public institutions were rigidly segregated by race. Any individual who tried to cross the color line could be singled out for attack. In some cases, these attacks were carried out by masked men in secret. But in a shockingly large number of cases, murders were carried out in public, as a public rite of human sacrifice as well as an act of terrorism. When private or public attacks on isolated individuals are not enough to maintain the social hierarchy, the system can react more violently, as it did in Tulsa, Oklahoma in 1921.

Oklahoma was settled largely by Southerners, many of whom had been slaveholders before the Civil War. Oklahoma became a state in 1907. One of the first things that the Oklahoma state legislature did was to pass racial segregation laws, which are commonly called Jim Crow laws. State laws about voter registration prevented black men from registering to vote, and thus from serving on juries or taking office in local government. There were also dozens of lynchings, nearly always of black men and boys. Nevertheless, a prosperous black community managed to arise in Tulsa.

In 1921, Tulsa was booming. Because of a surge of oil discoveries in Oklahoma in the early 20th century, Tulsa was called the Oil Capital of the World. Tulsa's Greenwood District was called the Black Wall Street because it was the wealthiest black community in the United States—until May 31, 1921. On that date, a white mob armed with machine guns attacked the Greenwood District. According to some accounts, the attackers used airplanes to keep track of what was happening and even to drop some bombs. An area of 35 city blocks, including 1256 homes, was destroyed by fire, leaving 10,000 black people homeless. Two black hospitals were destroyed, and more than 800 injured black people were admitted to white hospitals. Six thousand black people were jailed. The official death toll was 39 persons, but other estimates of the number of black people who were killed range from 55 to about 300. The Greenwood District of Tulsa was targeted because its black residents posed a threat to the system of racial oppression, simply by having some money of their own.

Many people who have benefited from a system of social hierarchy instinctively want that system to remain unchanged. However, many thoughtful people who have enjoyed unearned privileges want to correct things that they find to be fundamentally wrong and immoral. In 1785, Thomas Clarkson, who was a student at Cambridge University, entered a Latin essay competition. He was assigned the topic *Anne liceat invitos in servitutem dare* (Is it lawful to enslave the unconsenting?). In his research for the essay, Clarkson read everything he could find on the subject, including the works of a Quaker abolitionist named Anthony Benezet. Clarkson also interviewed people who had seen the slave trade and slavery first-hand. Clarkson's essay won the prize. Appalled by what he learned from his research, Clarkson dedicated himself to abolishing the slave trade. Likewise, in 1791, the Marquis de Lafayette urged the French National Constituent Assembly to abolish the slave trade, asserting that he considered black men to be men.

During the mid 20th century, the Civil Rights Movement lobbied for laws to undermine the race-based social hierarchy in the United States. The Civil Rights Act of 1964 outlawed racial segregation in public facilities, such as restaurants and cinemas. The Voting Rights Act of 1965 was passed to enforce the voting rights guaranteed by the Fourteenth and Fifteenth Amendments to the Constitution. The Fair Housing Act of 1968 made it illegal to refuse to sell or rent real estate to people because of their race, religion, sex, or national origin. Up until that point, many deeds included clauses that forbade the owner of the property from selling to nonwhites or to Jews. These clauses were called restrictive covenants. Some older deeds still contain restrictive covenants. However, the restrictive covenants are no longer legally binding.

I was a child when the major civil rights laws were being passed. I went through puberty during the heyday of the Women's Liberation Movement. If it were not for the Vietnam War and the looming threat of nuclear war, it would have seemed as if my parents' generation was solving the world's problems. I assumed that racism and sexism and other problems of social inequality would soon become things of the past. Yet here we are, still engaged in the same struggles!

I spent most of my childhood in a suburb that was more than 95% white, and where nearly every family considered itself middle class. Technically, most of the families should have been considered working class. Many of the parents (often just the father) worked in a factory or in some other blue-collar job. However, many of those blue-collar jobs were secure, union jobs that paid well. Thus, I had little opportunity to see conflicts over race and class while I was growing up. I had to learn about such conflicts from reading novels and history books. Many novels deal with the conflicts between rich and poor, and even between "new money" and "old money." For example, in F. Scott Fitzgerald's *The Great Gatsby*, Jay Gatsby had recently become so wealthy that he can take his pick of beautiful chorus girls. But he yearns for the well-bred Daisy Buchanan.

In the United States, many people have a strange reluctance to talk or even think about matters of social rank. We tell children that the United States of America is the Land of Opportunity, where everyone is created equal. Nevertheless, human rights activists are still struggling to right the wrongs of racism and sexism. Many white children who have a sheltered upbringing in Northern suburbs grow up blissfully unaware of these struggles. They may have heard about slavery, but it seems like ancient history to them. The only way for most of these children to engage with those issues is by learning about them in history or English class or by reading books or watching documentaries in their spare time. Young people could engage with these issues by studying sociology or political science in college. Unfortunately, most children are worried that if they take any course of study that is not strictly vocational, they will be unable to find a decent job after graduation.

For most people in the United States, status is a matter of wealth and occupation. Often, there is no real difference between the two: many high-status jobs pay well, and having no job pays nothing at all, at least after your unemployment insurance runs out. Today, many people seem to worship celebrities, who are people who have achieved fortune and fame in the commercial media, usually because of their work as entertainers or athletes.

The National Opinion Research Center compiled a list of more than 800 occupations. Survey data from 1989 were then used to rate the prestige of each occupation. The results showed that Americans generally considered the higher-paying occupations to be more prestigious. However, a Harris poll from 2014 found that most Americans respect the people whose occupations involved helping other people: doctors, firefighters, scientists, nurses, engineers, police officers, and members of the clergy. In contrast, the respondents felt that people who deal with money—union leaders, stockbrokers and bankers, and accountants—had low prestige.

In the United States today, we do not have titled aristocrats. Even the old-money families from Boston and New York and Virginia have largely fallen from prominence. Old money has lost its influence, yet big money still exists. A tiny percentage of the population controls a large and growing proportion of the wealth in society. Also, a huge portion of the workforce is engaged in a strictly hierarchical system: the typical corporation. Corporations are generally run as hierarchical systems with a strict top-down system of command, much like the military. The corporation has its own Order of Precedence. At the bottom of the hierarchy are the rank-and-file workers. They report to their managers, who in turn report to higher levels of management. At the top of the management pyramid are the C-level officers (CEO, COO, CFO), who report to the board of directors, who in turn must report to the shareholders.

We hear a lot about "free enterprise." Yet in the Land of the Free, most workers have remarkably little freedom at work. They must do exactly what they are told to do, exactly when they are told to do it, and exactly how they are told to do it. Unlike slaves, they can quit their jobs and their overseers cannot legally rape or beat them. Yet the weakness of the social safety net in the United States means that the workers often have to tolerate intolerable working conditions, if they want to provide for themselves and their children. Most of the people who are being graduated from college today have such a crushing burden of student loan debt that they must take practically any job under any conditions, just to pay off their loans. Thus, they are like indentured servants.

Like schools, workplaces provide bullies with targets who cannot escape. The difference is that the stakes in the conflicts are often higher. In school, the mean kids just want the other kids to think that they are cool. At work, adults must compete for bonuses and promotions, or even for keeping their jobs during a time of cutbacks. Anyone can become competitive in such a setting. However, a narcissist can be vicious even when there is no real competition going on, and nothing is at stake but the narcissist's own ego. A narcissistic boss can attack his or her subordinates for simply doing a good job. Narcissistic managers can thus drive good employees out of a company, and they can drive the company itself into the ground.

Chapter 4
Heroes and Villains, Virtues and Vices

~

Like storybook characters, real people have character traits. A storybook character's traits are expressed through what the character thinks, feels, says, and does in the story. As you read the story (or watch a movie), you start to form opinions about that character. Do you like or dislike that character? Do you trust or distrust the character? Would you look up to that character? (Narcissists want you to look up to them.) Or would you look down on that character? Your opinions about a storybook character or about a person you observe in real life will depend on your point of view.

Every story is told from a particular point of view. Thus, the storyteller tells what he or she knows, thinks, and feels about the characters, setting, and conflicts in the story. A fictional work may focus on a particular character. This character is called the focal character. Often, the focal character is also the protagonist.

The term *protagonist* initially meant the primary character. However, it has come to mean the character for whom the audience has the most empathy. Empathy is the ability to put oneself in someone else's position, to understand what someone else is experiencing. For example, Captain Ahab is the focal character but not the protagonist of Herman Melville's *Moby-Dick; or, The Whale*. Captain Ahab's fanatical search for the white whale drives the plot. However, the audience is supposed to feel empathy for the narrator, who asks us to call him Ishmael.

Readers of *Moby-Dick* know what Ishmael is thinking and feeling because he tells us what he thinks and feels. We have no such window into Ahab's thoughts and feelings. Thus, it may take a while for the reader to realize that Ahab is a madman. Melville chose those characters' names carefully. According to the Bible and the Koran, Abraham had rejected his son Ishmael, who was then miraculously saved from dying of thirst. Thus, the name *Ishmael* came to represent orphans, exiles, and outcasts but also survivors. According to the Bible, Ahab was an idol-worshipping king who died a horrible death. Melville wrote for an audience who had read the Bible. His audience would have understood what those names meant.

In a work of fiction, the characters face some sort of conflict. Often, the protagonist is in conflict with some sort of opposition, called the antagonist. The antagonist can be a character or group of characters. In detective fiction, the antagonist is the criminal or criminals who have committed the crime that the detective is trying to solve. But in a caper story, the protagonists are the criminals; the security guards and the police are the antagonists.

The antagonist can also be an institution, a concept, or a force of nature. For example, the primary antagonist in Hemingway's story *The Old Man and the Sea* was the giant marlin that the old fisherman was trying to bring to shore. As the old man fights the fish for two days and two nights, he begins to feel compassion and respect for the great fish. He begins to think of the fish as a brother and decides that no human beings deserve to eat that fish. At that point, the sharks that want to eat the fish before he can bring it to shore become the antagonist.

Some fictional characters are portrayed as good. The good characters are sometimes called good guys or white hats. Good characters may also be smart, brave, and strong. A smart, brave, and strong character who is willing to make some sort of sacrifice for the common good is called a hero. (A heroine is a female hero.) The best kind of hero is a champion. A champion is someone who fights on behalf of someone else.

A champion has the virtues of strength, courage, and selflessness. Unfortunately, most people today use the word *champion* to mean a person who has won a meaningless sporting contest, rather than a struggle for justice. Nevertheless, a few champions, notably Muhammad Ali, have used their championship in the sporting world as a platform that made them effective champions in the struggle for justice.

Of course, even the good characters have flaws, and strong characters have weaknesses. Thus, a hero must sometimes struggle to overcome his or her flaws and weaknesses. Otherwise, it would be hard for the audience to feel empathy for the hero.

In contrast, some other fictional characters are portrayed as bad. Bad characters are sometimes called villains, bad guys, heavies, black hats, or baddies. Bad characters may also be smart, brave, and strong. However, they are generally self-serving. A villain ought to have some weaknesses; otherwise, the hero has no chance of winning. However, it is also good for a villain to have some appealing traits. Evil is more interesting if it is seductive. A particularly sleazy type of villain is the confidence artist, also called a con man. A confidence artist works to gain your trust and then betrays you, often by stealing your money.

Sometimes, the protagonist of a story lacks the good qualities of a typical hero, such as idealism, courage, or good morals. These characters are sometimes called antiheroes. One example is Shakespeare's Hamlet, whose indecisiveness and rudeness make him less than heroic. Others include the protagonists of picaresque novels, which deal with the adventures of a roguish hero of low social standing who lives by his wits in a corrupt society, like Mark Twain's Huckleberry Finn. In the 20th century, existentialist writers created antiheroes that were alienated, indecisive, and bored. The morally ambiguous protagonists of many films from the 1970s have been characterized as antiheroes.

The "call me Ishmael" narrator of *Moby-Dick* can be viewed as an antihero. So can the protagonist of many antiwar and dystopian novels and movies. (A dystopia means a bad or defective world, just as a utopia means a good or ideal world.) These antiheroes are everyman characters who are caught up in events that have spiraled beyond their control. In some cases, the antihero's problems started because he lightly made some decision that turned out to be a grave mistake. For example, Ishmael willingly signed on to work on the *Pequod* because of a combination of alienation, boredom, and wanderlust.

Dystopian works often focus on the antihero's struggle to survive or to maintain sanity and dignity. In some stories, the antihero must sacrifice his sanity and dignity in order to survive, or he may risk his life in order to maintain his dignity. In the darkest novels, none of these things are possible. In Joseph Heller's novel *Catch-22*, men can be excused from flying combat missions if they are insane, but the fact that they want to avoid flying combat missions proves that they are sane. In George Orwell's *Nineteen Eighty-Four*, the antihero Winston Smith ends up losing his sanity, his dignity, and then his life.

Like a classical Greek tragedy, these antihero novels and movies convey a political message. The classical Greek tragedies were warnings to the powerful: if you disrespect the gods or mistreat other people, you will come to a bad end. The modern dystopian and antiwar novels and movies provide a different kind of warning. They warn us that there is something fundamentally wrong with how our society is structured and that these structural flaws are causing sane people to behave like lunatics.

Whether a major character is depicted as a hero, a villain, or an antihero depends on the storyteller's point of view. For example, the soldiers who are fighting for "our" side are considered heroes, while the enemy soldiers are typically considered villains. As my husband often says, "No army ever went to war believing that God was on the other side." Of course, in Homer's Iliad, the great men on both sides of the Trojan War were depicted as heroic. The ancient Greeks believed that there were many gods, and that the gods were often in conflict with each other. Thus, Homer could view human wars as an extension of the family squabbles of the Olympian gods. For that reason, his audience could easily feel admiration for heroic Trojans as well as heroic Greeks.

Many fictional characters have supernatural powers. Others are more or less realistic. However, any type of character can serve the purpose of teaching moral lessons. What kind of character traits make someone good? What kind of flaws can a person have and still be good? What kinds of character traits make someone bad? What kind of redeeming qualities might even a bad person have? (To redeem something means to make it acceptable.) What kinds of sins are forgivable? You can learn a lot about a society by studying its heroes and its villains.

The ancient Greeks and Romans gave a lot of thought to the question of how a man ought to behave. They felt that a man should be a good citizen. He should be trustworthy: strong, brave, and reliable during wartime and honest and companionable during peacetime. The characteristics of a good man were called virtues, after the Roman word *vir*, which meant man. Eventually, the word *virtue* was used to refer to good characteristics in general. The ancient Greeks and Romans also thought a lot about the things that a man should not do. These were called vices. The word was derived from the Latin word *vitium*, which mean failing or defect.

Some of the heroes from ancient Greek literature would not be considered heroic today, because of changes in attitudes about morality. For example, the main theme of Homer's Iliad is the wrath of Achilles. Yet to a modern audience, Achilles' wrath comes across as peevish. If Achilles were in a modern army, his refusal to fight would have been dereliction of duty. Even the cause of Achilles' wrath might make modern audiences uneasy. Achilles was insulted because he did not get to take his pick of the female prisoners of war, who became sex slaves. Achilles returned to the battle only because Patroklos, a man with whom Achilles presumably had a sexual relationship, was killed in his stead.

Likewise, a modern audience would have limited sympathy for Odysseus, the protagonist of the Odyssey. When Odysseus finally makes his way home from the Trojan War, he finds that his wife is being wooed by many suitors, who all believe that Odysseus died in the war. Rather than simply revealing himself and sending them packing, Odysseus kills them. Also, the audience is supposed to feel sympathy for Odysseus, who has been held captive far from his home. Yet we are supposed to think that it is okay for Odysseus to keep slaves—who are likewise being held far from their homes, by Odysseus himself! Modern audiences might be repelled by this double standard. However, Homer's audience accepted it because Odysseus was supposedly a descendant of one of the Olympian gods. As a result, he had some special privileges.

Odysseus and Achilles did many scandalous things that would be illegal today. As a result, they are unsatisfying as heroes to a modern audience. We want our heroes to be good, but how should we decide what is good? Should we turn to religion or to secular philosophy to answer those questions? Plato dealt with that question in the Socratic dialogue Euthyphro. The dialogue was between Socrates and a man named Euthyphro. Euthyphro believed that he had a clear understanding of piety, which means dutifulness in religion. In contrast, Socrates was about to be brought into court to be tried on charges of impiety.

In the dialogue, Socrates asks Euthyphro to tell him what makes pious things pious. Euthyphro says that piety is what is pleasing to all of the gods. After asking a series of other questions, Socrates poses the pair of questions called the Euthyphro Dilemma. Monotheists state it as follows: Are moral acts good because they are willed by God, or are they willed by God because they are good? If things that are good are good only because God commands them, then morality means just following orders. There are no moral principles besides obedience. But if that were true, then what does it mean to say that God is good? Yet if God commands good things because they are good, then human beings might be able to think through the moral principles for themselves. If that were true, why would human beings need divine commandments?

The question of whether something is a virtue or a vice can be difficult. The answer may depend on the situation. For example, we usually think that truth telling is good and lying is bad. Yet sometimes it would be better to lie. For example, if a man with senile dementia keeps asking where his wife is, it would be kinder to say that she is out getting her hair done, rather than continually reminding him that she is dead. The branch of philosophy that deals with questions of right and wrong is called ethics. Philosophers and theologians from various traditions have written about virtues and vices. Despite differences in theology, thinkers from many different traditions have come to some surprisingly similar conclusions. One is a consensus that pride can be dangerous and that humility can be an admirable quality.

In Roman Catholic theology, pride is one of the seven capital sins. The others are lust, gluttony, greed, sloth, wrath, and envy. The word *capital* refers to the head, as in the head (source) of a river. The capital sins are forms of self-worship that are a source of sinful behavior. For example, lust can lead to adultery and greed can lead to theft. The seven capital sins are sometimes called the seven deadly sins because they are believed to destroy the life of grace and charity within a person. Each of the seven capital sins has an opposing heavenly virtue.

Many philosophers and theologians have considered pride (*superbia*) to be the worst of the capital sins because it is the source of the others. According to St. Isidore of Seville, "A man is said to be proud if he wishes to appear above (super) what he really is." A related concept is vainglory, which is excessive elation or pride over one's own achievements, abilities, etc. The opposite of pride is humility. Humility means the act of lowering oneself in relation to others or at least having a clear perspective and respect for one's position in a given context.

Lust, gluttony, greed, and envy are forms of uncontrolled desire. Although we often use the word *lust* to refer to sexual desire, the sin of lust could also refer to uncontrolled desire for money, food, fame, and power. The opposite of lust is chastity, which meant moral wholesomeness. In modern usage, people often use the word *chastity* to mean sexual abstinence. However, it was really intended to mean the abstinence from illicit sex, such as extramarital sex.

Today, many people use *gluttony* to mean overconsumption of food. However, gluttony originally meant any kind of overconsumption or waste. In particular, it implied that someone was taking more than his or her fair share. The opposite of gluttony is temperance. Temperance means the practice of self-control, moderation, and deferred gratification.

Greed has also been called avarice, cupidity, and covetousness. Like lust and gluttony, it involves excessive desire. However, greed refers specifically to an excessive desire for material possessions. The opposite of greed is charity. Originally, charity meant far more than benevolent giving. It also encompassed generosity and self-sacrifice.

Envy is an uncontrolled desire for someone else's traits, status, abilities, or rewards. Jealousy is a related concept. If you are envious of someone, you want what they have: their looks, their money, their talents, etc. If you are jealous of someone, you have bad feelings toward the person who has the things you desire. The opposite of envy is benevolence, which means unselfish love and voluntary kindness.

Wrath means a desire for vengeance. The opposite of wrath is patience, which means resolving conflicts and injustice peacefully, instead of through violence.

Of course, the seven capital sins are not the only kinds of problems that can give rise to bad behavior. Ignorance (lack of knowledge), stupidity (poor skills in problem solving), and fear can also lead to bad behavior. They may be viewed as personal weaknesses, but they are not forms of self-worship.

Many modern psychologists point out that high self-esteem is not always bad. Nor did the ancient Greeks think that pride was always a sin. Aristotle argued that whether pride or humility was a virtue or a vice depended on whether it was an accurate reflection of a man's worth. Aristotle used the word *megalopsychia* (magnanimity, or greatness of soul) to describe the kind of pride that was appropriate for a great man. He felt that a potentially great man would not live up to his potential unless he had *megalopsychia*. (Aristotle was the tutor to the boy who grew up to become Alexander the Great.) Aristotle also thought that lower self-esteem was a virtue for a lesser man. "If he both is and thinks himself to be worthy of small things he is not proud but temperate."

In contrast, Aristotle thought that inappropriately high or low self-esteem was a vice. "A person who thinks himself worthy of great things when he is unworthy of them is vain, whereas a person who thinks himself worthy of less than he is worthy of is pusillanimous." (Pusillanimous means lacking courage and resolve.)

Aristotle thought that a great man should be moderately pleased to receive well-earned honors from good people, but he should despise honors that are given casually or on trifling grounds. (In other words, he should not seek narcissistic supply from submissive underlings.) Aristotle thought that a great man should be dignified around the great and the good, but he should be unassuming around people of the lower classes. It is a difficult and lofty thing to be superior to great people, but it would be vulgar to show off in front of humble people.

This concept of megalopsychia raises an important issue. Whether someone is being virtuous or vicious is often a judgment call. That judgment is made in a social context, and it is based on the concepts of virtue and vice that are accepted within that social context. People are considered vain if they have a higher self-esteem than other people think that they deserve. People are considered greedy if they want more than other people think they deserve. People are considered gluttonous if they consume more than other people think they should have. Perhaps we have an instinctual bias that tells us that lower-ranking individuals deserve less. As a result, poor people would be criticized for vanity or greed for doing things that would not raise eyebrows if a rich person did them. The Tulsa Riot of 1921 teaches us a grim lesson about how hierarchical societies can react when low-caste people acquire a little bit of property and prestige.

Chapter 5

The Struggle for Rank

~

A man who thinks that he is superior to women is called a misogynist. White people who think that they are superior to people of color are called racists. When a white man thinks that he is superior to other white men, he is called a narcissist. All of these terms are used to describe people with a false belief in their own superiority. This kind of problem is difficult to solve because human beings are always involved in some sort of struggle for social rank. Unless you are the last human being on earth, you will end up having to deal with this problem.

The title character in Daniel Defoe's novel *Robinson Crusoe* was stranded alone on a desert island. If you live alone on a desert island, like Robinson Crusoe, you do not need to worry about social rank. If you are the only person, then you never have to argue about who owns what. Also, you have nobody to boss around, and there is nobody to boss you around. So there are no power struggles. If there are no other people, you do not have to worry about what other people think of you—you do not have to worry about prestige. As soon as even one other person shows up, the three p's of property, power, and prestige start to become important. You have to work out how to share things. You have to decide who can or must do what. Also, you would probably want the other person to respect you.

Whenever there are two or more persons in a society, there will be social conflicts. Societies can be judged according to how they resolve these conflicts, and how the strong treat the weak. A just society has fair and reasonable ways to resolve conflicts over property. A just society would allow an individual to rise to a position of political power as long as he or she serves the public interest. A just society would also allow people to gain prestige through socially meaningful achievements, such as productive work or humanitarian work or achievements in the arts and sciences.

Even the best possible society will inevitably have some sort of hierarchy, and the existence of a hierarchy is not necessarily a bad thing. Personally, I would not mind if the people who are willing to work harder than everyone else, and those who have discovered or created something particularly important, are allowed to earn more money than other people. A society can benefit if it provides incentives for productive behavior. Also, I feel that high-status jobs should go to the individuals who are best able to do those jobs, instead of being given to people with the right pedigree or the best political connections. I want positions of public trust to be given to people who have shown that they are trustworthy. I want honors such as the Pulitzer Prize to be awarded for truly great work, and to the person who actually did the work. A system in which property, power, and prestige are given only to those who deserve them is called a meritocracy.

In contrast, an unjust society would allow idle people to inherit enormous fortunes while hardworking people earn practically nothing for their labor. An unjust society would allow the ruthless to exploit the weak. It would put untrustworthy people in a position of public trust and then fail to hold them accountable for their misdeeds. An unjust society would give special privileges to people who have done nothing to deserve them, while depriving others of basic human rights. An unjust society would grant celebrity status to people who have accomplished nothing of value, while failing to honor people who have made important contributions to society. Unjust societies remain unjust for two reasons: the powerful use every resource at their command to maintain the existing social order, and the weak remain weak because they do not stand together to demand justice.

Modern societies are far from perfect. But most modern societies are far better in most respects than they were a hundred years ago. The improvements were the result of reforms made by people who refused to accept injustice. As Frank Kameny, one of the pioneers of the Gay Rights Movement, explained, "I simply wasn't going to adjust myself to society. With considerable success, I have managed to adjust society to me. And society is much better off for the adjustments I've administered." To a large extent, these advances were made possible by widespread literacy. As Harvard professor Steven Pinker puts it, fiction is empathy technology. Reading fiction allows you to see the world from someone else's point of view. Thus, it helps people develop understanding and compassion.

Even small groups, such as families, have a social hierarchy. The parents control the resources (property) and have the physical power to set rules and force young children to obey them. Yet if parents choose to rule by force, their status will erode over time. As the children grow stronger, the parents must rely increasingly on negotiation, as opposed to force. To maintain their status, parents must therefore depend increasingly on prestige rather than on power. In other words, they must earn their children's respect.

Just as societies can be judged as just or unjust, families can be judged as functional or dysfunctional on the basis of how the strong treat the weak. In the famous opening line to his novel *Anna Karenina*, Leo Tolstoy wrote, "All happy families are alike. Each unhappy family is unhappy in its own way." Yet most unhappy families are unhappy for the same reason: adults who misbehave.

In a functional family, the members love and respect each other, and the strong care for the weak. Conflicts occur, but they are resolved peacefully. In a dysfunctional family, in contrast, some members disrespect others. The strong neglect or abuse the weak (children, the elderly, and the disabled). Conflicts are blown up out of proportion. Instead of resolving conflicts, the family members hold grudges. Often, the underlying problem in a dysfunctional family is an adult with a drug or alcohol problem, an untreated mental illness, or simply a warped idea of how family members should treat each other. Typically, the other adults in the family are in a co-dependent relationship with that deeply flawed adult. Thus, they allow the abuse, neglect, and pointless strife to go on. Children who grow up in dysfunctional families often go on to repeat the same patterns in their own families. They simply do not know any better way to relate to other people.

The pointless strife within a family often results from the struggle for dominance. Happy families have a dominance hierarchy, but it serves a good purpose. It allows the strong to protect and serve the weak. It allows older and wiser family members to guide the young and foolish ones. These power relationships will change over time, as the babies grow up and the parents' generation enters its so-called second childhood.

The adults in a dysfunctional family either do not understand or do not care about their children's feelings. Dysfunctional parents often use their power for their own gratification, rather than for the good of others. They may abuse or ridicule others because they enjoy humiliating other people. They may sexually abuse others because they care only about their own gratification. The ancient Greeks used the word *hubris* specifically to refer to a sort of crime, often sexual, in which a powerful person humiliates a less-powerful person. The ancient Greeks believed that the gods punish people for acts of hubris.

The parents in a dysfunctional family often play favorites. This problem, which psychologists call differential parenting, is the main theme of the fairytale of Cinderella. A woman wants her stepdaughter to serve as a scullery maid while her biological daughters get to go to the ball to meet the prince. The stepdaughter goes by a nickname (Aschenputtel in the German version and Cinderella in the French version) that mocks her for being dirty from handling ashes and cinders while cleaning the fireplaces. But thanks to help from a fairy godmother, the unloved stepdaughter is able to go to the ball and eventually marry the prince. In the folk versions of the story, her stepsisters meet a gruesome end.

A fairytale stepmother does not have a mother's love for her stepchildren. In real life, many dysfunctional parents treat some or all of their biological children like fairytale stepchildren. Dysfunctional parents often play favorites with one or more of their children for no good reason. Sometimes, they care too much about one child, or even a pet, who is perceived to have special needs. Meanwhile, they have little or no concern for other children's feelings and needs. Often, a dysfunctional parent decides that one child can do no wrong, while another can do no right. Favoritism may also be based on birth order or gender. The dysfunctional parent may prefer the firstborn or the baby of the family, or the only girl or the only boy. Sometimes, the dysfunctional parent prefers the children who are better looking or more athletic. Sometimes, the dysfunctional parent simply prefers girls to boys, or vice versa.

There are many ways for parents to play favorites with their children. A parent may lavish attention, affection, and gifts on some children, while neglecting or abusing others. Sometimes, the favored child simply gets less abuse than the others get. In some families, the favored children are encouraged to take part in the abuse of the unlucky child who serves as a scapegoat for the family's problems.

Unfortunately, even good parents must sometimes treat their children unequally. Newborns need more care than older children do. Sick or disabled children need more care than healthy children do. While struggling to care for a sick or disabled child, parents sometimes fail to meet the needs of their healthy children. Also, parents might not be able to afford the same kind of education for all of their children. Thus, they may make that kind of investment only for the child who seems most promising. This kind of differential parenting may breed resentment, but it is often unavoidable. In contrast, dysfunctional parents play favorites for no good reason.

The adults in many dysfunctional families are continually fighting over religion, politics, money, or material possessions. This discord results from two basic causes: mutual disrespect and poor social skills. They do not care about each other's feelings, and they do not know how to have reasonable, productive discussions. Sometimes, the participants in these fights actually enjoy hurting the other person's feelings. Typically, the participants do not know how to learn from other people or to settle disagreements amicably and productively. In particular, they lack the basic skills that are needed for two important types of conversation: dialectic and negotiation.

Dialectic is a process in which people pool their knowledge and correct each other's errors in thinking. Through this process, individuals can learn more than they could learn independently. The purpose of dialectic is to seek the truth. In contrast, the purpose of negotiation is to resolve conflicts. The goal is to find some solution that is acceptable to everyone involved. The members of a dysfunctional family do not pool their knowledge and learn from each other, and they do not work or play well with each other. Instead, they peck at each other like chickens.

Like all other social animals, a flock of hens establishes its own Order of Precedence, called a pecking order. Hens fight for social position within their flock by pecking (using their beak to poke or bite other hens). At first, the hens in a newly assembled flock will have many fights over small things. But through those fights, each hen learns which hens are stronger than she is and which ones are weaker than she is. As a result, the flock will quickly develop its pecking order.

At the top of the pecking order is the toughest, meanest hen. She will not hesitate to peck any other hen who steps out of line. Other hens will generally defer to her, while feeling free to peck at the hens who are weaker than they are. Once the hens can predict the likely outcome of any particular fight, they do not have to bother to fight. Often, hens will simply defer to larger hens, without bothering to fight it out. Once the pecking order has been established, there is generally a lot less fighting within the flock. As a result, the hens conserve energy and reduce their risk of injury. Of course, in a badly managed flock, the higher-ranking hens can peck the lowest-ranking hens to death.

The term *pecking order* is commonly used to describe dominance hierarchies in human societies as well as in flocks of chickens. The people who are at the top of the pecking order may use any number of strategies and tactics to get what they want. They may viciously attack lower-ranking individuals for real or imagined offenses. Public executions (including lynchings and stonings) and public rituals of humiliation (such as gang rapes) serve the purpose of demonstrating that the high-ranking people have power over other people.

An abusive parent can attack a child directly. Parents can also abuse a child indirectly, by allowing other people to torment that child. In a society, the high-ranking people often delegate this policing task to lower-ranking people. The rulers of a terror state give the police and paramilitaries a free hand to use force and terror as political weapons against the lower classes. For example, Stetson Kennedy revealed in his book *The Klan Unmasked* that in the 1940s and 1950s, some wealthy industrialists were providing financial backing as well as political protection to the Ku Klux Klan. In exchange, the Klan used a combination of propaganda and terror to suppress labor unions and to reinforce the system of racial hierarchy.

Hens have simple needs. They need food, water, comfortable places to sit, and safe places to lay their eggs. They use simple tactics when they fight over those things. Human beings have much bigger brains and much more complicated needs. As a result, human beings have a lot more to fight about, and they can use subtle tactics and sophisticated strategies. Yet one important principle can apply to both species. Like hens, human beings often engage in petty squabbles over minor things in order to compete for social rank. Perhaps they feel that if they work out the pecking order over petty things, then they will not risk injury by fighting over things that really matter. Yet many people will refuse to engage in petty squabbles but will stick up for themselves when the stakes are high enough.

Hens cannot talk, but human beings often view seemingly casual conversations as some sort of struggle for dominance. Narcissists may be particularly likely to view ordinary conversations as an opportunity to struggle for dominance. Linguist Deborah Tannen has explained that men are often more aware of this hidden purpose of conversation than women are. Men are more likely than women to view conversation as a contest in which they have to compete for the "one-up" position or keep other people from pushing them around.

This need to maintain the "one-up" position explains something that puzzled many women back in the days before nearly everyone had global positioning system navigational devices. Many men would refuse to stop and ask for directions, even when they were clearly lost. Tannen explained that many men would rather drive around aimlessly than put themselves in a "one-down" position relative to a stranger by asking for directions. To most women, that would seem to be a silly reason to refuse to ask for directions. (I once met a man who did not hesitate to ask for directions when lost. So I married him.) Yet a lack of awareness and concern for social dominance can put women at a disadvantage in many situations. By being "nice," they may be allowing themselves to be pushed into a subordinate social position.

Narcissists try to occupy a higher position in the pecking order than the people around them feel that they deserve. As a result, the narcissist may end up attacking many other people. If someone in your family or at work is narcissistic or has some other serious personality disorder, you may feel that you are "walking on eggs" a lot of the time. (The implication is that you have to step very softly to avoid breaking the shells.) If you do or say anything that puts the narcissist in a one-down position, the narcissist may feel narcissistic injury and respond with narcissistic rage.

Unfortunately, by walking on eggs around the narcissist, you are exhibiting the submissive behavior that reinforces the narcissism. The narcissist learns through experience that temper tantrums are an effective way to solve problems. Indeed, many people will choose to defer to a narcissist rather than risking a pointless squabble, at least when the stakes are small. Thus, the narcissist may feel gratified and emboldened by a series of tiny victories. To prevent the narcissist's obnoxious behavior from escalating, you may need to draw a firm line over a seemingly trivial issue. The problem is not the stakes in the conflict but the narcissist's behavior. Because of their poor social skills, narcissists seldom realize the true cost of their tiny victories: low prestige. Ironically, narcissists' rages and tantrums may actually prevent the narcissists from achieving the social standing that they so desperately desire.

Narcissists want to be in the one-up position (smarter, prettier, more popular, richer, more accomplished, more admired, etc.) relative to people whom they consider to be beneath them on the social ladder. For bigots, this social ladder is based partly on gender and race. A bigoted white man might not mind being beneath some other white men in the social order, as long as he is above all women and all black men. He might be annoyed at the higher-ranking white men for being snobs, but he may become violent if his wife or children step out of line or if a black person gets "uppity."

For example, in the novel *The Adventures of Huckleberry Finn*, Huck's drunken and dissolute father ("Pap") resented that Huck was becoming better educated than he was, and that Huck had money that Pap could not take away from him. Pap was positively infuriated that in Ohio, a "free n—r" (although one almost as white as a white man) was allowed to have fine clothes and a silver-headed cane. People said that the man was a college professor, and that the man was even allowed to vote when he was home. When Pap heard that such men could vote, Pap vowed never to vote again. Attitudes like Pap's led to lynchings and to pogroms such as the Tulsa Riot of 1921.

If you had been born into a feudal society, your social position would have been largely determined by your birth. The identity of your parents mattered, as did your sex and your birth order. First-born legitimate sons of the titled nobility would inherit their father's title. The younger sons had to seek their fortune in the church or the military. Daughters of the nobility or even the landed gentry had a relatively high social status; but to maintain it, they had to marry well. In contrast, the children of serfs were likely to remain serfs. Likewise, a child born to an enslaved woman was also a slave, even though many of those children were the offspring of the master of the house. Thus, under slavery, men often sold their own sons and daughters as if they were cattle.

In contrast, modern societies give many people many opportunities for social advancement. Many of these opportunities come through education. The right sort of education can allow you to have the kind of high-status job that would pay well and give you prestige. Yet when I was a child, a shockingly high percentage of my classmates did not want to engage with their schoolwork. In fact, I was often mocked and shunned for taking an interest in what we were learning in school. Aristotle wrote, "All men by nature desire to know." Yet many of my classmates thought that it was far more important to be ignorant and "cool" than to prepare for their own future.

When I was a child, I was mocked for being freakishly intelligent and for knowing facts about history and science and so on. Up until I was in my mid 20s, I would cringe whenever somebody complimented me for being smart or knowledgeable. Yet now that I am middle aged, an astounding number of people seem to think that they are far smarter and better informed about everything than I am. For example, when my first book (*Not Trivial: How Studying the Traditional Liberal Arts Can Set You Free*) went to press, my friends were thrilled. Some highly educated people (college professors, psychotherapists, and editors) gave me encouragement and useful critiques of the manuscript before it went to press. Many of them ended up buying several copies to give to their relatives and friends and students. However, many less-educated people had a completely different reaction.

When I mentioned that I had written a book about educational policy, several of my acquaintances instantly began telling me that the things that I wrote in the book were wrong. These were not people whose opinion I had sought out. They had no teaching experience, and they knew nothing about educational policy. Besides, they had not yet read my book, so they were not in any position to give me useful feedback. Instead, they were just trying to establish their dominance over me. As I listened to their attacks, I was stunned by how poor their skills in logic and rhetoric were. In the book, I lamented that the public schools in the United States had neglected to teach logic and rhetoric. Yet I am always disappointed to see that the problem is as bad as I suspected.

In *Not Trivial*, I explain a problem called the Dunning-Kruger effect. David Dunning and Justin Kruger are psychologists who studied how people rate their own abilities. Dunning and Kruger found that people who have poor intellectual and interpersonal skills tend to be unaware of their own incompetence. People with the worst skills tended to rate themselves as above average. People with poor skills cannot spot their own mistakes. As a result, they cannot judge their own level of skill. Nor can they judge other people's level of skill. For that reason, incompetent people are generally unaware that they are incompetent.

The solution to this problem is simple: give the unskilled people some training in the skills they lack. As their skills improve, their ability to judge their skills improves. So does their ability to judge other people's skills. As they become more skilled, their overconfidence decreases. In other words, as their skills improve, they become more humble, less narcissistic. At the opposite end of the scale, people with excellent skills tend to underrate themselves. They become acutely aware of their own mistakes, and they find it hard to imagine that other people lack skills that they take for granted. In other words, incompetent people tend to be overconfident, while highly skilled people tend to be humble.

Dunning and Kruger's results lead to a disturbing conclusion. If you give children a genuinely good education, you may deflate their self-esteem. However, it is better for a person to be skilled yet humble, rather than ignorant and arrogant.

Because of the Dunning-Kruger effect, ignorant people do not realize that they are ignorant. Nor are they able to judge whether someone else is knowledgeable and wise. You can see this phenomenon on the Internet, where uneducated people try to "debunk" the work of the world's greatest scientists. It would be comical if it were not sad.

At practically every Web site that allows comments, the comment threads quickly become dominated by Internet trolls: arrogant, foolish people with appallingly bad manners. Regrettably, the Internet gives people who otherwise have few social outlets the opportunity to engage in bullying and inflammatory behavior without any consequences. I do not tolerate such behavior on my own Web sites. I remove comments that contain false statements about scientific topics, as well as comments that are abusive or pointlessly argumentative. Like a judge in a court of law, I allow only qualified experts to serve as expert witnesses, and I insist on decorum.

Commenters are often surprised to find that I deleted their offensive comments. Often, they seem to feel that their comments were actually a form of meaningful intellectual exchange. Sometimes, they complain that I have deprived them of their Constitutional right to free expression. They do not grasp that the U.S. Constitution forbids *governments* in the United States from censoring speech or other forms of expression. The Constitution does not force scientific journals to publish articles that do not meet the editors' scientific standards. Nor would the Constitution grant someone the right to enter your house to scream insults at you.

Internet trolls seem to want admiration. They want other people to think they are cool. Unfortunately, they keep using the tactics that worked on the playground when they were 9 years old: willful ignorance and bad manners. They may believe that they are winning a long series of tiny victories, but they are just making fools of themselves. As a result, they lose prestige rather than gaining it.

Most people would like to have the three p's of property, power, and prestige. However, some people want those things more than other people do. Ambitious people are willing to work harder and make greater sacrifices in order to achieve those things. Some ambitious people are willing to stick to honest and decent means to earn a high social rank. Others are willing to step on other people as they claw their way to the top. Unfortunately, many ambitious people lack the talents, self-discipline, and interpersonal skills that they would need in order to achieve their goals honestly. As a result, they may use other kinds of tactics to achieve their goals. Thus, they can become dangerous. The desire for power and control can lead to appalling behavior. It is the underlying cause of domestic violence and workplace bullying. It is an underlying cause of mass shootings.

For years, many policymakers believed that they could solve the problem of domestic violence by sending the offenders to anger-management classes. When my sister, who has a degree in psychology, heard about that, she was disgusted. She pointed out that the offenders were not beating up their boss at work. Instead, they were beating up their wife and kids at home. Also, the abuse was often cold and premeditated, not the product of blind rage. The problem clearly was not anger. It was the offender's sense that he or she had the right to use violence against people beneath him or her in the pecking order. My sister was right. Research eventually showed that anger management programs are ineffective at decreasing domestic violence. In fact, the anger management programs are so ineffective that the U.S. Department of Justice's Office of Violence Against Women will not allow its grants to be used to fund them.

Like domestic abusers, the bullies who stalk the halls at school and at work are also struggling for social rank, and for the power that goes with it. Like predatory animals, school bullies usually attack the weak: children who are unable or unwilling to fight back and have no allies to protect them. School bullies generally want control and attention, but they do not know acceptable ways to obtain either one. Thus, the school bullies should be regarded as socially incompetent, rather than evil.

Although school bullies often pick targets with apparent weaknesses, such as children who have physical or mental disabilities and children who have no friends, adult bullies in the workplace often pick targets who have strengths or other good qualities that make the bully look bad in comparison. Often, the bully picks the most skilled person in the workgroup, someone with high ethical standards and good interpersonal skills. Sometimes, the bullying is part of some Machiavellian attempt to compete for a promotion or merely to avoid being laid off in a time of cutbacks. Other times, the bullying is motivated by pure jealousy. Like Snow White, the bully's target may have no idea that he or she is being targeted.

The struggle for rank within a school or a workplace can descend into violence. This violence occurs because the perpetrators have not completed their coming-of-age character arc. Violence is a perfectly natural way for toddlers to try to achieve their goals or simply to express their emotions. Toddlers hit. They bite. They scratch. They pinch. People who study violent behavior in toddlers generally count the number of offenses per hour of observation. As children grow, they develop better ways to express themselves and to solve problems. As a result, they become less and less violent. People who study violent behavior in adolescents may count the number of offenses per month. Yet even though individuals become less prone to violence as they mature, they grow stronger. Yet as they grow stronger, their violence becomes increasingly serious, even deadly. The easy availability of firearms, and especially automatic weapons, has made the potential consequences even more deadly. The result has been a rash of mass shootings.

Starting in the 1980s, there has been an epidemic of mass shootings in the United States. In many of these events, the shooting ended with the suicide of the shooter. During the 1980s and 1990s, several mass shootings were committed by disgruntled postal workers. Thus, someone who committed such an offense was described as going postal. This outbreak of violence in the Postal Service occurred in the wake of changes in management. The shooters in these cases typically had no criminal record or history of mental illness. Instead, these shooters seemed to be responding to bullying and humiliating treatment by management, which occurred in the wake of changes in how the Postal Service was being run. Since then, there have been mass shootings at other public places, including high schools and colleges, churches, and movie theaters, and even at elementary schools. The easy access to firearms, and especially to large-magazine automatic weapons, which tend to raise the death toll, is clearly part of the problem. Yet we must also look at the psychology of the shooters.

Why would someone commit a mass shooting? The explanations seem to vary from case to case. Some perpetrators clearly have a brain disease that could explain their behavior. One example is Charles Whitman, the former marine sharpshooter who used the clock tower at the University of Texas at Austin as a sniper's nest on August 1, 1966. Before the shooting, Whitman had been having increasing difficulty in controlling his emotions. Autopsy showed that Whitman had a tumor in an area of the brain associated with outbursts of rage. Another example is James Huberty, the perpetrator of the mass shooting at a McDonald's restaurant in San Ysidro, California on July 18, 1984. His autopsy revealed no alcohol or drugs, but his body contained shockingly high levels of lead and cadmium, which he probably absorbed during his career as a welder. Cadmium toxicity is known to cause mental problems and violent behavior. Yet another example is Sylvia Seegrist, who shot 10 people at a shopping mall in Springfield, Pennsylvania on October 30, 1985. Seegrist had a long history of violent outbursts and had been hospitalized numerous times for her severe case of paranoid schizophrenia. At the time of the shooting, she was so out of touch with reality that she did not understand that the three people she killed would stay dead.

Some of the perpetrators of mass shootings were either unable to tell right from wrong or unable to control their own behavior. Nevertheless, many people who have committed mass shootings or serial murders seem to have freely chosen to do something that they know is wrong. Most of the perpetrators of mass shootings and serial killings are young men who have been jilted, fired, or humiliated. The youthful offenders tend to be boys—usually white but sometimes Asian—who felt rejected and despised. Nevertheless, most of these youths had at least some friends. Many commentators suspect that the problem is a malignant form of narcissism. Many of the perpetrators publish manifestos, in which they complain that they are not getting the popularity, power, and sex that they deserve. Their goal is typically to commit suicide in such a way that makes them infamous. I suspect that many political assassins also want to achieve notoriety. It is an ugly form of prestige, but it is prestige nevertheless. If they cannot inspire admiration, they can at least inspire fear.

Assassination of public officials is rare in the United States because it is ineffective as a political strategy. Because of our system of checks and balances, power is so widely distributed that the death of even a high-ranking official would have little effect on government policy. In fact, the public's sympathy for the victim of such an attack could actually increase public support for the victim's political agenda. For example, Congress passed important civil rights legislation in the wake of John F. Kennedy's assassination. Thus, it is likely that most of the people who try to kill public figures in the United States are pursuing some personal agenda, rather than using assassination as a political instrument. Their main goal is probably notoriety. They want to become household names. Unfortunately, they often achieve that goal.

Often, the assassins are found to have compiled a list of potential targets who were chosen simply because they are famous, not because they were united by any political cause. For example, seven months before the John F. Kennedy assassination, Lee Harvey Oswald had attempted to assassinate a prominent man whose politics were far different from Kennedy's: Maj. Gen. Edwin "Ted" Walker, USA, Ret., who was an ardent segregationist and a member of the John Birch Society, whose members considered Kennedy to be a traitor.

I do think that Oswald shot Kennedy and that he acted alone. Oswald had decided many years earlier that he wanted to become famous. Also, he had already tried to assassinate some other famous person. It was sheer bad luck that Kennedy's motorcade was scheduled to pass by the building where Oswald worked. Vincent Bugliosi, the famed prosecutor of Charles Manson, documented that all of the forensic evidence points in Oswald's direction. But even if you are not an expert on ballistics or other forensic sciences, just look at Oswald's facial expression in his mug shot. His face has clearly been bruised because of rough treatment by the police, but he looks smug. He does not look angry or frightened or confused, as I would expect a wrongly accused person to look. Oswald's brother commented that after his arrest, Lee Harvey Oswald looked like a cat that has just swallowed the canary. He looks smug because he had finally succeeded in his lifelong goal of making a big mark on history—indeed, people are still talking about him more than half a century later. If mass shooters really are being motivated by a desire for infamy, we must stop giving it to them. We must stop broadcasting their names and their photographs. We must stop feeding the narcissists. Unfortunately, that is an impossible dream in the era of the Internet.

As social animals, human beings are naturally inclined to struggle for social rank. The things that people do as part of such struggles can be judged in terms of their effectiveness as well as in terms of their morality. When we label someone as narcissistic, we are giving them failing grades in either or both domains. If someone has earned your respect, either through accomplishments or through virtuous behavior, you would not consider that person's high self-esteem to be narcissism. In contrast, if you feel that someone should be ashamed of him- or herself, then his or her high self-esteem may make you feel contempt. The label of narcissism is an expression of that contempt.

Chapter 6

Art and Science

The members of any group of social animals will struggle amongst themselves for social rank. Hens mainly use their beaks for that purpose. Yet some other species use inventiveness as a way to earn rank. To woo their mates, a male bowerbird will build and decorate a lair. Only the males with the most spectacular lairs will succeed in attracting mates. Of course, human beings have a crucial ability that no other species has: language. Human beings must have developed the ability to use language more than fifty thousand years ago. About five thousand years ago, some people in what is now Iraq learned to use marks impressed into soft clay as a way to record language. In other words, they invented writing. The concept of writing then spread to Egypt. The idea may also have been carried to China, or the Chinese may have come up with it on their own. A few thousand years later, some people in Central America came up with the same idea on their own.

The development of writing was a watershed moment in human history. It allowed people to hear from the past and speak to the future. Modern scholars can still read texts that were written several thousand years ago. Writing allowed human beings to preserve poetry and dramatic works, thus creating literature. In fact, some scholars believe that the Greek alphabet, which was the first one with vowels, was developed for recording the poetry of Homer. Yet that simple, clear system of recording speech enabled the Greeks to make and share great advances in philosophy and the sciences.

When I was a toddler, my parents read many books to me. Shortly after my fourth birthday, I decided that I wanted to read books by my-self. By analyzing the spelling of the rhyming words in my Dr. Seuss books, I realized that writing was simply a way to use letters to repre-sent the sounds in spoken words. That discovery enabled me to read books on my own. As a result, I read countless books while I was grow-ing up. Early on, I realized that some stories are true and some are make-believe. Any story that involved magic or talking animals had to be make-believe. Yet some stories were clearly make-believe, even though they had no magical elements. As I grew older, I realized that no story can be perfectly true. All stories are told from a particular point of view. Even if I were trying to tell a perfectly true story, that story would be shaped by what I knew and how I felt. For example, I might include details that made sense to me and leave out the details that did not seem important. Yet those details might seem important to someone else.

Human beings are the only living species that can tell stories. Of course, other animals can communicate with each other. Much of the communication in the animal kingdom is done through chemical sig-nals, such as pheromones. Some of the communication is through be-havior. When a foraging honeybee returns to her hive, she instinctively does a dance that tells other honeybees where she found her load of nectar and pollen. Animals can even communicate with each other through vocalization or other sounds. Puppies cry for their mother, and older dogs bark and growl. Prairie dogs make warning calls that warn other prairie dogs about predators. They can even make a specific call that represents a coyote, as opposed to a domestic dog. But no other animal can explain what happened yesterday, or what it plans to do tomorrow. To be able to do that, a creature must understand certain grammatical principles that only human beings can grasp. (I explain those underlying grammatical principles in detail in *Not Trivial: How Studying the Traditional Liberal Arts Can Set You Free*.)

Only human beings can tell stories, and all human societies value storytelling. By telling stories, we share information that can save lives. In traditional societies, young people hold their elders in high esteem because of the stories that old people can tell. Back in the mid 1990s, I spent some time in the Bahamas. While I was there, an elderly Bahamian man told me an exciting story. When he was a child, a hurricane passed through the Bahamas. At some point during the storm, he and his friends noticed that the ocean had retreated from their island. So he and his friends walked out onto the reef and started picking up shell-fish. While they were out there, an elderly woman came running down to the beach. She told the boys to run as fast as they could to high ground. She knew that the water was likely to come back in a mighty rush. The boys obeyed her and thus avoided drowning. That event took place in the 1920s. He told it to me in the 1990s. I just told it to you now.

In the old days, old people were valued as the storehouses of knowledge. But today, even young people can serve that role if they are well educated. On December 26, 2004, a 10-year-old girl named Tilly Smith was vacationing with her family at Maikhao Beach in Thailand. She had learned about tsunamis in school two weeks before. When she saw the early warning signs of a tsunami at the beach (water receding from the shoreline and frothing bubbles on the water's surface), she told her parents, who warned the other people on the beach and the hotel staff. As a result, the beach was evacuated. Unlike other beaches on the island that day, Maikhao Beach had no reported casualties. The people on Maikhao Beach that day were saved because some adults respected what a little girl had learned in school.

Stories help us teach important lessons about our environment and about other people. When we think, we often create stories in our own minds to help us make sense out of our experiences. In that sense, scientific theories are like stories. But like all stories, scientific theories contain some element of make-believe, typically in the form of over-simplification. Yet even a scientific theory that has some flaws can still be useful, if it allows us to make accurate predictions. The value of a scientific theory depends on the accuracy of the predictions it allows us to make.

I feel a bit sheepish about using storybook characters, such as Winne-the-Pooh, to explain how real people think and behave. Yet fictional characters can serve as models that can help us make sense out of the real world. In fact, many stories are written specifically to teach us lessons that will help us understand reality. Also, like the dead, story-book characters cannot sue me for libel if I say something unflattering about them. I read all of A. A. Milne's Pooh books when I was a child. As a result, I learned about depression from Eeyore and about mania from Tigger.

The study of literature can be of practical value because literature sometimes deals with themes and conflicts and aspects of character-ization that we are likely to encounter in real life. Thus, literature can provide models that can help us make sense out of our own experiences. Yet art does not always imitate life. Often, the elements of the story are chosen and shaped to serve artistic ends, rather than scientific ones. The story may be intended to thrill us or amuse us, as opposed to instruct-ing us or warning us. Thus, we can allow art to expand our minds and give shape to our thoughts; but if we really want to know what is going on in the real world, we must use science. The branch of science that deals most directly with narcissism is psychology, which is the study of the mind and behavior. Yet to study psychology, we must draw on many interrelated disciplines, starting with the classical liberal arts.

In my book *Not Trivial*, I explained that the ancient Greeks devel-oped a curriculum of seven basic subjects. The Romans called these subjects the liberal arts because they were considered appropriate for freeborn men, as opposed to slaves. The seven classical liberal arts in-cluded three verbal arts, called the trivium. The trivium consisted of grammar, logic, and rhetoric. Grammar is the study of how words are altered and combined to form meaningful sentences. Logic is the study of how sentences are combined to form arguments. Rhetoric is the art of persuasion. There were also four arts of number, space, and time. Together these four subjects made up the quadrivium. Mathematics is the study of number. Geometry is the study of number and space. Music is the study of number and time. Astronomy is the study of number, space, and time. By studying these seven subjects, the student learns to think rationally and to express him- or herself persuasively.

The liberal arts were highly valued in ancient Athens, which had a form of government that was called democracy, which means rule by the people. (In contrast, monarchy means rule by one person such as a king or dictator and aristocracy means rule by the "best people.") The liberal arts were also valued in ancient Rome, especially during the period of the Roman Republic. A republic is a society ruled by elected officials, rather than by someone who inherited power or gained power by force. Training in the liberal arts prepares a person to take a meaningful part in public affairs. Thus, the liberal arts have always been highly valued in societies with a democratic or republican system of government. They have always been repressed in societies in which the people are ruled by force rather than by reason.

In Western Europe, interest in the liberal arts declined during the Dark Ages that followed the collapse of Rome. But during the High Middle Ages (the 11th through 13th centuries), a new type of institution arose: the university. The first true university, the University of Bologna, was chartered by the City of Bologna, which is in northern Italy, in the year 1088. Other universities arose out of monastic and cathedral schools. The early universities embraced the classical liberal arts and other writings from the ancient Greeks and Romans. At the time, those writings were filtering back into Continental Europe from Ireland and from the Muslim countries.

The classical liberal arts curriculum was developed largely in ancient Athens, where it served the purpose of strengthening Athenian democracy. During the Renaissance, the wealthy families of northern Italy developed an enriched curriculum that they called the *studia humanitatis* or studies of humanity. The humanities included philosophy, history, literature, languages, and art. Like the classical liberal arts curriculum, the humanities curriculum of the Renaissance served a political purpose. It enabled the men and women of the ruling class to learn how to have productive and even pleasant discussions about practically any subject.

Philosophy is a broad subject. It can be broken down into several branches. For example, metaphysics deals with questions about the general features of reality, such as existence, time, the relationship between mind and body, and the relationship between cause and effect. One of the branches of metaphysics is ontology, which deals with questions of what is real as opposed to what is imaginary, and how to sort things into categories and hierarchies. Epistemology is another branch of metaphysics. It deals with the nature and scope of knowledge. It deals with questions of what can we know, how can we know it, and how sure can we be. Aesthetics is another branch of philosophy. It deals with questions of beauty and matters of taste and sentiment. Ethics or moral philosophy deals with questions of how to decide what is right and wrong.

In a serious study of narcissism, we must draw on many branches of philosophy. We must answer the ontological questions of what we mean by narcissism and how to decide whether a particular person is narcissistic. We must also deal with questions of ethics because we are concerned about how we think people ought to think and behave. We must also deal with questions of epistemology. What can we know about another person's thoughts and feelings? What can we really know about why people think and behave as they do? What kind of evidence would we need to test whether our hunches are correct?

The modern sciences grew out of what was originally called natural philosophy. Natural philosophy originally meant the study of nature, or things in the observable world (in contrast, mathematics deals with theoretical patterns, and theology deals with the supernatural). However, modern scientists are far different from the medieval natural philosophers. Not only do modern scientists have far more impressive equipment at their command, they also have more disciplined ways of working and thinking. Modern science can draw on any branch of philosophy except theology. (Although some scientists are religious, divine revelation does not count as scientific evidence.) In other words, modern scientists are expected to follow the scientific method.

In the scientific method, you first develop a theory about some aspect of the observable world. Next, you formulate some hypotheses that relate to that theory. Then, you then gather data through observation and experimentation, to test those hypotheses. If the results of your experiments do not match the predictions of your theory, you must reject or alter your theory. Thus, the scientific method involves observation and experimentation, but it also requires the disciplines of logic and mathematics.

The exact methods that scientists use depend on the kind of phenomena that they are trying to study. There are many different branches of science, each devoted to studying a different set of problems. For example, there are the physical sciences, such as physics and chemistry. Then, there is biology, which is the study of living things. Then there are the social sciences, such as psychology, sociology, anthropology, economics, and so on, which are studies of human beings and society. To study narcissism, you will draw mainly on the works of psychologists, along with some of the works of sociologists and anthropologists.

For a theory to be accepted as scientific, it must be logical and well supported by evidence. A theory can be rejected because it is illogical or because it is poorly supported by evidence. For example, the idea that narcissists are suffering from low self-esteem is illogical because it involves a contradiction. A contradiction involves two statements that cannot both be true at the same time. For example, the statement "X has high self-esteem" and "X has low self-esteem" cannot both be true at the same time if they refer to the same person. In contrast, a paradox is something that only seems to pose a contradiction but can actually be explained. For example, a person who thinks he deserves an unrealistically high social rank may seem insecure because he throws a screaming tantrum when he receives even the mildest constructive criticism. Yet that paradox is easily explained. The person may think that he deserves a high social rank, and he may realize that other people are not willing to grant him that high social rank. His temper tantrums are not necessarily a sign of personal insecurity. They may simply be attempts to bully other people into giving him the power that he desires.

In psychology, there are many debates about the underlying cause and nature of a psychological phenomenon. These debates often take the form of a psyche-versus-soma problem. Debates of this kind have been going on since the days of ancient Greece. Some problems that were initially believed to be somatic (i.e., due to a physical disease of the body, including the brain) have turned out to be a result of psychological or social factors, and vice versa.

In the 1920s, a problem that was being called congenital word blindness broke out among children in the public schools of Iowa. Many of the children in Iowa's public schools were failing to learn to read, even though they had normal sight and hearing and normal intelligence. Today, psychologists and educators no longer use the term *congenital word blindness*. Congenital means present at birth, and all newborns are illiterate. Instead, psychologists and educators use the term *dyslexia*. The word came from the Greek prefix *dys-*, which meant bad or defective, and the Latin root *legere*, which meant to read. Thus, *dyslexia* was intended to mean bad reading. Originally, it was intended to mean the loss of the ability to read, in someone who had suffered from a stroke or other injury to the brain. For example, someone who has an injury in the visual part of the brain may lose the ability to read even though he or she can still write. Using the neurological term *dyslexia,* as opposed to the educational term *illiteracy*, suggested that the problem is in the child's brain, as opposed to the child's school. Yet the problem in Iowa was clearly due to a problem in the schools.

The Rockefeller Foundation sent Dr. Samuel Orton to Iowa to figure out why so many of the children in Iowa were failing to learn to read. Orton found that the problem resulted from a bad method of teaching reading. Instead of teaching children that letters stand for sounds and helping them learn to sound words out from left to right (phonics), schoolteachers had been told to have children memorize whole words as shapes (sight words). The more sight words the children in a school had been asked to memorize, the worse the children's problems with reading seemed to be. The solution to this problem was to stop using sight words and teach phonics instead. Orton noted that the children who were having trouble with reading also tended to become frustrated, angry, and depressed. As a result, they tended to misbehave. Orton found that a child's mood and behavior problems tended to clear up after the child finally learned to read.

Dyslexia is a result of bad teaching, but some psychological problems really are due to some disorder of the brain. In the 1940s, a psychiatrist named Leo Kanner described a problem that he called autism. Children with this problem were lost in their own world. They had trouble in communicating with or emotionally connecting with other people. At first, Kanner believed that autism was caused by mothers who were emotionally cold to their children—refrigerator mothers. This theory was then popularized by Bruno Bettelheim, a University of Chicago professor who ran a residential school for troubled children. The tendency to blame autism on poor parenting—and poor mothering, in particular—went largely unchallenged until 1964. Then, Bernard Rimland, a psychologist with an autistic son, published *Infantile Autism: The Syndrome and its Implications for a Neural Theory of Behavior.* Leo Kanner wrote the foreword to the book. By that time, Kanner had come to believe that autism was a brain problem, rather than the result of poor parenting.

Even if everyone agrees that autism must have some underlying biological cause, there can still be serious disagreements about what the cause is. In 1998, the medical journal *The Lancet* published an article suggesting that the measles component of the measles-mumps-rubella vaccine could be responsible for causing a gastrointestinal problem as well as autism. Although the evidence in the article seemed flimsy, the journal editors published the article because any potential safety problem associated with a childhood vaccine is taken very seriously. However, the evidence was worse than flimsy, it was completely fraudulent. When the sordid details of the fraud were finally made public, the journal retracted the article and the lead author lost his license to practice medicine in the United Kingdom. I discuss this story at length in my book *No More Measles!* However, a few points are relevant here.

The suggestion that vaccines might cause autism created a panic, mainly because the number of cases of autism seemed to be rising dramatically at the same time that children were receiving more vaccines. However, the rise in autism diagnoses was due to an ontological problem, not necessarily an increase in the incidence of a neurological problem. (Remember, ontology deals with how things are named and categorized.) The increase in autism diagnoses was driven mainly by changes in what was meant by the word *autism*, as well as changes in how mental health professionals decided who is autistic and who is not. In 1970, the word *autism* meant a severe disorder that occurred in only about 1 out of every 5000 children. Since then, the concept of autism was expanded into a spectrum that included children with classical autism at the severe end of the spectrum and essentially normal children at the mild end of the spectrum. Whenever you broaden the definition of a diagnostic label, the number of people who would qualify for that label would rise, even if there is no actual change in the health of the population.

The problem that we now call autism certainly existed before doctors started calling it autism. However, children who had this problem in the 1930s were generally given a diagnosis of childhood schizophrenia or mental retardation. In 1970, the diagnosis of autism would have been given only to severely disabled children. Today, the label of autism is being applied to many children would not have been given any psychiatric diagnosis in 1970. However, the changes in the diagnostic criteria were not the only possible reason for an increase in autism diagnoses.

Beginning in 1970, federal and state laws started requiring public schools to provide education to children with disabilities, including mental retardation and autism. As a result, more and more children with disabilities started getting a proper diagnostic workup from a mental health professional, as opposed to just getting a diagnosis of mental retardation from the family doctor. Consequently, a growing number of children may have received a correct diagnosis of autism, as opposed to an incorrect diagnosis of mental retardation. Such an improvement in case finding can create the false impression that a condition is becoming more common, even if it is not.

The number of autism diagnoses rose even further because of changes in the reasons why the children were being evaluated. According to US federal law, schools must develop an individualized education program for every child who has a disability and meets federal and state requirements for special education. As a result, there may now be an incentive for parents and school administrators to seek a diagnosis that would enable the child to get additional educational services, even if the child does not have a true medical problem. Thus, some autism diagnoses may be faux diagnoses—false diagnoses made for a nonmedical purpose, such as an administrative or educational purpose.

By 2010, the estimated incidence of autism-spectrum disorders in American children had risen to 1 in 68. Some of the increase may have been due to improved case finding (e.g., a correct diagnosis of autism as opposed to an incorrect diagnosis of mental retardation). Perhaps some of the increase in autism diagnoses was due to a rise in faux diagnoses. However, most of this increase was due to the broadening of the definition of autism. The diagnosis of autism started being given to children who would not previously have been considered to have any serious mental problems. In the meantime, other kinds of studies were showing that autism has a strong genetic component, which suggests that the problem is not becoming more common.

If autism were completely genetic, like hemophilia or Huntington's disease, then you would expect the incidence of the disorder to stay stable from one generation to the next, at least until genetic counseling to prevent the disease becomes available. Because the genetic component in the cause of autism is so strong, the real rate of autism has probably been rising little, if at all. Nevertheless, the rise in the number of autism *diagnoses* was frightening, and it was occurring at the same time that the number of required vaccinations was going up. Thus, it was only natural that members of the antivaccination movement would try to use the specter of autism to frighten parents away from vaccinating their children.

We still know very little about autism, but we do know that it is not caused by vaccines. Extensive studies have shown that autism is not more common in vaccinated children than in unvaccinated children. Properly designed studies have shown that there is no relationship between autism and any vaccine or combination of vaccines or any vaccine additive. Thus, there is strong scientific evidence to believe that vaccination has nothing to do with autism.

Like studies of autism, a study of narcissism must begin with an ontological question. What do we mean by narcissism? How do we define it, how do we decide who has it and who does not. Is narcissism a binary variable—a yes-or-no proposition, like pregnancy? You cannot be a little bit pregnant. Either you are pregnant or you are not. But perhaps you can be a little bit narcissistic. Is narcissism something you can measure on a scale, like intelligence? Is narcissism a consistent trait, like your blood type; or is it something that goes up and down, like body temperature? Is narcissism something that is expressed only in certain situations? If so, is it nonexistent or only dormant in other situations? Once we work out the ontological questions related to narcissism, we can start to develop theories about what causes it and what, if anything, we could do about it. To do that, we have to relate narcissism in some way to other concepts that we can define and phenomena we can observe and measure.

In science, the word *theory* can be used in two different ways. Sometimes, people use the word *theory* to mean any idea or set of ideas that is considered to be possibly true. For example, you may have a theory that giving children too much praise may make them narcissistic. However, scientists often use the word *theory* in a grander sense, to mean a set of general principles. For example, the germ theory of disease is the idea that some diseases result from infection with a particular germ (e.g., a bacterium or virus). When doctors talk about the germ theory of disease, they do not mean that they are still unsure about whether the smallpox virus caused smallpox. Likewise, when they talk about the theory of evolution, they do not mean that they are still unsure about whether evolution happens.

The so-called hard sciences give us more reliable results than the soft sciences do. Physics is the hardest of the hard sciences. It has given us clocks that are so accurate that they would be off by less than 1 second per 138,000,000 years. In contrast, psychology and other social sciences are soft sciences, simply because human beings are so complex and unpredictable. Nevertheless, the questions that psychologists and sociologists study are so important that even the tentative answers that they give us are often far better than nothing at all.

The pure sciences deal with questions of what is true or false, and what is likely to happen. The applied sciences, such as engineering and medicine, apply the knowledge gained from the pure sciences to solving practical problems. Similarly, the professions of law and accounting also use specialized knowledge to solve practical problems.

To be scientific, a theory must provide the simplest logical explanation of all of the available evidence. Over the years, I have heard many people, including some psychiatrists, claim that theories about the human mind do not have to be logical because human beings are often illogical. Yet that would be like saying that a theory about the human mind can be stupid because human beings are often stupid.

To develop a useful theory of narcissism, you need to understand the concept of mental illness. In particular, you need to understand how people use the concept of mental illness to solve practical problems, whether those are medical problems, problems in living, or legal problems. The first question to grapple with is the question of what is normal and what is not.

Chapter 7

Normal and Abnormal

Many people are concerned that narcissism is becoming more common in the United States today. In fact, some people are convinced that it is becoming so common that it is becoming normal. This raises the question of what we mean by normal and abnormal.

The word *normal* means pertaining to a norm. In the social sciences, a norm is an expected pattern of belief and behavior. Norms differ from one society to another, and they change over time. They can even differ between social groups within the same geographic area. When I was a child in the 1960s, my family lived in an area with a large Amish population. If was normal for my mother, as an "English" (non-Amish) person, to drive a car to the supermarket. In contrast, it was normal for Amish people to drive an old-fashioned horse and buggy to the supermarket. Likewise, life aboard the whaling vessel *Pequod,* as depicted in Melville's novel *Moby-Dick*, represented several shocking departures from a North American white man's idea of normality, especially with regard to assumptions about freedom and equality.

Fictional works, such as novels and movies, often deal with characters and settings that would strike the audience as abnormal. For example, some fictional characters are extraordinary people, such as superheroes and supervillains. Some fictional settings involve extraordinary circumstances such as wars and natural disasters. However, many fictional characters are everyman characters, who represent normal people. Also, many fictional settings are also ordinary. Of course, many works of fiction deal with everyman characters who encounter strange people in strange settings. To the intended audience of *Moby-Dick*, Ishmael was an everyman character. Ishmael was the sort of person Melville's readers might know socially, yet Ishmael was telling a story about strange people (a maniacal one-legged ship captain and a friendly cannibal from the South Pacific) in a strange setting (a whaling ship on the high seas). Thus, Ishmael is the sort of person that Melville's readers would consider normal, while Captain Ahab and Queequeg the harpooner were clearly exotic.

Melville was writing for an audience of people like himself: well-to-do white men in North America in the 1850s. These men had a great deal of freedom in their personal lives. However, they also benefited from having a relatively high status in an oppressive racial and class hierarchy. Melville's intended readers would be shocked to read of the dictatorial power that a sea captain had over everyone else aboard ship, including the white men. Melville's readers would also have been surprised to read that nonwhite pagan harpooners like Queequeg clearly outranked the white Christian able-bodied seamen like Ishmael. Also, the degree of equality among the common seamen, despite their differences in race and national origin, would have been astonishing.

To Melville's intended audience, Queequeg was an exotic character. Yet Queequeg's oddity was clearly a result of his exotic cultural background. Queequeg came from the far side of the planet, from a society with cultural practices and religious beliefs that were strikingly different from those of New Englanders. In contrast, Captain Ahab was a New Englander, though one who had spent many years on the high seas. Yet by the end of the novel, it becomes clear that Queequeg is sane, and Ahab is a madman. Queequeg's strange beliefs and customs are normal for someone from his background, and Queequeg could respond to reason. Ahab, on the other hand, is a dangerous fanatic who sacrifices his ship and the lives of nearly all of his men in his maniacal mission to kill the white whale that had bitten off his leg. Thus, the reader is led to realize that Queequeg is normal and Ahab is abnormal.

Seeing life aboard the *Pequod* from Ishmael's point of view gives Melville's readers the opportunity to imagine what it would be like to live at the bottom of an unjust society. The novel shows that horrible things can happen when a powerful man uses other men as instruments of his will. *Moby-Dick* depicted the horrors of a kind of slavery that could be inflicted even on white men. At one point, Ishmael poses a rhetorical question, "Who ain't a slave?" Yet in 1851, slavery was an extremely divisive political issue in the United States. Thus, it is not surprising that *Moby-Dick* was a financial flop during Melville's lifetime. However, it became popular in the 20th century, after the end of slavery and the closing of the American frontier. Many high schools added *Moby-Dick* to the curriculum in the mid 20th century, when Ishmael's broadmindedness with regard to race and culture and his disenchantment with a dangerous tyrant had become more acceptable.

When readers allow themselves to see the world from Ishmael's point of view, they experience an altered sense of self. The ability to experience any sense of self is evidently a rare gift that has been given to only a few species. Only a few creatures besides human beings seem able to understand that their reflection in a mirror represents their own body. Thus, they seem to have a concept of self. Some social animals also seem to have some sense of empathy, which is the ability to understand or feel what other people understand and feel. For example, Frans de Waal showed that capuchin monkeys were happy to do a simple task in exchange for a slice of cucumber—until they saw that another monkey was being rewarded with grapes for the very same task. At that point, the monkeys would throw their slice of cucumber back at the experimenter, rather than eating it. Of course, the monkeys would not mind if other monkeys were being paid in cucumbers while they were being paid in grapes.

We human beings can develop our sense of fairness to a far greater degree, partly because we are generally smarter than monkeys, but mainly because we can use language. Our ability to understand the basic principles of grammar allows us to make abstract rules, complete with if-then statements, about what people should or should not do in a given situation. As a result, we can develop an abstract concept of right and wrong, as well as the concept of extenuating circumstances. In short, we can develop a moral code.

The uniquely human ability to tell stories and especially to read stories allows human beings to develop their ability to empathize with human beings from other walks of life. For example, Harriet Beecher Stowe's bestselling novel *Uncle Tom's Cabin* persuaded many people to oppose slavery. Stories can even help people develop empathy for animals. Anna Sewell's 1877 novel *Black Beauty*, which was the story of a horse, told from the horse's point of view, inspired the passage of many laws against cruelty to horses and other animals.

Because of our ability to develop a self-concept and to imagine the world from other people's point of view, we human beings can develop theoretical models of how we think someone ought to think, feel, and behave in a given situation. We can even make adjustments for a person's special circumstances, such as their age. When a toddler hits you, you might simply say, in a serious tone of voice, "We don't hit people!" But if a strange adult walked up to you on the street and hit you, you might call the police and press criminal charges for aggravated assault. Likewise, legal systems may handle juvenile offenders differently than they handle adult offenders.

During everyday life, you will naturally develop opinions about what someone else ought to have thought or felt or what that person ought to have done in a particular situation. If a substantial proportion of the population agrees with that opinion, the opinion becomes a social norm. In other words, a norm is a social consensus. People who adhere to the norm are normal. People who deviate from the norm are abnormal. Notice that the words *deviant* and *abnormal* sound frightening, whereas *normal* sounds reassuring. Most people are reassured when things meet their expectations and disoriented or even afraid when things do not meet their expectations. Yet being normal is not always good.

Abnormal has bad connotations, but so does the word *mediocre*. The word *mediocre* came from a French word meaning halfway up a mountain. Today, the word *mediocre* is used to mean that someone or something is average instead of being particularly good. If you want to be normal, it usually means that you aspire to being mediocre. Mediocrity is not always bad. A person who has been injured in an accident might go to great lengths to regain the ability to walk as well as an ordinary person. Yet there is also a downside to normality and mediocrity.

If a society has bad norms, then a good person would be abnormal. When slavery was accepted as normal, abolitionists were abnormal. Society advances only when people discard bad norms and accept good ones. Yet social norms always represent some sort of consensus. That truism raises important questions: Whose opinions should prevail? Who is to decide what should be normal? What, if anything, should be done to enforce social norms? Laws are social norms that are written and enforced by the government. In a dictatorship, the dictator makes the rules and relies on his supporters to carry out his wishes. But in a republic, the laws are made by elected officials and enforced by civil servants who are also subject to the rule of law. The Civil Rights Movement in the United States was an attempt to improve social norms as well as laws. The main goal was to ensure that everyone in the United States would really have equal protection under the laws—a promise that had been made in the Fourteenth Amendment to the Constitution but that has yet to be fully realized.

Medical doctors also deal with questions of normal and abnormal. There is a great deal of natural variation within the human species. Healthy adults can differ significantly from each other in terms of color and size. For example, the iris of the eye can be various shades of black, brown, green, or blue. All of those colors are considered variations of normality. But if the sclera (the white of the eye) is yellow, it is a sign of liver disease. Thus, a yellow sclera is considered an abnormality.

Physicians have achieved a consensus on many aspects of how the human body ought to look and function. For example, physicians agree that normal human body temperature ranges from 36.5–37.5 °C (97.7–99.5 °F). They know from long experience that if the body temperature drifts too far from that range, the patient is in serious trouble.

Body temperature is one of the four vital signs. The others are pulse, blood pressure, and respiration rate. Vital means pertaining to life. The vital signs are the signs that show that you are alive, as opposed to freshly dead. When people die, they stop breathing, which means that their respiration rate drops to zero breaths per minute. Their heart stops, which means no pulse and no blood pressure. Their body temperature will then drop to match room temperature. Of course, people who are near death from hypothermia (low body temperature) may have a breathing rate and heart rate that are so low that they are hard to detect. Fortunately, their oxygen consumption is also low, because of their low body temperature. As a result, they might get CPR until they warm up. One of the basic rules of emergency medicine is that no hypothermia patient is dead until he or she is warm and dead.

The four vital signs are signs. A sign is something that you can observe or measure in object, such as another person's body. Thus, it is objective. The word *objective* originally meant an observation of an object that is separate from the observer. The word *objective* has come to suggest that an observation is reliable because people can agree on it. For example, if different people measure the same person's body temperature at more or less the same time, they will probably come up with the same value.

A sign is something that an outside observer, such as a doctor or nurse, can observe. In contrast, a symptom is something only the patient can observe. A symptom is a subjective experience, which means the subject's perception of his or her own body and mind. For example, itching is a symptom, but scratching is a sign. You can see people or animals scratching themselves. From that, you can infer that they feel itchy. But you cannot feel their itch. Likewise, you can see someone behaving in ways that suggest that they are in pain or hallucinating, but you cannot feel their pain or experience their hallucinations. To evaluate someone's pain or someone's hallucinations, you have to watch what they do and listen to what they say.

This difference between signs and symptoms is particularly important in veterinary medicine and pediatrics. Animals and infants cannot talk. As a result, they cannot describe their symptoms, such as pain. (For centuries, many philosophers and even some veterinarians and physicians believed that animals and babies could not feel pain.) Today, we know that the nerve pathways and brain structures involved in the perception of pain are pretty much the same in a dog or a newborn baby as they are in an adult. So when we see an animal or a baby react to something that would be painful for us, we infer that it was painful for them, too.

When human babies are uncomfortable or simply lonely, they cry for help. But when adult animals are in pain, they may need to avoid expressing their pain. Such expressions would be a sign of weakness. Likewise, adult human beings may not always describe their symptoms accurately. They may complain of symptoms that they do not really have, and they may hide symptoms that they really do have.

Sometimes, healthy people pretend to be sick. Sometimes, this pretending amounts to fraud. If they are pretending to be sick in order to avoid work or to collect disability payments, the problem is called malingering. But if they are faking illness in order to seek unnecessary medical care (and the attention and sympathy that goes with it), the problem is called factitious disorder or Munchausen syndrome. If they cause illness in another person (such as their child) for the purpose of gaining attention and sympathy for themselves, the problem is called factitious disorder by proxy.

In one famous study, psychologist David Rosenhan and seven other healthy volunteers tried to gain admission to various mental hospitals in the United States. They called for an appointment with a psychiatrist. During the appointment, they told the psychiatrist that they were hearing voices that seemed to be pronouncing the words "empty," "hollow," and "thud." They were supposed to act normal otherwise. If they were admitted to the hospital, they were to act normally and report that they felt better and no longer heard the voices. All of these people were admitted to 12 different mental hospitals, ranging from run-down public hospitals in rural areas to psychiatric wards in university-based hospitals to exclusive private hospitals. At the public hospitals, they all received the diagnosis of schizophrenia. At one private hospital, the volunteer received a diagnosis of bipolar disorder, an illness with a better prognosis. The length of the hospitalizations ranged from 7 to 52 days. All of the volunteers were eventually released with a diagnosis that their schizophrenia was "in remission."

Many people felt that the Rosenhan study showed that psychiatrists cannot tell healthy people from mentally ill people and that a psychiatric diagnosis is therefore meaningless. But what the study really showed is that the psychiatrists cannot be expected to tell that a patient is lying about something that only the patient could know: his or her symptoms. Likewise, many other kinds of doctors have been fooled by cases of factitious disorder, which means that the patients are lying about their symptoms and possibly even producing fake signs of illness. It is reasonable for a psychiatrist at a mental hospital to admit someone who wants to be admitted and is complaining of the most obvious symptom of a common yet serious mental illness. Nor was the diagnosis of "schizophrenia in remission" unreasonable. Schizophrenia is a chronic disease whose symptoms often come and go.

Malingering and factitious disorder are forms of fraud. In contrast, hypochondriacs mistakenly believe that they are physically ill. As a result, the hypochondriacs tend to interpret normal sensations as symptoms of illness. Unfortunately, many people who truly are sick are dismissed as hypochondriacs if the correct diagnosis is not obvious.

Some healthy people pretend to be sick, but some sick people pretend to be healthy. They may hide their signs of illness or simply neglect to mention their symptoms. Sometimes, the person does not realize that he or she is sick. However, people often hide an illness that they think is unimportant or embarrassing.

Doctors cannot read minds. Thus, it can be hard to tell whether a patient is malingering. Also, many cases of factitious disorder and factitious disorder by proxy go undiagnosed for years. On the other hand, many patients who really were sick have been dismissed as hypochondriacs. Part of the art of medicine involves getting to the truth about the patient's signs and symptoms of illness. Unfortunately, physicians and mental health professionals get only a limited view of a patient's behavior and have to rely on what they patient says about his or her thoughts and feelings.

Most physicians focus on the body, but psychiatrists and other mental health professionals focus on the mind: the patient's thoughts, feelings, and behavior. Like other physicians, psychiatrists have tried to establish what is normal and what is not. For you to qualify for a diagnosis of a mental disorder, your thoughts, feelings, and behavior must differ significantly from those expected norms. For example, it is normal for people to grieve after a loved one dies. Thus, ordinary grief is not considered a mental disorder. The norms are based on what is expected for a person of that age, gender, and social background. For example, the ideas that a person learned in church are normal for someone of that background. Thus, the beliefs that someone learned in church are not considered to be evidence of a mental disorder. This rule of thumb is intended to prevent psychiatry and psychology from being used as tools of cultural oppression.

In 1974, the American Psychiatric Association decided to stop classifying homosexuality as a mental disorder. Homosexuality violated a social norm at the time. However, research showed that most gay people were content with being gay and that gay people appeared to be as well adjusted as straight people. Thus, homosexuality was not causing suffering or disability and was therefore not a mental illness. Since 1974, the public has become far more broad-minded with regard to issues of sexual orientation and gender identity. Most young people in the United States today consider homosexuality to be a variation of normality, as blue eyes are a variation of normality. Most of the human beings on Earth have brown eyes, but that does not mean that blue eye color is a disease.

A Hungarian-born American psychoanalyst named Thomas Szasz was one of the first psychiatrists to argue that homosexuality should not be classified as a mental illness. Yet he also wanted to discard the entire concept of mental illness, for reasons that do not hold up to careful scrutiny.

Chapter 8

What Is a Mental Illness?

Is narcissism a mental illness? To answer that question, you need to know what a mental illness is. To figure that out, you need some basic skills in ontology. Ontology is the branch of philosophy that deals with how to define terms and how to sort ideas, people, and objects into categories. Is mental illness valid as a category? Does narcissism belong in that category? If narcissism is a mental illness, does it mean that narcissists should not be held accountable for the behavior that results from their narcissism?

The concept of mental illness has been controversial for several reasons. One reason is the age-old metaphysical puzzle of the relationship between mind and body—between psyche and soma. How can we tell whether someone is suffering from a purely psychological problem, and how can we tell if the problem is really due to an underlying somatic problem, such as a disease of the brain? When is it reasonable to try a somatic treatment, such as a drug, to treat a seemingly psychological problem? Also, the concept of mental disorder implies abnormality. Should psychiatrists and psychologists have the power to decide what or who is normal? Yet another reason for the controversy is that the mental problems themselves seem abstract, and the criteria used to diagnose them may seem arbitrary. Of course, the mind itself is an abstraction, and the decision of whether anything is normal or abnormal is a judgment call.

To be considered a mental illness, an abnormal pattern of thoughts, feelings and behavior must cause suffering or disability. For example, you can have a phobia about climbing ladders. If you developed this phobia while working as a house painter, then your phobia could cause you distress or make it hard for you to do your job. It would therefore qualify as a mental illness. But if you never have to climb any ladders, then a ladder phobia would not be distressing or disabling. As a result, your ladder phobia would not qualify as a mental illness.

Like everyone else, psychiatrists and other mental health professionals develop expectations of how other human beings should think, feel, and behave. Those expectations typically depend on the age and social background of the person being evaluated. For example, in the United States it is normal for a three-year-old—but not for a 30-year-old—to believe in Santa Claus. Yet it is perfectly normal for a 30-year-old in the United States to feel that he or she has a personal relationship with Jesus Christ. To qualify as a mental disorder, a pattern of thoughts, feelings, and behavior must not only be distressing or disabling, it must be outside the range of normal variation for a person from that social background or in that social setting.

Many religions and political movements have teachings that may seem kooky to outsiders yet seem normal to believers. For that reason, psychiatrists are not supposed to regard someone's religious or political beliefs as evidence of a mental disorder. Likewise, the normal and expected reactions to typical life events are not supposed to be regarded as mental disorders. It is normal for a person to feel grief after the death of a loved one. Thus, ordinary grief is not a mental disorder, even though it causes suffering. On the other hand, normal reactions to abnormal experiences might qualify as a mental disorder. People can be broken mentally and emotionally by horrible events.

Thoughts, feelings, and behavior all originate in the brain. Yet the health of the brain depends on the health of the body as a whole. For example, low blood sugar and liver failure can cause serious problems with brain function. Also, no behavior can occur unless the rest of the body can follow the brain's commands. For this reason, it can be hard to figure out whether a particular mental illness is due to a physical problem (especially a brain disease) or due to some purely psychological or social problem.

Metaphysics is the branch of philosophy that deals with the relationship between body and mind. Likewise, psychiatry is the branch of medicine that deals with the mind-body relationship. The word *psychiatry* means mind doctoring. Psychiatrists are physicians (MDs or DOs) who have been specially trained in psychiatry. Psychiatrists can prescribe drugs. However, they can also provide psychotherapy, which is often called talk therapy or counseling. For many of their patients, psychiatrists offer some combination of medication and psychotherapy. Many nonphysicians, such as psychologists and social workers, can also provide psychotherapy. Members of the clergy also provide some kinds of talk therapy, such as marriage counseling and family therapy. Even conversations between laymen, such as between friends or between members of a support group, can be therapeutic.

Psychiatry is a branch of medicine because some psychological problems are the result of problems in the body, especially in the brain. Thus, some patients may need care from someone who has medical training and perhaps the ability to prescribe medications. However, it is possible for a person to have a mental illness without having any sort of underlying physical disease. For example, a person could suffer from disabling anxiety after living through some horrifying experience. Also, some kinds of mental illness could result from miseducation. Yet even if the cause of a mental illness is purely psychological, the emotional scars could leave some lasting imprint on the brain. The brain rewires itself in response to its experiences and activities. In short, the relationship between mind and body is never simple.

To get an accurate understanding of mental illness, you may have to unlearn some false ideas. In particular, you may have to unlearn some of the ideas that were spread by Thomas Szasz. Szasz was a prominent figure in the antipsychiatry movement. His ideas were taken very seriously in the 1960s and 1970s, but few people take them seriously today. Szasz's undergraduate degree was in physics, not philosophy. Also, his psychiatric training was based on psychoanalysis, which is more of a religion than a science. As a result, Szasz made many foolish mistakes with regard to metaphysics (including cause and effect as well as the mind-body relationship), ontology (how to define terms and categorize things), and ethics (right and wrong), and even basic logic. Thus, although he addressed some of the important questions that were facing the psychiatric profession in the 1960s and 1970s, his answers to those questions were often misleading. As a result, he championed some policies that did far more harm than good.

In his 1960 essay, The Myth of Mental Illness, Szasz admitted that some medical diseases, such as drug intoxication and untreated syphilis, can cause problems with personality, thinking, and behavior. But then he turned right around and claimed that central nervous system diseases could not produce such complicated symptoms. In particular, Szasz alluded to a problem that is called the Cotard delusion or the walking corpse syndrome, in which the patient is convinced that he or she is already dead. Szasz insisted that this kind of delusion could not result from a medical problem in the brain. Even in 1960, there was no reason to doubt that this illusion could result from a brain disorder. Today, we know that it can be the side effect of a common drug.

The Cotard delusion can be a side effect of the antiviral drug acyclovir. When you take acyclovir, your liver breaks it down into a chemical called CMMG. The CMMG is then supposed to be filtered out of the blood by the kidneys. But if acyclovir is given to someone with poor kidney function, the CMMG can build up to toxic levels in the bloodstream. The high levels of CMMG then cause some people to experience the Cotard delusion. Fortunately, the symptoms of the Cotard delusion go away after the person stops taking acyclovir. It goes away even faster if the patient undergoes dialysis treatment to remove the CMMG from the bloodstream. We still do not know much about how the brain works. As a result, we do not know why CMMG toxicity causes the Cotard delusion. Nor do we know why the Cotard delusion sometimes happens in people who have never taken acyclovir.

In numerous essays, Szasz claimed that mental illnesses (but especially schizophrenia) are a myth because they cannot be linked to particular disorders of the brain. However, that argument is misleading. By convention, psychiatrists use the terms *mental illness* and *mental disorder* to refer to psychological problems whose underlying basis in brain malfunction, if any, is still unknown. If scientists could trace schizophrenia to a particular problem in the brain, then schizophrenia would be reclassified as a neurologic disorder, as opposed to a mental illness. If scientists could show that schizophrenia is due to a particular gene or combination of genes, then it would be classified as a genetic disorder. The nature of the problem would remain the same, but medical doctors would put the problem into a different category in their classification system.

Even if we found out what was going wrong in the brain of someone with schizophrenia, the patients might still be treated by psychiatrists, and they might still benefit from the same combination of medication and psychotherapy that is currently being used. Likewise, we now know that Huntington's disease is due to a mutation in a particular gene. Thus, Huntington's disease is classified as a genetic neurological disorder as opposed to a mental illness. Yet people with Huntington's disease might still get some benefit from some of the drugs that are used to treat schizophrenia or major depression and may get some benefit from psychotherapy as well as speech therapy or occupational therapy. (Unfortunately, Huntington's disease still responds poorly to any available treatment.)

Szasz frequently claimed that schizophrenia is not a brain disease because it had not (and still has not) been linked to a particular disorder of the brain. However, that argument is an example of an argument from ignorance (*argumentum ad ignorantiam*): X must be false because X has not been proved true. Nobody knows precisely what is going wrong in the brain of someone with schizophrenia. But even in the 1960s, we had compelling evidence that the brains of people with schizophrenia are not working properly. People with schizophrenia have problems with logical thinking, and they often hear voices when nobody is talking. The nature of those symptoms suggests that there is a problem in the brain. Yet the nature of that underlying problem is still a mystery.

Szasz claimed that mental illnesses are not medical problems. He argued that mental illness is just a metaphor for problems in living. Yet psychiatrists are not supposed to classify ordinary problems in living as mental illnesses. The diagnosis of a mental disorder means that the patient has something more serious than a simple problem in living.

Szasz often complained that psychiatric diagnosis is illegitimate because it involves some sort of judgment by the psychiatrist. For example, to judge whether a patient's beliefs are delusional, the psychiatrist must compare those beliefs to his or her own beliefs and the prevailing beliefs within society. In The Myth of Mental Illness, Szasz wrote, "He might state that he is Napoleon or that he is being persecuted by the Communists. These would be considered mental symptoms *only* if the observer believed that the patient was *not* Napoleon or that he was *not* being persecuted [sic] by the Communists." Of course, an American mental patient in 1960 was *certainly not* Napoleon and *almost certainly not* being persecuted by the Communists.

Many mental illnesses involve delusions, which are ridiculous false beliefs that the person continues to hold even when shown that the belief is untrue. For example, back in the late 1980s, a friend of mine told me that her brother was horribly depressed because he was convinced that his wife was having an affair—with an 18-inch tall man who lived under the bed. No such man existed or could exist. Yet nothing could shake my friend's brother from his concern about the little man and his anger at his wife. His belief in the little man was clearly a delusion. Fortunately, he did consent to psychiatric care. The psychiatrist concluded that my friend's brother's beliefs about the little man were delusional. This delusion was a feature of a mental disorder called psychotic depression. After my friend's brother had been on antidepressant medication for a while, his mood lifted and he stopped talking about the little man.

All delusions are false beliefs. However, not all false beliefs are delusions. For example, it is normal for people to hold firm political or religious beliefs that are not accepted by people outside their social circle. If you hold some sort of unpopular belief because you learned it in church or from some political movement, you would not be considered mentally ill, even if your belief is causing distress or disability. In contrast, if you are distressed or disabled because of some strange idea that you came up with on your own, you probably would qualify for a diagnosis of a mental illness. The diagnosis of a mental disorder is based not just on what you think but how and why you came to think that way.

My friend was fortunate. Her brother was willing to accept psychiatric care. He took his medication, and he responded reasonably well to it. Unfortunately, many people with psychiatric disorders are unwilling to accept even basic shelter.

In the early 1980s, I went to college in Philadelphia. On my way to classes, I often walked past homeless people who were clearly mentally incompetent. It was obvious, even to my untrained eye, that many of these people had serious brain disorders. Not only did they have problems with thoughts, emotions, and behavior, but many of them seemed to have problems with movement and coordination. These were not like hippies or Amish people who had chosen an alternative lifestyle for philosophical or religious reasons. These people were so ill that they could not take care of themselves. I suspect that many of them had schizophrenia, and some of them probably had Alzheimer's disease or other form of senile dementia.

Back then, I was shocked to learn that a surprising number of educated laymen and even many psychiatrists stoutly resisted the idea that serious mood problems and/or disabling hallucinations and delusions might result from a brain disease. In the mid 1980s, the psychiatric profession in Philadelphia was still under the grip of Freudian psychoanalysis. Back then, psychiatrists did not have to undergo periodic re-certification. As a result, many of the older psychiatrists were still basing their practice on nonsense that had been popular in the 1950s. In particular, many of them were convinced that schizophrenia resulted from bad mothering.

It baffled me that educated people could be so resistant to the idea that the major mental illnesses, such as schizophrenia and bipolar disorder, probably resulted from some underlying disease of the brain. Everyone knows that drugs such as alcohol and amphetamines can alter your mood. That is why people take those drugs recreationally. So it seemed reasonable to me to suspect that some disorder involving brain chemistry could be responsible for major depression and bipolar disorder. Furthermore, anyone who lived through the 1960s knew that even a tiny dose of LSD would give people hallucinations and delusions. So it seemed obvious to me that the street people who were talking to invisible people were probably suffering from brain disorders.

I concluded that some mentally disabled people needed to be taken into care, even if they did not want to be. I also knew that psychiatric medications were sometimes beneficial. I had met a few people who had worked in mental hospitals when Thorazine, the first antipsychotic drug, became available. They dispelled the notion that Thorazine was just a chemical straightjacket. However, Thomas Szasz was strongly against involuntary treatment and especially involuntary hospitalization for the mentally ill. His views were often cited as justification for refusing to provide care for the mentally ill.

Most Philadelphians seemed to accept it as normal for mentally disabled people to die of exposure and malnutrition on the sidewalks of the City of Brotherly Love. When I suggested that some of the mentally ill street people needed hospital care, I was told that involuntary hospitalization would be a violation of human rights. Yet the real reason for refusing care to these people was tight-fistedness, not concern for human rights.

In the late 19th and early 20th centuries, a large number of mental hospitals were built throughout the United States. Some were privately run, but many were run by the state governments. Many of the inmates in these institutions were held there against their will. Some of the inmates had major mental illnesses, such as schizophrenia or bipolar disorder. Others had been railroaded into the hospital by corrupt psychiatrists or hateful family members. Others were there simply because they had nowhere else to go. Up until the 1970s, many people who had no need for hospitalization sometimes remained trapped in the hospital for years because the institution depended on their unpaid labor to sustain itself. In fact, the healthier the patient was, the more valuable his or her work was to the institution and the less likely he or she was to be discharged. The practice of exploiting the unpaid labor of inmates was called institutional peonage.

In 1973, a federal district court declared in *Souder v Brennan* that patients at nonfederal institutions had to be paid at least the federal minimum wage whenever they performed any activity that provided economic benefit to the institution. As a result, the cost of running the institutions rose sharply and there was extreme pressure to release as many patients as possible. In the 1960s, John F. Kennedy and his brothers had hoped that mental patients could be discharged from state institutions to receive outpatient treatment at community mental health centers. However, too few of those centers had been built to meet the flow of patients. Furthermore, many of the people who ended up working at those centers often did not want to serve the people with the most serious mental disorders.

The end of institutional peonage freed many people who should not have been incarcerated in a mental hospital. Yet it also led to a massive wave of deinstitutionalization, including the refusal to provide residential care for people who desperately needed it. As a result, many severely mentally ill people ended up incarcerated in prisons, where they often received no psychiatric care and where the basic living conditions were often even more inhumane. Others ended up on the sidewalks, where many of them died of exposure and malnutrition.

Many people who are in the grip of a psychotic episode or suffering from severe depression or mania resist care of any kind. As a result, their families may try to get them committed involuntarily to a hospital. Fortunately, Pennsylvania had a process that was supposedly designed to ensure that civil commitments were not being used inappropriately. According Pennsylvania state law, a person could be committed to inpatient psychiatric treatment only if he or she had shown clear evidence within the past 30 days of dangerousness to self or others. Yet the judges seemed to be ignoring such evidence.

If you refuse to take shelter during freezing weather, you are likely to die of exposure. In fact, many street people did die of exposure. Nevertheless, many judges did not think that people who refused to take shelter during freezing weather were a danger to themselves. I met one woman whose brother lost his feet to frostbite after he had been allowed to sign himself out of the hospital while he was still dazed from electroshock treatments—yet was somehow considered not a danger to himself.

People who are trying to kill themselves are clearly dangerous to themselves. Yet some judges did not consider a suicide attempt within the previous 24 hours to be evidence of dangerousness to self within the past 30 days. One judge decided that the daughter of a friend of mine posed no danger to herself, even though she was in the emergency department receiving life-saving treatment for a suicide attempt. Some judges did not consider aggravated assault to be evidence of dangerousness to others. For example, before Sylvia Seegrist carried out her deadly assault at the Springfield Mall, a judge decided that she posed no threat to others, even though she had just stabbed a psychologist. Even if you were lucky enough to get your mentally ill family member committed to a psychiatric ward, the commitment period generally did not last long enough for antipsychotic medications to take full effect.

These cases involved people who seemed to be suffering from brain disorders, but the judges seemed to be suffering from a different kind of madness—or perhaps from stupidity or ambition. At the time, I wondered how people who were so immune to evidence and logic had managed to get through law school and pass the bar exam. Years later, I learned that you do not have to be a member of the bar, or even a law school graduate, to become a judge in Pennsylvania. In fact, you would need more hours of training to become a hair stylist in Pennsylvania than to sit on the bench of many of the lower courts. Hair grows back, but a bad judgment can ruin lives.

Why were the judges so reluctant to commit mentally ill people to treatment? Were they really taken in by the idea that mentally disabled people had a "right" to freeze to death? Or was money the real concern? Commitment of an indigent person to the state hospital would cost the state government about $300 per day. It was much cheaper for the state to throw the severely mentally ill people onto the sidewalk to freeze to death.

When I first got involved in advocacy for the mentally ill, I thought that a few patients were "falling through the cracks" of the system. Eventually, I realized that the people with the most expensive problems were being forcibly shoved through the cracks. One commonly used tactic was called motor coach therapy: mentally ill people would be put on a bus to a completely different catchment area, often a completely unfamiliar city where they had no family or friends. At the same time that these desperately ill people were being thrown to the four winds, there was an increasing trend to send healthy but rebellious teenagers to inpatient psychiatric facilities. They would stay there as long as their insurance lasted.

Of course, the people who were running the mental health system did not admit that they were simply sending psychotic and demented people to their deaths to save money. Instead, they claimed that they were protecting the individuals' civil rights.

We do need to have proper legal proceedings to keep psychiatric hospitalization from being used for political purposes. Involuntary mental hospitalization was often used as a tool of political repression in the Soviet Union. Szasz claimed that it was serving the same role in the United States, particularly in the case of Edwin A. Walker—the man whom Lee Harvey Oswald had tried to kill before killing John F. Kennedy. Yet Walker was not being hospitalized for political reasons, he was awaiting trial for serious federal crimes.

Walker had been a major general in the U.S. Army. However, Walker resigned his commission in 1961 after the Joint Chiefs of Staff scolded him for trying to influence the votes of his troops. In 1962, Walker was arrested on four federal charges, including sedition and insurrection, for his role in inciting the Ole Miss Riot of 1962. The rioters were armed segregationists who fought against federal marshals and federal troops who had been sent to guard a black army veteran, James Meredith, as he enrolled as a student at the University of Mississippi. During the riot, 166 of the federal marshals and 40 of the soldiers and National Guardsmen were injured and two civilians were killed.

While Walker was awaiting trial for his role in inciting the riot, Attorney General Robert F. Kennedy ordered him to be sent to a psychiatric facility for observation, to determine whether he was fit to stand trial. Kennedy's order was understandable, given that Walker was insisting that the U.S. government had been thoroughly infiltrated by communists, a belief that smacks of paranoia. (Some film critics believe that Walker was one of the models for the insane Gen. Jack D. Ripper in Stanley Kubrick's movie, *Dr. Strangelove, or How I Learned to Stop Worrying and Love the Bomb*.)

Walker's belief that the federal government was thoroughly infiltrated by communists was clearly false, but it would not have qualified as a delusion. That belief was widely shared by members of the John Birch Society, of which Walker was a prominent member. Since his political ideology was learned from a political movement, it would not have qualified as evidence of a mental illness.

Szasz complained that Walker was being persecuted for his political beliefs. The American Civil Liberties Union took Szasz's side in the dispute, and Walker was released after only a few days. The charges against Walker were eventually dropped after a sympathetic U.S. attorney persuaded a federal grand jury in Mississippi not to indict him.

By sending Walker to a psychiatric facility for observation, Kennedy was making it easier for Walker to offer an insanity defense, if his case went to trial. The insanity defense might have discredited Walker politically, but it could have kept him out of prison and allowed him to keep his military pension. But besides being opposed to involuntary psychiatric hospitalization, Szasz was opposed to the insanity defense. Thus, he was not only opposing contemporary psychiatry, he was going against principles of humane jurisprudence that date back to Roman times. Insanity is a legal concept, not a medical diagnosis.

Ancient Greek physicians believed that imbalances of the chemical makeup of the body could cause a person to become irrational. The ancient Romans accepted this idea, along with the idea that strong emotions could lead to problems in the body. Roman society was brutal in many ways, but Roman law allowed for humane treatment of the mentally ill. Thus, someone who was not of sound mind (*non compos mentis*) might not be held responsible for a criminal act.

In the United States today, a criminal case cannot be tried if the defendant is not mentally competent to stand trial. *Competent* means that the defendant can adequately assist his or her attorney and is capable of making informed decisions about trial strategy, such as whether to plead guilty or accept a plea agreement. Competency deals with the defendant's mental state at the time of the trial, not at the time of the crime in question.

My husband feels that people with major mental illnesses such as schizophrenia are being railroaded into prison because of the way that criminal cases are handled. The trial cannot start until the defendant is competent to stand trial. But by that time, the jury cannot see how floridly psychotic the defendant was at the time of the offense. Most laymen have never seen anyone in the throes of a psychotic episode. As a result, most jurors have no understanding of the effects that a major mental illness can have on someone's behavior. As a result, people in the modern-day United States have become less humane to the mentally ill than the ancient Romans were.

Our prisons in the United States today are full of people with major mental illnesses. Yet less than 1% of criminal defendants plead not guilty by reason of insanity. The insanity defense is seldom tried because it seldom succeeds. Although Thomas Szasz complained about the use of psychiatrists and psychologists as arbiters of who is mentally ill, mental health professionals do not actually get to decide whether a criminal defendant is sane or insane. That decision is made by the jury. All that the psychiatrist or psychologist can offer is expert testimony.

Different jurisdictions use different rules for deciding who is not guilty by reason of insanity. One of these rules is the M'Naghton test. Under this rule, a defendant should not be held responsible for his actions if he did not know that his act would be wrong or if he did not understand the nature and quality of his actions. Another rule is called the product test: a defendant is entitled to acquittal if his offense was the product of his mental illness (i.e., would not have been committed if the illness were not present). According to yet another rule, called the Model Penal Code test, a defendant is not responsible for criminal conduct "if at the time of such conduct as a result of mental disease or defect he lacks *substantial capacity* either to appreciate the criminality of his conduct or to conform his conduct to the requirements of the law."

Psychiatry focuses on the poorly understood borderland between purely somatic problems and purely psychological problems. Some mental illnesses almost certainly do result from some as-yet mysterious underlying disorder of the brain, but others probably do not. Psychiatrists are particularly interested in the mental illnesses that do reflect an underlying problem in the brain. Yet once the underlying problem is clearly understood, the disorder would be reclassified as a medical problem. Thus, it might be classified as a neurological disorder, as opposed to a psychiatric disorder.

In general, physicians classify a problem as a mental disorder only if the nature of the underlying brain disorder, if any, is unclear. By saying that narcissism is a mental disorder, I am not saying that it is a disease of the brain. Nor am I saying that there is nothing wrong with the person's brain. In fact, I am saying nothing about the underlying cause. Instead, I am simply saying that the person's problems with thoughts, emotions, or behavior are not within the expected range for that person and are leading to suffering or disability.

Since mental illnesses involve thoughts, feelings, and behavior, they overlap with some of the concepts that theologians classify as sin. Sin is an English word. In English translations of the Bible, the word *sin* is used for Hebrew and Greek words that came from archery. These words literally meant that the arrow hit the target but did not land in the bull's-eye at the center of the target. In other words, the person has fallen short of perfection. The concept of sin cannot be separated from the concept of free will. Free will is the ability to choose between different possible courses of action. The ancient Romans understood that some mental illnesses can undermine a person's ability to make good choices. As a result, they would excuse people for offenses committed while the person was *non compos mentis*, or not of sound mind.

Psychosis means a loss of contact with reality. People who are suffering from a psychotic episode may not understand the consequences of their actions. For example, Sylvia Seegrist was so out of touch with reality that she did not understand that the people she killed would stay dead. Other kinds of offenses can result from an irresistible impulse due to a brain disorder. Charles Whitman, who used the clock tower at the University of Texas in Austin as a sniper's nest, had a brain tumor that was undoubtedly causing murderous impulses that he could no longer resist. Yet a mental illness is not always an excuse or even an explanation for bad behavior.

Many people feel that a psychiatric diagnosis is an excuse for misbehavior. Sometimes it is, and sometimes it is not. It would be cruel and pointless to punish a psychotic person for behavior that was purely a product of the psychosis. Yet it would also be a bad idea to use a label of mental illness to excuse any or all bad behaviors. In fact, people with some kinds of mental illness need to be held strictly accountable for their bad behavior. The founders of Alcoholics Anonymous (AA) understood that concept. They felt that alcoholics cannot blame all of their problems on alcohol. The founders of AA felt that the alcoholic's life has gone off the rails because of problems in how the alcoholic thinks about the world and relates to other people. Thus, they concluded that a drunk cannot put his or her life back together without addressing those problems, which have probably gotten worse because of the drinking.

Alcoholics Anonymous grew out of a Christian evangelical movement called the Oxford Movement. Many of the steps of their 12-step program represent attempts to atone for misbehavior that stems from capital sins, such as pride and wrath. Some of the steps involve admitting and making amends for misbehavior, whether or not you were drunk when you misbehaved. People who simply stop drinking without making these fundamental improvements in their character are described as dry drunks. As one wag put it, "If you take the rum out of a fruitcake, you still have a fruitcake."

Alcoholics Anonymous is essentially a religious organization, and it has always been fiercely protective of its members' privacy. As a result, there were remarkably few scientific studies of the effectiveness of AA's 12-step program for recovering alcoholics. Thus, many scientists were skeptical of its value. But in the 1990s, a large study called Project MATCH showed that the 12-step approach seemed to work as well as the other kinds of psychotherapeutic approaches for alcoholism. Unfortunately, all of these approaches have only modest success.

Since Alcoholics Anonymous is a religious organization, it may not receive taxpayer funding in the United States. Nor may a judge order people to attend religious programs, including AA meetings or other religious 12-step programs. Judges can order people to attend a drug or alcohol rehabilitation program only if a secular alternative is available.

We are still at a primitive stage in our understanding of the mind-body problem. Scientists still know little about how the brain works, or about what can cause it to malfunction. Also, nobody is really sure of the extent to which brain malfunction is responsible for some mental illnesses. Meanwhile, our educational system neglects the humanities in ways that makes it hard for modern people to learn time-tested nonmedical solutions for psychological and social problems. As a result, the available treatments for mental illnesses are often ineffective and sometimes do more harm than good. We know that the results of drug treatments for mental disorders are sometimes disappointing. Yet so are the results of some kinds of talk therapy. As Albert J. Bernstein, PhD explained in his book *Emotional Vampires: Dealing with People Who Drain You Dry,* people with personality disorders tend to prefer therapeutic approaches that make them worse, not better. "People who throw tantrums like two-year-olds hardly need to be encouraged to get their feelings out into the open or, God forbid, get in touch with their inner child."

Chapter 9

Defining and Classifying Mental Disorders

Before you can begin figuring out how to prevent and treat mental illnesses, you need to find some reliable way to figure out who is mentally ill and who is not, as well as a reliable way to sort cases of mental illness into meaningful diagnostic categories. By definition, a mental illness is a problem that involves abnormal thoughts, feelings, or behaviors and that leads to suffering or disability. A diagnosis of a mental disorder supposedly means that the psychiatrist thinks that the patient's thoughts, feelings, and behavior are outside of the range that would be expected, given the person's social background and circumstances. When a patient receives a diagnosis of narcissistic personality disorder, it means that the psychiatrist thinks that the patient's abnormal thoughts, feelings, or behaviors are following a particular, defined pattern.

Psychiatrists group mental disorders according to whether the biggest problem seems to be in the domain of thoughts, feelings, or behavior. Of course, a person who has problems in one domain is likely to have problems in the other two, as well. For example, even if someone's most obvious problem seems to be abnormal thought patterns, that person can also have problems with feelings and behavior. Likewise, a person whose most obvious problem seems to be abnormal emotions can have less-obvious problems with thoughts or behaviors. Also, a person whose behavior seems to be the main problem can also have less-obvious problems with thoughts and feelings.

Over the years, several classification systems for mental illnesses have been developed. In the United States, the most influential system for classifying mental illnesses is the American Psychiatric Association's Diagnostic and Statistical Manual (DSM). So far, there have been five editions of the DSM, with some minor revisions between editions. The DSM is often called the psychiatrist's bible. However, it is not a bible. It is something that is more fundamental than that. It is a dictionary. The purpose of the DSM is to ensure that psychiatrists all mean the same thing when they use a particular diagnostic label, such as schizophrenia or narcissistic personality disorder.

Some pious people might be shocked by my suggestion that a dictionary could be more important than a bible. Yet the gospel according to John starts off by saying, "In the beginning was the word." Unless you know the meaning of words, any text is gibberish. Likewise, all scientific endeavors start with definitions and classifications. That is why the names for practically all branches of science end in the suffix –*logy*, which is derived from the Greek word for word. Biology is the study of *bios* (life), psychology is the study of *psyche* (mind), and sociology is the study of society. Nosology is the branch of medicine that deals with classification of diseases.

Some of the words used for describing and classifying mental illnesses were around before the first edition of the DSM was compiled: neurosis, psychosis, and personality disorder. The word *neurosis* originally meant nerve disease. It came to mean mental problems that were mainly disturbances of emotion, in people who were more or less in touch with reality (no hallucinations or delusions). In contrast, the word *psychosis*, which originally meant mind disease, was used for cases in which people had lost touch with reality. A psychosis typically involved hallucinations (which means seeing, hearing, feeling, smelling, or tasting things that are not real) and delusions (which are strongly held beliefs that are clearly false). Of course, a person with a psychosis may also have problems with mood and behavior. The other kind of mental illness seemed to be mainly a problem with behavior, in cases where the person's problems with thoughts and feelings were not obvious. These behavioral problems were the sort of thing that the ancient Greek philosopher Theophrastus described in his Characters: problems with how the person relates to other people or to society as a whole.

There have been two basic approaches to the classification of mental disorders. One was based on the idea that mental illnesses are primarily the result of biological (somatic) problems, including brain injuries and genetic disorders. This approach tended to appeal to the administrators of mental hospitals, whose patients tended to have severe and disabling mental illnesses, such as schizophrenia, which probably reflected an underlying disease of the brain. The other approach to the classification of mental disorders was based on the idea that mental illnesses are primarily the result of psychological problems. This approach appealed to office-based psychiatrists who mainly saw outpatients. The caseload of an office-based psychiatrist tended to include many people with relatively mild psychological problems. As psychotherapy became popular in the United States, many psychiatrists started seeing many patients who would not have qualified for the diagnosis of any mental illness at all. These patients were seeking psychotherapy to deal with problems in living or for personal growth, as an athlete might seek coaching or someone who wants to grow spiritually might seek out a guru.

The most famous proponent of the biological approach to the classification of mental illnesses was a German psychiatrist named Emil Kraepelin. Americans may be surprised to hear that Kraepelin, rather than Sigmund Freud, is regarded as the father of modern scientific psychiatry. Kraepelin believed that the major mental illnesses result from some defect in the soma (body or brain), as opposed to the psyche (mind). As a colleague of Alois Alzheimer, Kraepelin was a co-discoverer of Alzheimer's disease. Kraepelin's laboratory discovered the defects in brain tissue that are the hallmarks of Alzheimer's disease. This success led Kraepelin to believe that the biological basis of other major mental disorders would eventually be discovered. However, the brains and brain tissue of people who had died with a major mental illness did not necessarily look abnormal at autopsy. Even today, advanced imaging techniques are sometimes finding only subtle abnormalities in the brains of people with major mental illnesses.

Kraepelin understood that the first step in identifying the underlying cause of a mental disorder would be to find some way to categorize patients, so that two patients with the same underlying disease would receive the same diagnosis and two patients with different underlying diseases would receive different diagnoses. By the late 19th century, psychiatrists had come up with hundreds of diagnostic labels, most of which were based on the presence or absence of a particular symptom. Yet from long experience, Kraepelin knew that such an approach could be misleading. Often, patients who seemed to have completely different problems would have many symptoms in common. What mattered most was the overall pattern of the patient's symptoms. Instead of focusing on individual symptoms, he considered the overall pattern of symptoms: the syndrome.

Kraepelin is most famous for differentiating two important syndromes. At the time, many psychiatrists believed that all forms of psychosis were just different manifestations of the same underlying problem. But Kraepelin saw that there seemed to be at least two major categories of psychosis. He called one of them manic-depression and the other dementia praecox. Today, psychiatrists have divided the category of manic-depression into several different categories, including bipolar disorder and major depressive disorder. Dementia praecox, which originally meant the premature loss of memory and thinking skills, is now called schizophrenia.

In his textbook on psychiatry, Kraepelin also addressed problems that appeared to be moral defects. Kraepelin suggested that some people had a "lack or weakness of those sentiments which counter the ruthless satisfaction of egotism." In other words, some people seem to be particularly weak in resisting the seven deadly sins. Yet rather than considering this weakness to be a purely spiritual problem, Kraepelin recognized that it could sometimes be due to some underlying disease of the brain.

Kraepelin's discussion of these moral defects, which are now called personality disorders, has been criticized because it simply seems to be a list of behaviors that Kraepelin found objectionable, rather than being descriptions of true medical problems. Of course, that criticism can be applied even to the modern classification of personality disorders. Again, a mental illness can be a mental illness whether or not it results from a brain disease, and the personality disorders are illnesses in which the most obvious problems are behavioral.

Kraepelin's classification of mental disorders was extremely influential in Europe. But in the United States, it was eclipsed by Freudian psychoanalytic views of mental illness. But by the end of the 20th century, American psychiatry was abandoning Freud and embracing the kinds of ideas that Kraepelin had proposed. In 1990, President George H. W. Bush declared the years 1990 to 1999 to be the Decade of the Brain. During that decade, the Library of Congress and the National Institute of Mental Health undertook an educational campaign to raise public awareness of the benefits to be derived from research on the human brain.

The United States Census Bureau started keeping statistics on mental illness in 1840, when the census workers were instructed to count the number of "insane" and "idiotic" people, as well as the number of people who were "deaf and dumb" and the number of people who were blind. During World War II, the War Department wanted to know how many men were unfit for military service because of mental illness and how many men became mentally ill while they were serving in the military. In 1943, the Surgeon General issued a technical bulletin that gave guidelines for how military psychiatrists should make diagnoses. The army, navy, and Veterans Administration adopted modified versions of those guidelines. After the war, the World Health Organization started including mental disorders in its International Statistical Classifications of Diseases (ICD). In response, the American Psychiatric Association developed its own classification system. Its first *Diagnostic and Statistical Manual of Mental Disorders* (DSM-I) was published in 1952. It included the definitions of 106 mental disorders.

The DSM-I split mental disorders into two separate categories, according to whether the cause of the problem was believed to be primarily somatic or primarily psychological. Because of the influence of psychoanalysts within the APA, the psychotic disorders (including schizophrenia) were classified among the primarily psychological disorders. In the early 1950s, the American Psychiatric Association was dominated by psychiatrists who were interested in psychoanalysis and other forms of psychodynamic psychotherapy. For that reason, many of the mental disorders were described as reactions. The idea was that these problems were the person's psychological reaction to psychological, social, and biological factors. For example, schizophrenic reactions were supposedly "marked by strong tendency to retreat from reality, by emotional disharmony, unpredictable disturbances in stream of thought, regressive behavior, and in some, a tendency to 'deterioration.'" Unfortunately, the idea that someone with schizophrenia was "retreating" from reality implied that the person was choosing to be ill. This idea that mental illness is some sort of choice explains why so many supposedly sane people could be so callous to the mentally ill.

The DSM-II was released in 1968. It included 182 mental disorders. Despite significant challenges from behaviorists and the antipsychiatry movement during the 1960s, there were few changes between DSM-I and DSM-II. Although the term *reaction* was dropped, mental disorders such as schizophrenia were still being seen as reflections of broad underlying conflicts or maladaptive responses to life problems. The DSM-II also continued to categorize homosexuality as a mental disorder.

In the early 1970s, American psychiatry was under attack from many different angles. One important critique came from the Gay Rights Movement, which mounted an ultimately successful campaign to persuade the APA to remove homosexuality from the list of mental disorders. (In its place, the APA added a category called ego-dystonic homosexuality, which meant that the person was unhappy with his or her sexual orientation.) A broader critique of the DSM-II came from an important article by a psychiatrist named Robert Spitzer and a biostatistician named Joseph L. Fleiss. Spitzer and Fleiss showed that the DSM-II was failing to serve its primary purpose: to guide psychiatric diagnosis.

Spitzer and Fleiss explained that there are two important criteria for judging any system of classification: reliability and validity. If a diagnostic system is reliable, then a case of mental illness would always get the same diagnosis, regardless of which doctor is making the diagnosis. Validity, in contrast, means that the classifications are useful for some practical purpose, such as figuring out why the patient is sick or what can be done to restore the patient's health. A classification system can be reliable but invalid. For example, if you decided to sort psychiatric patients according to their astrological sign, you could get practically 100% agreement among the psychiatrists. However, the patient's astrological sign is not useful information. Thus, the classification system would be invalid, even though it is reliable. In contrast, any unreliable system is automatically invalid.

Spitzer and Fleiss showed that the DSM-II was unreliable. Two psychiatrists who were using the DSM-II would not necessarily come up with the same diagnosis for the same case. Many of the diagnoses in DSM-I and DSM-II were based on the psychiatrist's speculations about what was going on in the patient's subconscious mind—something that neither the psychiatrist nor the patient could actually observe.

In 1974, the APA made some important decisions. It dropped homosexuality from an updated printing of the DSM-II. It also decided to make a major revision of the DSM. Robert Spitzer was chosen to chair the task force. Spitzer set some ambitious goals for the task force. He wanted to make the DSM more useful for scientific research. Thus, it would have to provide reliable criteria for sorting patients into meaningful diagnostic categories. The DSM-II allowed psychiatrists to base diagnoses on speculations about the patient's subconscious mental processes. In contrast, the diagnoses in the DSM-III were based on things that could be observed: the signs that the psychiatrist could observe directly and the symptoms that the patient would report.

By making the new DSM more useful to scientists, Spitzer was also making it more useful to the Food and Drug Administration (FDA). In 1962, Congress gave the FDA the power to refuse to allow a drug to be marketed in the United States unless the drug had been shown to be effective as well as safe. In the 1970s, the FDA started demanding higher scientific standards in drug research. If you wanted to market a drug for the treatment of a particular mental illness, you had to submit data on the effects of that drug in people with that particular mental illness. However, no such research could be done unless there were some reliable way of deciding who had that mental illness and who did not. To make the DSM-III user-friendly for government regulators, as well as for psychiatrists, Spitzer wanted the diagnostic criteria to be phrased in plain English, as much as possible.

The DSM-III was designed to be noncommittal with respect to the cause of most mental disorders. This neutrality seems reasonable, given the fact that so little is known about the cause of mental illnesses. However, it was also politically necessary, given the political struggles between biologically oriented and psychodynamically oriented psychiatrists. From 1977 to 1979, the National Institute of Mental Health sponsored field trials to test the reliability of the new diagnoses. Then, after much squabbling over the use of the word *neurosis*, the DSM-III was finally published in 1980. A revised version, the DSM-IIIR, was issued in 1987. The DSM-IIIR was 567 pages long and included contained 292 diagnoses.

The next major revision to the DSM, the DSM-IV, was published in 1994. The DSM-IV introduced a multiaxial system of diagnosis, to encourage psychiatrists to look at the patient's condition from many different perspectives. The Axis I diagnosis was the principal disorder that needs attention, such as schizophrenia, an episode of depression, or a flare-up of panic disorder. The Axis I diagnosis was often, but not always, the reason why the psychiatric evaluation was being done. Axis II included the personality disorders or intellectual disorders (such as mental retardation) that could be shaping the response to the Axis I problem. Axis III included the purely medical disorders, such as pregnancy or cancer, that could affect someone's mental well-being. Axis IV included the psychosocial stressors, such as divorce or unemployment, that the person had recently experienced. Axis V was the level of functioning that the person had attained in the past year. The DSM-IV was larger than DSM-III. It was 886 pages long and included 297 disorders. However, some of the personality disorders from DSM-III had been removed to an appendix. A "text revision" of the DSM-IV (DSM-IV-TR) was published in 2000. Most of the categories and criteria remained the same, but the descriptions were updated. Also, some of the codes were adjusted to reconcile with the latest version of the ICD.

The DSM-5 was published in 2013. It discarded the multiaxial system of diagnosis. Instead, the first three axes were incorporated into a single section. It replaced Axis IV with significant psychosocial and contextual features. It dropped Axis V. Instead, it suggests that the WHO's Disability Assessment Schedule could be used to assess functioning.

The publication of the DSM-5 has sparked controversy, but so has the publication of every system of classification of mental disorders. Some of this controversy emerges from scientific disputes, and some of it reflects social or economic concerns. The fundamental scientific problem is the fact that we still know little about the human brain and the relationship between body and mind. For example, we still do not know why people get disorders like schizophrenia, or why the symptoms of schizophrenia can wax and wane. Since schizophrenia is a syndrome, it might represent a group of unrelated diseases that all produce similar symptoms.

In other branches of medicine, doctors can order laboratory tests and diagnostic imaging to aid in diagnosis. As a result, a general practitioner can order a laboratory test to see if the patient's flu-like illness is really due to influenza. The general practitioner can also have the patient's chest x-rayed to see if the patient has pneumonia. Unfortunately, there are remarkably few reliable tests to aid in the diagnosis of mental illness. Psychiatrists must rely on the impression that they get of the patient's symptoms during the brief amount of time that they can actually spend with the patient. Also, as Kraepelin understood, the symptoms of any given mental illness can vary over time, and the symptoms of the various mental illnesses overlap so much that it can be hard to sort cases into meaningful categories. For those reasons, any system of classification of mental illnesses is bound to have problems with reliability and validity.

Another reason for controversy is the questionable role that psychiatrists have played in establishing social norms. If a mental disorder is, by definition, an abnormality, then psychiatrists would seem to be the people who get to decide what is normal and what is not. Unfortunately, psychiatrists have not always used this power wisely or humanely. For decades, psychiatrists considered homosexuality to be a mental disorder. Many psychiatrists have tried to "cure" homosexuality, and the treatments they have used have often amounted to physical and psychological torture. Gay rights activists have complained that such treatments have caused serious mental health problems and have even driven many gay people to suicide.

At the APA's 1971 conference, gay rights activist Frank Kameny grabbed the microphone and yelled, "Psychiatry is the enemy incarnate. Psychiatry has waged a relentless war of extermination against us. You may take this as a declaration of war against you." In 1973, the APA invited Kameny to the meeting where it announced that homosexuality had been struck from the list of mental disorders. Kameny described it as "the day we were cured en masse by the psychiatrists." In 2001, U.S. Surgeon General David Satcher issued a report that declared that there is no scientific evidence that sexual orientation can be changed. Some legislatures in the United States and elsewhere have passed laws against providing so-called conversion therapy, which is intended to change the sexual orientation or gender identity, to minors.

Psychiatry deals with the baffling relationship between brain and mind and the complicated relationship between the individual and society. Thus, psychiatrists can make one of two basic kinds of error. On one hand, psychodynamically oriented psychiatrists have tended to blame psychological or social factors for problems that really result from brain disease. On the other hand, biologically oriented psychiatrists may wrongly blame the brain for problems that are really psychological or social in origin. Either of these errors can cause problems. For example, a child who is suffering from depression may be punished for behaviors that are actually just a symptom of the depression. On the other hand, parents may be told that a child's problems are the result of a brain disorder when the real problem is bad schooling.

Every edition of the DSM was produced by committee and then approved by the membership of the APA. As a result, each edition of the DSM represents some sort of compromise with respect to the ideological views and economic interests of various factions within contemporary American psychiatry. The American Psychiatric Association was originally an organization that mainly represented the administrators of mental hospitals. Their caseload consisted mainly of people with severe, disabling illnesses such as schizophrenia and major depression. After World War II, the APA increasingly came to represent a large number of office-based practitioners of psychodynamic psycho-therapy. Their caseload was mainly outpatients, many of whom would not have qualified for the diagnosis of any particular mental illness. Many healthy people had begun to seek out psychoanalysis or some other form of psychotherapy as a form of spiritual quest. Thus, there was considerable pressure from that faction of the APA membership to have the DSM serve office-based practitioners, as opposed to hospital administrators.

Since the 1950s, the economic pressures have changed dramatically. Health insurance companies became less willing to reimburse for treat-ment for mental illnesses, even for the mental illnesses that are un-questionably medical problems. Also, office-based psychiatrists became more interested in using medications to treat mental illnesses. The de-velopment of expensive new drugs for treating mental illnesses meant that lobbyists from the pharmaceutical industry started pressuring the APA to rewrite the DSM in ways that supported the marketing efforts of the drug companies. One possible consequence of such pressure is called disease mongering.

The word *monger* came from a Latin word meaning a trader. It was originally used to mean someone who sold things. For example, a fish-monger is someone who sells fish. Over the years, the word *monger* start-ed to take on negative connotations, such as in scandalmonger (some-one who spreads rumors) and warmonger (someone who promotes war). Disease mongering involves efforts to promote the overdiagnosis of disease, in hopes of profiting from the sales of treatments. One way to promote overdiagnosis is to broaden the diagnostic criteria, so that a large number of healthy people would qualify for the diagnosis.

Within psychiatry, disease mongering could result in patients be-ing labeled with diagnoses for disorders that they do not have and then being given treatments that they do not need. For example, there has been an explosion in the number of children who have received a diag-nosis of attention-deficit–hyperactivity disorder (ADHD). Does this ex-plosion in diagnoses represent a real increase in the number of chil-dren with this condition? How could a population have such a massive increase in the prevalence of hyperactivity among children at the same time that it is experiencing a massive increase in childhood obesity? The epidemic of obesity is clearly real. The children's height and weight can be measured objectively. But is the hyperactivity epidemic real, or is it the result of unrealistic expectations about how children (especially boys) should behave? If both of these epidemics are real, might they both result from the same cause: lack of exercise? If so, is the hyperactivity merely a symptom of lack of exercise in some cases, as opposed to a disease to be treated medically?

Objective tests, such as blood tests and x-ray imaging, can be used to confirm or rule out many common medical diagnoses. However, mental illnesses cannot be confirmed or even ruled out by laboratory tests. Instead, the clinician must rely on his or her impression of the patient's symptoms. That is a challenge for several reasons. Patients may not report their symptoms accurately. Symptoms may change over time. Also, many mental illnesses have overlapping symptoms. For those reasons, there will always be problems with the reliability of psychiatric diagnoses.

Members of the antipsychiatry movement have made many criticisms of psychiatry. Some of these criticisms were valid, but many were way off base. The claim that mental illness is a myth is silly. Nobody can convincingly deny that some people are suffering or disabled because of abnormal patterns of thoughts, feelings, and behavior. Yes, we should be concerned about how that judgment of normal versus abnormal is being made. However, even an abnormal pattern would have to lead to suffering and disability before it can be considered a mental illness. Scientists and the public really should take a critical view of the role that psychiatrists might play in deciding what is abnormal and what is not, but the fact that it can be difficult to draw the lines between normal and abnormal does not invalidate the entire concept of mental illness. No one can say exactly how many hairs a man must lose before he is considered bald, but that fact does not mean that baldness is a myth.

The claim that the lack of objective laboratory tests invalidates the concept of mental illnesses is also nonsense. There have always been diagnoses in general medicine that are based on a constellation of symptoms and signs, even though doctors had no laboratory tests to confirm the diagnosis and no understanding of the cause of the problem. For example, the diagnosis of migraine headache is based purely on the patient's reports of the characteristic symptoms. That does not mean that migraine headache is a myth. The same principle applies to mental illnesses.

Some critics have claimed that it is inappropriate to use a medical model when one is addressing psychological problems. They have claimed that the concept of mental illness is just a metaphor for a problem in living. However, ordinary problems in living do not meet the definition of a mental illness. Mental illnesses are abnormal patterns of thought, feelings, and behavior that lead to suffering or disability. Sometimes, these abnormal patterns could cause (or result from) a problem in living. But by definition, normal responses to ordinary problems in living are not mental illnesses.

The DSM-I was published in 1952, which was the heyday of psychoanalytic psychiatry in the United States. Psychoanalysts had achieved powerful positions within the American Psychiatric Association, and Hollywood had embraced psychoanalysts and psychoanalysis. As a result, many people believed that psychoanalysis could help individuals solve their personal problems and that the psychiatric profession as a whole could help guide society in solving social and political problems. These expectations were not met. Some people claim that the problem was the limitations or inappropriateness of the medical model.

The term *medical model* has been used in many confusing ways, often by people who never bother to define the terminology that they use. (I suspect that some of them do not even think about the meaning of the words they use.) The term *medical model* can be used to mean two different things. In one sense, it can be used to refer to the nature of the underlying problem to be addressed. In the other, it refers to the doctor-patient relationship. In the former sense, the term *medical model* is used to mean that a mental problem is regarded as if it is the result of an underlying medical problem. The more bizarre someone's behavior is, the more reasonable this presumption seems to be. The latter sense of the term *medical model* implies that a patient is presenting a problem to a professional, who then draws on his or her expertise in addressing the problem, just as a mechanic might find and fix a problem in your car.

Sometimes, when people talk about the medical model, they are referring to a doctor-patient relationship. If your car is not working properly, you take it to a mechanic, who is supposed to find and fix the problem. Likewise, when people are suffering from a physical illness, they may seek help from a doctor, who is supposed to find and solve the problem. When people are suffering from a mental illness, they may seek help from a mental health professional, who is supposed to help them find and solve the problem. This form of medical model is appropriate if the doctor or mental health professional can figure out what is going wrong with your body or in your life and offer you effective ways to solve your problem.

When you hear someone from the antipsychiatry movement sneering at the medical model, ask yourself what alternative model that person would apply. Let us pray that the demonic possession model is off the table. Another alternative is the educational model, which presumes that the person is suffering from a lack of knowledge or skills and would benefit from instruction and coaching. Such training can be a form of *habilitation*, rather than *re*habilitation. In other words, it teaches people to learn skills that they never had, as opposed to relearning skills that they have lost. That model might be useful for some problems, especially educational problems. But it would be of minimal use for people with psychoses. You cannot train someone to stop hallucinating, and education cannot cure delusions.

Another term that crops up in debates about psychiatry is *Cartesian dualism*. Unfortunately, this term is typically used by people who do not seem to have read Descartes. Descartes was not dealing with the question of the relationship between body and mind so much as the relationship between body and soul. The soul is a supernatural entity. Modern science does not deal with questions about the soul or any other supernatural entity. Since the 1840s, scientists have been guided by a principle articulated by the great physiologist Rudolf Virchow: "Life itself is but the expression of a sum of phenomena, each of which follows the ordinary physical and chemical laws." This principle is sometimes called reductionism. Thus, modern scientists assume that the mind represents the activity of the brain. So unless someone is dealing with the supernatural, Cartesian dualism does not apply. Nor does reductionism mean that someone is being overly simplistic. Nothing about the brain is simple.

Another model, which was popular in the 1960s, was the shamanic journey. Scottish psychiatrist R. D. Laing believed that people who were suffering from mental distress were undergoing some sort of spiritual transformation and would emerge wiser and more grounded. For example, he once wrote, "Madness need not be all breakdown. It may also be break-through. It is potential liberation and renewal as well as enslavement and existential death." Eventually, Laing's own problems with alcoholism and clinical depression became so bad that the United Kingdom's General Medical Council forced him to stop practicing medicine. Evidently, he never broke through.

One idea that is often attributed to Laing is the notion that insanity represents a sane reaction to an insane society. Certainly, individuals can do odd things in odd circumstances. Also, psychiatry and mental hospitalization have sometimes been used to discredit political dissidents. But that does not mean that all mental illness is just political nonconformity.

It is obviously important to pay attention to the social context of anyone's thoughts, feelings, and behaviors. One of the pioneers of that approach was the French sociologist Émile Durkheim, whose 1897 book *Le Suicide* explored how the rates of suicide differed between countries and between groups within a country. For example, he found that Protestants were more likely than Catholics to commit suicide. (Later critics suggested that Protestants were simply more likely than Catholics to record certain kinds of deaths as suicide.) Thus, Durkheim showed us that it is important to look at behavior in its broader social context.

During the mid 20th century, the antipsychiatry movement made important criticisms of the kinds of care that had been provided to mental patients, often against their will. Many of these treatments were ineffective and dangerous. Today, many of them seem barbaric. On the bright side, lobbying from the antipsychiatry movement helped to put an end to the use of insulin shock, straightjackets, and frontal lobotomy. Yet on the other hand, rhetoric from the antipsychiatry movement was often used to refuse basic care, including food and shelter, to seriously disabled people.

Some members of the antipsychiatry movement have claimed that medical treatments, including drug treatments and electroconvulsive treatment (shock treatment), for mental problems are never appropriate. Yet a staggering amount of research has shown that these treatments do provide at least modest benefits for some patients, and that these benefits often outweigh the risks. Likewise, there is considerable evidence that some forms of psychotherapy can be beneficial in some circumstances. However, it would be irresponsible for a psychiatrist to offer nothing but talk therapy for a condition that is known to respond well to medication. The challenge for psychiatrists is to provide the right treatment to the right patient at the right time—whether that treatment involves medication, psychotherapy, or some combination of the two. Yet before the psychiatrist can provide the right treatment, the psychiatrist must come up with a reasonable diagnosis. For that reason, scientists and consumer advocates must pay careful attention to how the definitions of the mental disorders are written.

Scientific understanding of the brain is still at a primitive stage. As a result, even the most accomplished researchers and best-trained clinicians in the field of psychiatry are still largely fumbling around in the dark. We still do not know what causes the major mental illnesses such as schizophrenia and major depression. Although the psychiatric profession is far better equipped to treat those diseases than it was in 1950, the currently available treatments often have limited effectiveness and sometimes have unacceptable side effects. The current emphasis on brain malfunction as an underlying cause of mental illness is appropriate for dealing with major mental illnesses like schizophrenia, but it could be misleading in the search for solutions to other kinds of problems, such as poor performance in grammar school.

The diagnoses in the DSM-5 were written for researchers and

practicing psychiatrists. These diagnoses were supposedly designed to help mental health professionals provide the appropriate kind of care to people who are suffering because of their abnormal thoughts, feelings, and behavior. To this day, there are heated debates about the reliability and validity of many of the diagnoses in the DSM. Yet even if those diagnoses are reliable and valid for use by scientists and mental health professionals, they may not be useful for ordinary people because ordinary people have a different set of problems to solve.

The concept of mental illness is defined in such a way that it deals with abnormalities—deviations from what is considered normal for that person within that social setting. It deals with the scientific question of how people generally think, feel, and behave—not with the moral question of how people ought to think, feel, and behave. Psychiatry is a branch of medicine. As such, its focus is on providing diagnosis and treatments for people who are suffering or disabled because of some abnormality. As a result, psychiatry is simply not designed to deal with questions of whether normal is good. For that, you need a philosopher, not a psychiatrist. Also, psychiatry focuses on people who seek out treatment for themselves or who are presented for treatment. As a result, it tends to cater to people who recognize that they have some sort of problem, or people whose problems are so obvious that someone else calls in a psychiatrist. Thus, psychiatrists generally work with people who have problems, not so much with people who make problems for others. Many of the people who cause problems for others have personality disorders, such as narcissistic personality disorder.

Chapter 10

Personality Disorders

~

It is usually easy to tell when someone is having a psychotic episode. A psychotic person's speech and behavior and even his or her facial expressions can be noticeably odd. You might also be able to tell when someone is suffering from a major mood disorder, such as depression or mania, just by watching his or her facial expressions and behavior. However, even a trained observer can easily miss even a severe case of personality disorder. Many people with a personality disorder seem to wear what psychiatrist Hervey M. Cleckley called the mask of sanity. At first, they may seem normal. They may even seem to be intelligent and charming. Some of them even seem to be remarkably calm and collected, even in stressful situations. Eventually, however, the mask may slip—to reveal serious flaws in character.

If someone's character flaws are serious and persistent, are different from what society expects from that person, and are causing suffering or disability, the person would qualify for a diagnosis of a personality disorder. The DSM-5 defines personality disorders as "a class of mental disorders characterized by enduring maladaptive patterns of behavior, cognition, and inner experience, exhibited across many contexts and deviating markedly from those accepted by the individual's culture. These patterns develop early, are inflexible, and are associated with significant distress or disability." As I have explained in previous chapters, a psychological problem has to cause distress or disability to qualify as a mental illness. Also, psychiatrists do not consider a mental illness to be a mental disorder unless it is outside the range of what society expects from that person.

In other words, psychiatrists apply the label *personality disorder* only to cases in which the person's character flaws are particularly severe and particularly resistant to correction. Some researchers suspect that this resistance to correction means that the person has brain defects that cannot be fixed. Yet in some cases, the person might simply have failed to learn good problem-solving skills. Some people simply fall into the habit of using tactics that seem to work in the short run but are ultimately self-defeating. Perhaps all of us deal with both problems, to some degree. We all struggle against the limitations of our own brains, and we all are held back by the limitations of our knowledge and skills.

To receive a diagnosis of a personality disorder under the DSM, you have to be an adult, but your mental problem has to have begun early. For that reason, I view personality disorders as failures of normal development. It is normal for toddlers to engage in magical thinking or to throw tantrums when their wishes are not instantly fulfilled. Parents call that stage of development the terrible twos. But when grown-ups behave like toddlers, we suspect that they are mentally ill. For that reason, healthy people who are working on their own coming-of-age story arc can learn some important lessons from studying people with personality disorders.

Everyone has character flaws. So how is an ordinary person different from someone who would qualify for a diagnosis of personality disorder? Is it a difference of degree or a difference of kind? Or is it a difference of degree that is so extreme that it might as well be a difference of kind? Scientific studies of personality disorder often focus on individuals who are in prison because they have failed to meet even minimal standards of civilized behavior. In contrast, the Greek philosopher Theophrastus wrote about the commonplace character flaws and social gaffes that could make an ordinary person irritating.

Theophrastus wondered why individual Greeks could be so different from each other, even though they lived under the same sky and were educated alike. Even today's top psychiatrists are still puzzled by that question. However, they have come up with a few partial answers. One involves genetics. Some traits predictably result from the genetic hand of cards that the person was dealt at conception. Genetics explain why identical twins look and often behave so much like each other, even if they were brought up separately from birth. Yet even identical twins who were reared together can differ from each other in important ways.

Every human being has traits that are different from those of a chimpanzee or an elm tree. The differences between species are clearly the result of the genetic differences between the species. However, not all differences between individuals within a species are due, even in part, to genetic differences between those individuals. During the development of every individual, genes interact with environmental influences. Like a tree, each human being is nourished and held back by influences in his or her environment. A tree that is given the optimal conditions may develop into a magnificent, fruitful specimen. In contrast, a tree that is subjected to harsh conditions may end up stunted and twisted like a bonsai. It can be hard to tell whether the stunting and twisting of a personality resulted from a genetic flaw, a harsh environment, or some interaction of the two.

All mental illnesses involve some combination of problems with thoughts, feelings, and behavior. In a case of psychosis, the most obvious problem is in the domain of perception and thought. Yet a psychotic person may also have abnormal emotions and behavior. In a case of a mood disorder, the most obvious problem is in the domain of emotion. Yet a person with a mood disorder may also have problems with perception, thought, and behavior. In a case of personality disorder, the most obvious problem is in the domain of behavior. Yet the person may also have some serious problems with thoughts and emotions. To understand the abnormal behavior of someone with a personality disorder, such as narcissistic personality disorder, you need to understand how that person thinks and what (if anything) that person feels. From studying people with personality disorders, we may learn lessons about how to help them and how to keep them from harming others. We may even learn some lessons about how to help ourselves. To correct your own character flaws, you need to learn the lessons that people with personality disorders have somehow failed to learn.

The medical model often falls short when it comes to explaining personality disorders. Many cases of personality disorder, especially the milder cases, are probably not due to disease of the brain. Instead, they could represent failures of social learning. Perhaps the person has simply learned maladaptive patterns of thinking, emotion, and behavior. Thus, the problem could result from miseducation or even from lack of education. The person might have been taught bad behavior, or the person may never have been taught good behavior. Yet in other cases, the individual might simply be a slow learner. Some people find it hard to learn certain kinds of lessons, perhaps because of some problem in their brain. In those cases, neither the medical model nor a standard educational model is entirely appropriate. The best model for those cases is special education: lessons designed to help someone overcome handicaps in learning.

The medical model can also fall short if a problem is unlikely to be diagnosed in the context of an office visit and is unlikely to respond well to any treatment that a doctor or other mental health professional can offer. On the other hand, there is probably a great deal that can be done, on an individual or societal level, to help children develop properly (an educational model or perhaps a special education model) and to keep people from becoming stunted and broken by life experiences (a public health model).

The ancient Greek philosopher Theophrastus wrote 29 character sketches that describe ways in which ordinary people can be annoying. In contrast, the DSM-5 defines 10 specific personality disorders, which are grouped into three clusters, labeled A, B, and C. Cluster A is described as the odd, bizarre, or eccentric personality disorders. It includes three disorders: schizotypal personality disorder, paranoid personality disorder, and schizoid personality disorder. Cluster B is described as the dramatic and erratic personality disorders. It includes histrionic personality disorder, narcissistic personality disorder, antisocial personality disorder, and borderline personality disorder. Cluster C is described as the anxious and fearful personality disorders. It includes avoidant personality disorder, dependent personality disorder, and obsessive-compulsive personality disorder. The DSM-5 also gives a diagnostic code for a personality change due to another medical condition and two codes for personality disorders that do not fit neatly into one of the 10 main categories.

Any system of classification must be judged by two criteria: reliability and validity. To be valid, a system must be reliable. But reliability may hinge on technical problems. For example, a personality disorder is defined as a problem that can be seen in many contexts. Yet the psychiatrist may see a patient only in the context of an office visit. In that setting, the patient may be careful to wear his or her mask of sanity. For that reason, psychiatrists rarely have the opportunity to learn enough about a patient to make a reliable assessment of that patient's personality.

Diagnostic categories must also be valid. In other words, they must be useful for some practical purpose. People who get the same diagnosis should have something important in common with each other. They should also differ in meaningful ways from the people who get a different diagnosis. Likewise, the personality disorders that are grouped into the same cluster should have something important in common with each other. If you analyze the three clusters, you can see that each cluster involves problems with a particular kind of relationship. In Cluster A, the main problem seems to be in the person's relationship with reality. In Cluster B, the main problem seems to be in the person's relationships with other people. In Cluster C, the main problem seems to be in the person's relationship with his or her environment.

The Cluster A personality disorders seem to be mainly problems in relating to reality, possibly because of something going wrong in the brain. However, these problems with reality can end up causing problems in how the person relates to other people. People with schizotypal and schizoid personality disorder tend to be cold and aloof, while people with paranoid personality disorder can be hostile and suspicious.

Many psychiatrists feel that schizotypal personality disorder is really a mild form of schizophrenia. (The World Health Organization puts it in the same category as schizophrenia, rather than classifying it as a personality disorder.) The symptoms of schizotypal personality disorder are similar to those of schizophrenia, but milder. Also, the two disorders tend to run in the same families.

The prefix *schizo-* means split. Schizophrenia literally means split mind, but it does not mean multiple personality disorder. Instead, the thought patterns of someone with schizophrenia may be disrupted and incoherent, like a reflection in a shattered mirror. The symptoms of schizophrenia include hallucinations, delusions, and general incoherence of thought, as well as odd or inappropriate emotions. The diagnosis of schizotypal personality disorder is given to people who have odd or eccentric behavior, are prone to magical thinking and paranoia, and tend to be cold and aloof and socially withdrawn. However, their condition is never severe enough for them to qualify for a diagnosis of schizophrenia.

People with schizotypal personality disorder may benefit from some of the same medications that are used for treating schizophrenia. However, these people also need a lot of social support and counseling to improve their social skills and their thinking skills. You cannot use reason to persuade a schizophrenic person to give up his or her delusions. However, people with schizotypal disorder can sometimes be persuaded to reject some of their weird beliefs.

Despite the similarity in name, schizoid personality disorder is not related to schizophrenia or schizotypal disorder. Instead of having a shattered mind, the person with schizoid personality disorder is split off from society. People with schizoid personality disorder simply seem to have a lack of interest in social relationships. They may seem cold, secretive, and apathetic. However, they may have a rich fantasy life. Many are particularly creative, especially in writing fiction and in creating visual art. Some psychiatrists have argued that schizoid personality disorder should be removed from the DSM. They feel that it does not qualify as a mental illness because the people with the condition are not necessarily suffering from it.

Paranoia, which is the irrational belief that other people want to harm you, is a common feature of schizophrenia and schizotypal disorder. It is also the prominent feature of paranoid personality disorder. Paranoid personality disorder consists of pervasive, long-standing suspiciousness and general mistrust of others. People with this problem tend to take things personally, and they are continually on the lookout for evidence to confirm their suspicions. Because of their suspicious, hostile nature and their tendency to hold grudges, they usually have limited social interactions. In that respect, they may become as socially isolated as someone with schizoid personality disorder.

The prognosis for paranoid personality disorder is poor. People with the condition rarely seek out treatment, and they rarely choose to take part in it when it is offered. Medication does not seem to help much —possibly because the patients are too suspicious to take their prescribed medication. Psychotherapy does not seem to help much, either. The feelings of paranoia are based on delusion and cannot be reasoned away, even if a therapist could somehow gain the paranoid person's trust.

The Cluster A personality disorders probably do represent some underlying problem with how the brain functions. However, even mentally healthy people often have problems with interpreting reality, and these problems can undermine their relationships with other people. Psychotic people often suffer from delusions, which are ridiculous false beliefs that are firmly held despite clear evidence that they are false. However, even someone who is generally regarded as mentally healthy could hold some religious beliefs that may seem ridiculous to other people.

Religious people hold strong beliefs that they learned from trusted authority figures. You may have to profess some odd beliefs in order to be accepted within a particular social group. For that reason, psychiatrists do not consider a religious belief to be a delusion, even if the belief is illogical or flatly contradicted by evidence. A religious person's commitment to doctrine can be a way of expressing loyalty to a social group. In contrast, a psychotic person's delusions tend to undermine his or her social relationships. Thus, religious beliefs are sometimes socially adaptive while psychotic delusions are socially maladaptive.

Psychoses and to a lesser extent the Cluster A personality disorders represent some failure in the person's ability to create a workable mental model of reality. All of us human beings make mental models to help us navigate our physical and social environments. However, the model that we make of the physical environment may have to be adjusted to allow us to navigate our social environment. In other words, human beings often have a social or political need to believe things that have no basis in fact or reason.

Back in the 1930s and 1940s, American Socialists would criticize American Communists for holding beliefs that were "politically correct," as opposed to factually correct, when they stuck to the Communist Party line on issues. The implication was that false beliefs would give rise to bad politics. (Today, the term *political correctness* is usually used to disparage the tactful use of nonsexist, nonracist language. However, it is sometimes used to discourage people from raising any sensitive topic in conversation or even in college classrooms.)

The pressure to hold politically correct beliefs occurs in practically any social setting. That fact has been recognized since ancient times. In *The Republic*, the Greek philosopher Plato used the Allegory of the Cave to describe the personal and social resistance to true but unorthodox ideas. Plato asked his audience to imagine a group of prisoners who had lived for their entire lives chained up in a cave, so that all they can see are the shadows cast on the back wall by events outside the cave. To the prisoners, those shadows are reality. However, a prisoner who escapes from the cave would come to see the outside world in three dimensions and in full color. If he then went back into the cave, he would be temporarily blind as his eyes adjusted to the dim light. Yet the other prisoners would think that he had been harmed by his experiences. As a result, they would kill anyone who tried to drag them out into the light. History is full of accounts of people who have been dealt with harshly for telling an unfamiliar or unpopular truth.

Like all higher animals, all human beings make mental models that help them survive in their environment. However, human beings can make more elaborate models of reality and can think about the validity of their mental models. As a result, human beings can correct and refine their mental models in ways that other animals cannot. With the rise of literacy, civilized people started describing their mental models in writing. They also started writing about ways to correct and improve mental models. The purpose of a classical education was to teach people how to address the questions of what is true and what is good. Thus, an educated person would be better able to develop accurate models of reality and better able to make good choices.

People with Cluster A personality disorders are unusually bad at making accurate mental models of reality, possibly because something is going wrong in their brain. However, people with a healthy brain can improve their own ability to make and apply accurate mental models by studying the classical liberal arts, including logic and rhetoric, and then studying the physical and social sciences. I explain the nature and purposes of this kind of education in detail in *Not Trivial: How Studying the Traditional Liberal Arts Can Set You Free.*

The four Cluster B personality disorders are predominantly problems in how the person relates to other people. Histrionic people regard other people as an audience. Narcissists regard other people as underlings. Sociopaths regard other people as things. People with borderline personality disorder regard other people as either angels or devils, with no middle ground in between. All of these Cluster B personality disorders have one thing in common: people with these disorders do not seem to know how to relate to other people as equals. For some mysterious reason or combination of reasons (whether it is bad wiring in their brain or bad upbringing or some combination of the two), people with Cluster B personality disorders do not know how to base their interpersonal relationships on mutual respect. Their emotional reactions to other people are abnormal. Because of an inability to relate normally to other human beings, people with some Cluster B personality disorders seem to suffer from some sort of emotional emptiness. Often, they try to fill the void with excitement, often from risky behavior such as skydiving or from booze, drugs, and anonymous sex. As a result, their lives can spiral out of control.

The word *histrionic* came from the Latin word for actor. People with histrionic personality disorder love to be the center of attention, appreciation, and excitement. The emotions that they express are dramatic, quickly changing, and possibly exaggerated. Their feelings are easily hurt, but they seem to lack concern for others. Histrionic people are often attractive and seductive and beautifully groomed. However, they tend to be intellectually and emotionally shallow. Fortunately, you can generally write yourself out of their dramas and walk away from their performances. Thanks to the Internet, they will always have an audience.

Some critics have suggested that histrionic personality disorder should be removed from the DSM because Western society has trained its young women to be histrionic. The media bombard young women with the message that they must be sexually attractive to gain men's approval, and that men's approval is the key to success. If seductiveness is not enough, a young woman may try theatrical behavior to attract attention. The goal is to be the leading lady in a great love story or at least a romantic comedy. As their looks fade, histrionic women may cast themselves in a motherly role. Thus, some histrionic behaviors are highly adaptive. Gay men may also internalize the same message. Thus, histrionic behavior would not violate a social norm for gay men and may not be maladaptive. Among gay men, such theatricality is called camp. Within the gay community, camp is a subversive form of artistic expression, not a personality disorder.

People with narcissistic personality disorder tend to regard other people as underlings. According to the DSM-5, individuals with narcissistic personality disorder have most or all of the following attitudes, typically without having the talents or accomplishments to back them up:

- Having an exaggerated sense of self-importance
- Expecting to be recognized as superior even without achievements that warrant it
- Exaggerating your achievements and talents
- Being preoccupied with fantasies about success, power, brilliance, beauty or the perfect mate
- Believing that you are superior and can only be understood by or associate with equally special people
- Requiring constant admiration
- Having a sense of entitlement
- Expecting special favors and unquestioning compliance with your expectations
- Taking advantage of others to get what you want
- Having an inability or unwillingness to recognize the needs and feelings of others
- Being envious of others and believing others envy you
- Behaving in an arrogant or haughty manner

All of these attitudes reflect excessive ambition. A person with narcissistic personality disorder expects and demands the power, property, and prestige that go along with a high social rank. The drama starts when other people do not provide the admiration and special privileges that the narcissist thinks that he or she deserves. Of course, if you really did have a high social rank, nobody would think you were crazy if you had such expectations or made such demands. They might think that you were a snob, but they would not think that you were nuts.

Histrionic people create drama because they love the attention. Narcissistic people create drama because they are continually battling unsuccessfully for social dominance. Narcissists are sensitive to real or imagined threats to their social rank. Like Snow White's stepmother, they can become furious if someone is simply beautiful in their presence. The narcissist wants to be the beautiful one, the popular one, the rich one, the smart one, etc. Thus, narcissists can become filled with hatred for anyone who could outrank them in any way, even if that other person has no interest in competing.

Narcissists want to dominate other people, rather than connecting with them as equals. In other words, narcissists behave like an overly ambitious hen that is struggling to maintain an unrealistically high position within the pecking order. A powerful hen takes what she wants from the lower-ranking hens. The brain circuits that are involved in this kind of social competition are primitive. Chickens can fight for dominance. However, chickens cannot understand or apply philosophical concepts like truth, justice, or solidarity. Likewise, when narcissists are battling for social rank, they tend to act like birdbrains. They tend to ignore higher philosophical concepts—unless they can use those concepts to gain some advantage. As a result, narcissists often seem shallow, callous, and hypocritical.

People with narcissistic personality disorder want to occupy a high social rank, so that they can look down on most or all of the people they encounter. In other words, they are ambitious, yet their reach exceeds their grasp. As a fan of boxing might put it, narcissists often try to punch above their weight. Yet since narcissists often judge their own matches, they often declare themselves the winner, even if onlookers would think that the narcissist has lost. Narcissists are regarded as mentally ill because their self-perceptions are inaccurate and because their strategies and tactics fail or even backfire.

Narcissists tend to have an unhealthy drive to win pointless victories. Many of their victories are pointless, and some may be pyrrhic. A pyrrhic victory means that someone won a battle but was damaged so badly in that battle that he ended up losing the war. As a result, the narcissist's struggles for dominance can be ultimately self-defeating.

Narcissists may be poor at spotting situational irony, which means a mismatch between the intended result of an action and the actual result. Their interpersonal skills may be so poor that they cannot judge whether they have won or lost in a competition. Also, their reasoning skills may be so poor that they are simply not good strategists, even if they are reasonably good tacticians. Tactics are the actual means used to achieve an objective, while strategy is the overall plan of a campaign. In other words, effective tactics win battles, while effective strategy wins wars.

For a patient to qualify for a DSM-5 diagnosis of narcissistic personality disorder, the attitudes described by the diagnostic criteria must be pervasive and persistent. In other words, the person must express these attitudes in many different situations over a long period. The attitudes must also be making it hard for the person to have meaningful relationships with others. Since narcissists insist on being treated as a superior, they cannot base their relationships on mutual respect. Instead, they seek out submissive followers (co-dependents) who will give them unearned praise.

Individuals are considered narcissistic when they expect or demand a higher social rank than other people are willing to give them. The diagnosis of narcissistic personality disorder is a social judgment. Many people are distressed by the idea that the diagnosis of narcissism is a personal judgment made in a social context. They want psychiatric diagnoses to be more like an ordinary medical diagnosis. They want the diagnosis of narcissism to be based on some objective criterion, such as the result of some laboratory test. However, the fact that a diagnosis of narcissism is a personal, social judgment does not mean that the problem being judged is unreal or unimportant.

Narcissism, like beauty, is in the eye of the beholder. For example, Italian fascists supported Benito Mussolini because they considered "Il Duce" (the leader) to be a great leader, deserving of admiration and a position of public trust. His admirers and supporters considered him a great man. In contrast, his detractors thought that he was a narcissistic fool. (A fool is a person with bad judgment.) Unfortunately, his critics turned out to be right. Mussolini turned out to be one of the most dangerous fools of the 20th century. In June of 1940, he declared war on Britain and France. He reportedly told his Army's Chief of Staff, "I only need a few thousand dead so that I can sit at the peace conference as a man who has fought." Unfortunately, about half a million Italians died in the war, and the country as a whole suffered terrible destruction and hardship. When the war ended in 1945, Mussolini tried to escape to Switzerland. However, he was captured and executed by partisans, who then hung his corpse, alongside that of his mistress, upside down in a gas station in Milan.

Fools can be dangerous if they achieve political power. However, narcissistic people can be dangerous even if they remain on the bottom of the social pyramid. When the narcissist's desire for power, property, and prestige is not met, the narcissist may lash out in anger. Because they feel that they are taking what is rightfully theirs, they seem to have no conscience. Because they feel that they are in the superior social position, they have no sense of shame. Shame is the emotion that corresponds to being in an *inferior* social position. (I will explain anger and shame in more detail in Chapter 11.) If narcissistic people fail in their attempts to gain status, they may do something appalling to make themselves infamous. That is how narcissism can motivate someone to commit murder in public, such as an assassination or a mass shooting. If the narcissist cannot gain respect, at least he can inspire fear.

Since narcissism is a problem related to social rank, it can occur only in a social context. As long as Robinson Crusoe is alone on his island, he cannot compete with anyone for social rank. Likewise, the diagnosis in a case of narcissism depends on which people the narcissist considers to be underlings. A man who considers himself superior to all women is called a misogynist. A white person who considers himself or herself to be superior to all people of color is called a racist. A religious person who looks down on all those who do not adhere to the One True Faith is called a religious bigot. A wealthy and privileged person who looks down on members of the lower classes is called a snob. A person who looks down on anyone with a superior education is called anti-intellectual. I consider each of these problems to be a serious mental defect. Yet if a person's superiority complex is restricted to these categories, he or she might not qualify for a psychiatric diagnosis of narcissistic personality disorder. Because sexism, racism, religious bigotry, and anti-intellectualism are so commonplace in the United States, such biases by themselves do not even qualify a person for a psychiatric diagnosis of a mental disorder. To qualify for a diagnosis of narcissistic personality disorder, a white man would have to consider himself superior to other white men—not just to women and people of color.

Many psychotic people suffer from delusions of grandeur, which means a false belief that one is famous, wealthy, and immensely powerful. Narcissists do not necessarily have delusions of grandeur. They may not *believe* that they are already famous, wealthy, and powerful. However, they do feel that they *deserve* more fame, wealth, and power than other people are willing to grant them. The solution to this problem seems straightforward. Teach the narcissistic person better strategies for achieving his or her goals, but make his or her status depend on good behavior. Ambitious people often respond well to this kind of carrot-and-stick approach. Unfortunately, narcissists may not take instruction from anyone whom they consider to be an underling. If you accept instruction from someone, you put yourself in a one-down position relative to that person. A narcissistic person may choose to remain ignorant, rather than humbling him- or herself in such a way. For that reason, a narcissist may seem to be as immune to reason as a delusional schizophrenic.

Theoretically, a narcissist's behavior could be corrected by someone whom the narcissist accepts as a superior. Unfortunately, the people who outrank the narcissist within the social hierarchy may not realize that there is a problem to be corrected. Ambitious people may be horrid to the people who are at or below their social rank. However, they can show fawning submission to the people they wish to impress.

What causes narcissistic personality disorder? Nobody really knows. It seems to be more common in some families than in others. Studies of identical twins have shown that the underlying problem could be at least partly genetic, perhaps because an unusually powerful drive for social dominance could be partly genetic. However, researchers have not been able to link any particular genes to the disorder. Also, narcissistic personality disorder seems to be far more common in modern societies than in traditional societies. So I doubt that the genetic studies will reveal much. Personally, I suspect that narcissistic personality disorder results from a combination of overweening ambition and poor interpersonal skills. There are two possible solutions to this problem: either accept the social rank that other people are willing to give you, or find an effective way to rise in other people's estimation.

The features of narcissistic personality disorder overlap with those of antisocial personality disorder, which has sometimes been called psychopathy or sociopathy. A sociopath can be just as egotistical as a narcissist. However, there is a key difference. A narcissist may view you as an underling, but a sociopath views you as a thing. According to the DSM-5, antisocial personality disorder consists of disregard for and violation of the rights of others:

- Failure to obey laws and norms by engaging in behavior which results in criminal arrest, or would warrant criminal arrest
- Lying, deception, and manipulation, for profit or self-amusement
- Impulsive behavior
- Irritability and aggression, manifested as frequently assaults others, or engages in fighting
- Blatantly disregards safety of self and others
- A pattern of irresponsibility
- Lack of remorse for actions

The diagnosis of antisocial personality disorder is reserved for adults who have been misbehaving since they were 15 years old and whose misbehavior is not the result of schizophrenia or bipolar disorder.

Sociopaths may seem at first to be charming, but they have no respect for other people and no concern for other people's rights or feelings. Sociopaths may even seem to have reckless disregard for their own safety. Because of this lack of concern for other people's feelings, sociopaths sometimes choose to break laws and violate other social norms. They can be manipulative or even predatory. They may lie, cheat, steal, rape, or kill—and feel no guilt or shame afterward. In rape, the rapist uses the victim's body as if it were a thing that belongs to the rapist. Murder literally turns a person into a thing. Sociopaths feel no guilt or remorse over such actions because they regarded their victims as things to begin with.

Many of the studies of antisocial personality disorder have focused on convicted criminals. Yet not all sociopaths are criminals, and not all criminals are sociopaths. Sometimes, the pressures of war can cause a seemingly normal person to behave like a sociopath, at least to people who are classified as the enemy. Yet engaging in or even just observing such behavior can take a terrible emotional toll on someone who is not really a sociopath. Veterans in the peace movement have told me that post-traumatic stress disorder (PTSD) actually represents a wounded conscience. As one combat veteran explained to me, "There are things you can't undo and can't unsee. You wrestle with them all night in your dreams." A nurse practitioner who works at a Veterans Administration hospital once told me that the nicest patients are the ones with the worst PTSD.

A sociopath's brain often fails to produce the normal kinds of emotional responses. For example, they may be capable of feeling fear, but they can be bad at judging threats. As a result, they may not feel fear in response to a physically dangerous situation. Sociopaths also lack empathy. For those reasons, sociopaths are not held back by feelings of concern for the wellbeing of themselves or other people. Nevertheless, many sociopaths are more or less law abiding.

Unfortunately, a sociopath's brain can also have some trouble with some kinds of advanced mental processes, especially with respect to planning and self-control. As a result, sociopaths often fail to think ahead and make proper plans. They can also act impulsively. As a result, they often end up in legal trouble. Much of the research on antisocial personality disorder has involved men who were in prison for some criminal offense. However, not all criminals are sociopaths, and not all sociopaths are criminals.

Sociopathy is a medical/psychological concept, whereas crime is a legal concept. Criminals are people who have broken laws. Many things that are illegal are not particularly evil, and many evil things are condoned by law. Arlo Guthrie deals with this concept in his song *Alice's Restaurant*. In the first part of the song, Guthrie tells the colorful tale of the Alice's Restaurant Massacre (he pronounces it "massaCREE"), in which he got caught dumping garbage outside of the town dump on Thanksgiving Day. (For some mysterious reason, the dump was closed on Thanksgiving). The second part of the song recounts what happened when Guthrie went to the Army Recruitment Center on Whitehall Street in Manhattan in response to his draft notice. During the selection process, he was asked whether he had a criminal record. Guthrie explained that he had once been convicted of littering. He recounts that he was then handed a form that asked, "Kid, have you rehabilitated yourself?" The song goes on:

> I went over to the Sargent, said, "Sargent, you got a lot a damn gall to ask me if I've rehabilitated myself, I mean, I mean, I mean that just, I'm sittin' here on the bench, I mean I'm sittin' here on the Group W bench, 'cause you want to know if I'm moral enough join the army, burn women, kids, houses and villages after bein' a litterbug."

The diagnosis of a mental disorder, such as antisocial personality disorder, can be given only when the problem is leading to suffering or disability. However, sociopaths may not always seem to be disabled. In fact, psychologists have found that the top executives of major corporations often have high scores on standard measures of sociopathic traits.

Yet for some reason, we are supposed to admire men who have millions or billions in ill-gotten gains, while despising honest people who are down on their luck. Thus, we often give prestige to the wrong sort of people. Yet sociopathy may not always be disabling. In his song *False Leader*, Gary Clail sings, "The real criminals of this world are not those in prisons, but those who steal the wealth of the world from the people."

Like narcissists, sociopaths seem to have a lack of empathy, which means that other people's suffering does not bother them. So how can you tell whether someone is a narcissist or a sociopath? Can a person be both of those things at the same time? I think that the difference between narcissism and sociopathy lies in where that person draws the mental boundaries between persons, animals, and things. A narcissist wants to dominate other human beings. A particularly dominant person may treat other people like animals. The famous movie director Alfred Hitchcock once quipped, "I never said all actors are cattle; what I said was all actors should be treated like cattle." In contrast, a sociopath regards other human beings as if they were inanimate objects.

To add to the confusion, an individual may regard only certain persons as things, and only under particular circumstances. For example, once serial murderer Ted Bundy started confessing to his crimes, he claimed that he could not kill any woman with whom he had ever had an extended conversation. After that kind of interaction, he started to think of a woman as a person. I think that Ted Bundy was primarily narcissistic. In his day-to-day life, he was preoccupied with impressing other people with his superiority. He viewed his relationship with the police and the courts as a game that he would ultimately win. Yet his homicidal rages were directed at women whom he did not know socially and could therefore regard as things rather than people. Thus, they could serve as objects to stand in for his first love, a beautiful and wealthy young woman who broke up with him when he seemed directionless. Like his first love, most of his victims were beautiful young women with long dark hair, parted in the middle.

Unlike a pure sociopath, Ted Bundy showed signs of embarrassment when he finally started confessing his crimes. By that point, he knew that he no longer had any hope of being set free. The best he could hope for was to persuade the governor of Florida to delay his execution. As a result, Bundy stopped proclaiming his innocence and started to describe his crimes in detail. Yet instead of simply laying out the facts, Bundy hemmed and hawed and used a lot of distancing language. Distancing language means indirect phrasing that a person uses to create psychological distance between him- or herself and the objects, persons, or activities that he or she is describing. For example, when the interviewer asked Bundy if he removed the front passenger seat of his Volkswagen Beetle so that he could transport bodies, Bundy became clearly upset. He objected to the word "body." Instead, he talked about "cargo." Bundy also became flustered when he described how the "cargo" sometimes regained consciousness and started talking.

These hesitations and the distancing language are signs of shame. Shame is the feeling that goes along with being in a subordinate social position—a position that narcissists often cannot tolerate. Privately, Bundy was proud of the murders, which he regarded as accomplishments. Yet when it came time to confess, he found it hard to admit to things that would make other people think less of him. In contrast, Richard Kuklinski, the mafia hitman known as the Iceman, showed no signs of emotion as he recounted his crimes. Like Bundy, he had nothing to lose by making those confessions. But unlike Bundy, he had very little to gain.

As a young man, Kuklinski had earned a reputation for his explosive temper: he would beat or even kill other men for getting on his nerves, often for a minor or imaginary reason. Often, allowed a long time to elapse before he killed the man. (Kuklinski insisted that he never killed any females.) Because of his enormous size and strength and his ruthlessness, he quickly became useful as an enforcer for organized crime. Kuklinski explained that he got relatively little pleasure from the act of killing. What excited him was the hunt: the stalking and the technical challenges of getting away with murder. In an extensive set of interviews with forensic psychiatrist Park Dietz, Kuklinski seemed remarkably calm as he described his offenses.

Unlike Bundy, Kuklinski did not hem or haw or use distancing language when he described how he murdered people. In fact, he seemed emotionally flat. He did show the occasional flash of anger in response to some questions. He also seemed to show genuine sadness when he reflected on his failure as a family man. Despite his criminal career, he had maintained a façade of normalcy at home. He had a wife and children, a nice suburban home with a pool. He sent his children to Catholic school, and he served as an usher at mass on Sundays. He took his kids to Disneyworld every year. In prison, he showed signs of genuine grief that his children no longer wanted anything to do with him.

> I've never felt sorry for anything I've done, other than hurting my family. The only thing I feel sorry for. I'm not looking for forgiveness, and I'm not repenting. No, I'm wrong. [Sniffles] I am wrong. I do want my family to forgive me. Oh boy. I ain't going to make this one. Oh shit. This would never be me. THIS would not be me. I feel for my family. You see The Iceman crying. Not very macho, but I've hurt people that mean everything to me, but the only people that meant anything to me.

Kuklinski was candid about his reasons for talking with Dietz. Kuklinski wanted to know what was wrong with him, why his life had turned out so badly. Park Dietz told Kuklinski that Kuklinski qualified for the diagnosis of two personality disorders: antisocial and paranoid. The sociopathy enabled Kuklinski to kill without remorse, and the paranoia helped him get away with murder. Because of his paranoia, Kuklinski kept his distance from other people, he was quick to anger, and he never forgave anyone who offended him. As a result, Kuklinski ended up killing most of the few people who knew about his criminal activities. Kuklinski was eventually caught because the police noticed that so many people around him were disappearing.

Dietz told Kuklinski that the sociopathy and the paranoia probably resulted from a combination of genetic and environmental factors. According to Dietz, the genetic aspect of Kuklinski's mental problems was probably his lack of fear of physical injury. As Dietz explained to Kuklinski,

The fact that you are born with a genetic predisposition to fear-lessness doesn't mean that it's inevitable for you to become a criminal, because some people who have that predisposition to fearlessness become pro-social risk-takers.

The environmental factor in Kuklinski's case was brutal treatment by his parents. Kuklinski's older brother Florian died at age 10. The official story is that the boy fell down the stairs, but Kuklinski claimed that his parents beat the boy to death. (The boy died many years before the medical profession started talking about battered child syndrome.) Kuklinski's younger brother Joseph was convicted of raping and murdering a 12-year-old girl. As Dietz explained to Kuklinski,

> The difference between the people who grow up to be risk-taking good guys with white hats and the people who grow up to be risk-taking bad guys with a long, long rap sheet and a lot of crimes has to do with how their parents raised them. If you raise a kid with love and kindness and affection, most of the time, you have a good shot at their growing up to be decent, caring, loving human beings and treating their own kids well. But if you raise a kid the way Stanley raised you: with no love, no affection, constant abuse, beatings for no reason, all you teach is hatred. You make it impossible for that child to grow up to form strong attachments and loving, caring relationships or to risk themselves to protect the world.

The other Cluster B personality disorder is borderline personality disorder. Borderline personality disorder is the hardest personality disorder to describe. The DSM-5 describes it as follows: "a pervasive pattern of instability of interpersonal relationships, self-image, and affects, and marked impulsivity, beginning in early adulthood and present in a variety of contexts." People with borderline personality disorder want to have close personal relationships. In particular, they are terrified by the prospect of abandonment. Yet their impulsive and irrational behavior tends to drive people away.

Borderline personality disorder is classified as a personality disorder because people with the condition tend to have serious problems with interpersonal relationships. Yet these problems may stem from problems with thinking and with emotion. For example, people with borderline personality disorder are prone to black-and-white thinking. As a result, they tend to regard another person as either an angel or a devil, rather than as an imperfect human being. Some evidence suggests that these people have problems with the frontolimbic networks in the brain. These networks play an important role in allowing reason to help regulate emotions.

The most famous case of borderline personality disorder is probably Susanna Kaysen's. Kaysen spent 18 months in a psychiatric hospital after she tried to commit suicide by swallowing 50 aspirin tablets. She described her experiences in her memoir *Girl, Interrupted*, which was adapted into a major motion picture in 1999.

The causes of borderline personality disorder are unknown. The problem seems to be more common among people who have a family history of other kinds of mental illnesses. It also seems to be more common among people who were abused or neglected in early childhood.

Borderline personality disorder is a life-threatening illness. Up to 10% of the people who qualify for this diagnosis eventually succeed in killing themselves. An even larger percentage of patients engage in other kinds of self-injury, such as cutting the skin on their arms and legs. So far, no drug treatments seem to be useful in managing the core symptoms of borderline personality disorder. The most promising approach for managing borderline personality disorder is called dialectical behavioral therapy (DBT). This approach is called dialectical because it is aimed at the middle ground between accepting the clients as they are and urging them to change. In its standard form, DBT consists of four components:

- A skills training group, in which a teacher provides lessons in a classroom setting and assigns homework in which the clients practice using their new skills in everyday life. The class usually meets once a week for two and a half hours. The course usually lasts 24 weeks.

- Individual therapy, which focuses on motivating the client and helping the client apply new skills to specific challenges. The client generally receives one session a week, to run concurrently with the skills training group.
- Phone coaching is available between therapy sessions. Clients can call their therapist between sessions to receive coaching when they need it the most.
- The therapist consultation team is intended to provide support for the therapists. The teachers and therapists usually meet once a week.

Dialectical behavior therapy is intended to teach four types of skills: mindfulness (being fully aware and present in the moment), distress tolerance, emotional regulation, and interpersonal effectiveness (how to negotiate effectively while maintaining self-respect and good relationships). DBT was developed in the late 1970s by Marsha M. Linehan, who was serving a clientele of women with repeated suicide attempts and nonsuicidal self-injury. These clients responded poorly to standard cognitive behavioral therapy. These clients had so many serious problems that the standard approach to cognitive behavioral therapy was impractical. Also, many of these clients would simply drop out of cognitive behavioral therapy. Others unwittingly trained their therapists to provide ineffective therapy. For example, the clients would throw tantrums if the therapists addressed uncomfortable topics but would engage warmly if the therapist changed the subject to a less-important topic. Like people with other personality disorders, people with borderline personality disorder tend to avoid the kinds of experiences that would help them outgrow their problem.

The Cluster C personality disorders are primarily problems in how the person responds to the environment. However, these problems can lead to conflicts with other people. There are three personality disorders in Cluster C: avoidant personality disorder, dependent personality disorder, and obsessive-compulsive personality disorder.

People with avoidant personality disorder have such poor self-esteem that they are shy and anxious in social situations, even though they have a strong desire for close relationships. They are highly self-conscious and hypersensitive to rejection or criticism. As a result, they are often highly uncomfortable in situations that they cannot control, and they often have problems with occupational functioning. Because of these problems, they may use fantasy as an escape mechanism. Some psychiatrists argue that this condition should not be classified as a personality disorder. Instead, they view it as just a severe form of generalized social anxiety disorder.

People with avoidant personality disorder may benefit from training to improve their social skills and their skills in reasoning. The challenge is to get them to participate in the therapy. People with avoidant personality disorder may avoid treatment if they distrust the therapist or fear rejection.

Dependent personality disorder refers to a pervasive and excessive need for care by other people. The person with dependent personality disorder may seem submissive and clingy and may have fears of separation. A study of twins suggested that this disorder has a genetic basis. However, this kind of submissiveness and dependency can be a perfectly reasonable reaction to a debilitating illness.

The other member of the Cluster C personality disorders is obsessive-compulsive personality disorder. I think I understand what life is like for people with this problem. Years ago, I worked as a copy chief for a company that published neurology and psychiatry journals. Then, I worked as an editor in the publications department of a drug company that was doing research on antidepressant and antipsychotic medications. Somewhere along the line, I realized that my job description was practically identical to the diagnostic criteria for a mental illness that I do not have: obsessive-compulsive personality disorder.

Obsessive-compulsive personality disorder is a general pattern of concern with orderliness, perfectionism, excessive attention to details, mental and interpersonal control, and a need for control over one's environment, at the expense of flexibility, openness, and efficiency. A person with obsessive-compulsive personality disorder is "preoccupied with details, rules, lists, order, organization, or schedules to the extent that the major point of the activity is lost." According to my job description, I had to enforce persnickety rules, fix even minor defects, and keep things on schedule. When I am working, I force myself to pay attention to those things. In contrast, people with obsessive-compulsive personality disorder engage in that kind of persnickety behavior naturally, even when it is inappropriate.

People with obsessive-compulsive personality disorder tend to be so overly conscientious that they refuse to delegate tasks or to work with anyone who does not do things exactly their way. As a result, they tend to be workaholics with a limited social life. Besides being rigid and stubborn at work, they tend to be rigid and scrupulous about ethics and morality. People with OCPD also tend to hoard money and objects.

Obsessive-compulsive personality disorder (OCPD) is not the same thing as obsessive-compulsive disorder (OCD), although the symptoms of the two disorders overlap. People with OCD have obsessions, which are thoughts that they cannot put out of their minds. To relieve the tension that is provoked by these thoughts, the person with OCD may feel compelled to perform some sort of ritualistic behavior. For example, they may feel compelled to wash their hands numerous times per day because they feel that their hands have been contaminated. Adrian Monk from the television show *Monk* showed a character with a comically exaggerated case of OCD. He had an extensive list of phobias, including dentists, germs, needles, milk, snakes, elevators, etc. He would avoid these things or use rituals to dispel the anxiety that these phobias provoked. Yet he was not a coward. He did not hesitate to confront murderers.

People with OCD know that their involuntary thoughts are irrational, and they generally want to be able to stop doing their compulsive behaviors. In contrast, people with OCPD feel that they are doing things the right way, and they can become aggressive in policing other people's behavior. Dana Carvey's character the Church Lady from *Saturday Night Live* is a caricature of someone with OCPD. People with OCPD view themselves as perfect people in an imperfect world. They have a tendency to believe that they are always right. Psychologists call this problem truth ownership. Because of their sense of intellectual and moral rectitude, they can seem narcissistic. Since they feel that they own the truth, they cannot be persuaded by reason. Thus, they may seem to be as unreasonable as a delusional schizophrenic.

Since people with OCPD believe that they own the truth about what is right and wrong, they can become aggressive toward people whom they perceive as wrongdoers. Like the Spanish Inquisition, they seem to delight in finding and punishing people who have broken their arbitrary rules. In a series of sketches in the British television comedy *Monty Python's Flying Circus*, the Spanish Inquisition would strike without warning. (Nobody expects the Spanish Inquisition!) Likewise, people with OCPD can strike without warning, but the effects are seldom funny.

People with OCPD love to play "Gotcha!" (colloquial for "I got you!"). They set up an elaborate system of pointless rules. They make and enforce the rules. Of course, they do not always give anyone advance warning about the rules. Then, they lie in wait for someone to break the rules. If they catch you breaking one of their rules, they "gotcha!" Now they have something that they can hold over your head forever!

Of course, any civilized person would feel dismay at having offended someone and may try to resolve the conflict. However, the people with OCPD actually want the conflict. They delight in holding grudges. For the person with OCPD, the purpose of the game is to establish that they are the master or mistress of the rules of proper behavior. If you try to negotiate over those rules, you pose a threat to your attacker's self-concept. In this respect, OCPD is similar to narcissism. Whether your attacker has OCPD or narcissism, you are being attacked for irrational reasons by a shameless person. For that reason, the standard approaches that usually work in resolving a conflict with a sane person will not work and may actually intensify the conflict.

I do not have OCPD. The central problem in OCPD seems to be mental inflexibility, but I score in the 99th percentile in tests of mental flexibility. I also dislike pointless conflict, so I am also slow to become angry and quick to forgive. Also, I do not enjoy pointing out other people's mistakes. That is just the sort of unpleasant thing I have to do to get paid for reading textbooks and scientific journal articles for a living. As an editor and proofreader, I have to enforce countless persnickety rules that do not matter to most people. So even though I do not have OCPD, my work experience has given me insight into how people respond to people with OCPD. It is normal to be irritated by someone who corrects your grammar, even if by doing so they keep you from looking stupid in public. However, narcissists seemingly would rather risk looking stupid in public than allow someone to fix their dangling participles.

As an editor, I had to correct all sorts of insignificant mistakes and enforce all sorts of seemingly arbitrary rules. Yet that activity served a higher purpose. The goal was to enhance the credibility of the work by making it look as if it had been prepared by a conscientious educated person. Many of the articles and book chapters that I have edited over the years needed heavy editing. Besides correcting typographical and spelling errors, I have had to correct problems like misplaced or dangling modifiers, errors in parallel structure, garden path effects, poor word choice, and even some errors of fact and errors in reasoning. Often, I had no choice but to edit the manuscript heavily. Many authors appreciated this kind of help. However, a few people felt that I was challenging them to engage in some sort of power struggle.

The people with the most impressive credentials tended to be truly grateful for heavy editing. They were busy people who did not have time to waste on things like dangling participles, and they were pleased with the improvements that I made in their writing. They also tended to learn from my editing. As time went on, their manuscripts became cleaner and cleaner. In contrast, the people who complained that I edited their work too heavily tended to be low-ranking people within the scientific community or writers who had no scientific credentials. I handled their complaints by going through their manuscript line by line, explaining why each of the changes I recommended was necessary. I would patiently explain the difference between a transitive versus intransitive verb, and the difference between an absolute phrase and a participial phrase. I explained the rules for modifier placement. I started taking that approach because I had been trained to suggest no change unless I could explain why it was necessary. I eventually realized that explaining my reasoning worked because I was establishing my social standing as an authority on grammar. It also helped bad writers become good writers.

If the author was a medical doctor or a veterinarian, I would point out that in a sane and rational world, they get to prescribe drugs and perform surgery, while I fix the grammar in manuscripts. That always lightened the mood, probably because it clarified that I considered them to have a higher social rank than I had. The most serious conflicts that I had were with people who had been English majors but were nevertheless bad technical writers.

To be a good technical writer, you need a clear understanding of the basic rules of syntax. The more complicated and arcane your topic is, the clearer your prose style has to be. Many people with English degrees were shocked when they saw how heavily I edited their work. To resolve these conflicts, I started writing handouts that explained how to use the basic rules of English grammar to improve your prose style. Once I taught someone how to use a dictionary, how to diagram sentences, and how to apply a few simple rules of syntax, that person's writing would improve to the point that it would need only minimal editing. My handouts became so popular that I was invited to write a grammar column for the *American Medical Writers Association Journal.* Those articles were so well received that I decided to write a book about grammar.

At first, I imagined that I should write a slim volume about the unintended comedy that can result from putting words in the wrong order. But then, I started wondering why so many people, especially people with college degrees in English, did not understand the basic rules of the grammar of their native language. These are concepts that they should have learned in grammar school. Yet an amazingly large percentage of American college graduates seemed to be completely unfamiliar with these concepts. So I started trying to figure out why American grammar schools stopped teaching grammar.

The answer was simple. Since the mid 1960s, prominent educators have been spreading the idea that formal lessons in grammar do no good and are probably harmful. I knew from personal experience that they were wrong about that. Yet because of that bad advice from prominent people, a huge percentage of the English teachers in public schools in the United States stopped teaching grammar. One obvious result of the suppression of grammar lessons was a severe and prolonged decline in verbal SAT scores. Other consequences were more subtle. Classics professor David Mulroy explained these problems in his book *The War Against Grammar.*

Mulroy asked the students in his elective class on mythology to re-write a complicated sentence in their own words. He chose the opening sentence of the Declaration of Independence:

> When in the Course of human events, it becomes necessary for one people to dissolve the political bands which have connected them with another, and to assume among the powers of the earth, the separate and equal station to which the Laws of Nature and of Nature's God entitle them, a decent respect to the opinions of mankind requires that they should declare the causes which impel them to the separation.

Mulroy did not identify the source of the sentence, which none of the students seemed to recognize. To his dismay, only a small percentage of his class understood the gist of the sentence, which is that when people are breaking a political tie, they should explain why they are doing so. The students' failure to understand the literal meaning of this sentence stemmed from their inability to identify the main clause in the sentence. In other words, the problem stemmed from their lack of understanding of English grammar.

Many of the students thought that the sentence was about a romantic breakup or about theology or the environment. Instead of rendering the actual meaning of the sentence in their own words, many students wrote elaborate essays that were actually just free-associations on some of the more colorful words from the sentence. To me, the students' thought processes represented a loosening of associations, which is a key feature of schizotypal personality disorder and schizophrenia. These were normal college students. Yet because of their ignorance of grammar, many of them seemed downright schizotypal when confronted with a long sentence.

Grammar was one of the seven basic subjects that made up a well-rounded education for a youth in ancient Greece. The other subjects were logic, rhetoric, mathematics, geometry, music, and astronomy. The ancient Greeks believed that studying these subjects helped a person become a better person: a more reliable citizen in wartime and a more pleasant companion during peacetime. These studies prepared one for the study of philosophy, which literally means the love of wisdom. The Greeks expressed contempt for the barbarians who had not been educated in philosophy.

If ignorance of grammar could make someone seem schizotypal, ignorance of logic could make the person seem downright schizophrenic. People with schizotypal personality disorder can be persuaded that some of their weird beliefs are not logical. In contrast, people with full-blown schizophrenia hold tightly to their delusions, despite all attempts at persuasion. Yet it is easy to find similar pigheadedness among people who are not regarded as mentally ill. Sometimes, the problem is that the person has never been taught the elementary principles of logic. Sometimes, the problem comes from a struggle over social rank. Some people do not want a lower-ranking person to win in any argument, even when the lower-ranking person has logic and evidence on his or her side.

Narcissism can be a side effect of ignorance. In the 1990s, psychologists David Dunning and Justin Kruger found that people who have poor skills in some domain, such as grammar or logic, tend to believe that their skills in that domain are above average. Their skills are so poor that they cannot spot their own mistakes. As a result, they cannot accurately judge their level of skill. For that reason, ignorant people can be arrogant and overconfident. The solution to this problem is simple. Teach the ignorant people the skills that they lack. As their skills improve, their ability to judge their level of skill improves. As a result, they start giving themselves lower but more accurate ratings. Ironically, the people who have the highest level of skill tend to underrate themselves. They take their own level of skill for granted, and they tend to assume that other people must have a similar level of skill.

People with Cluster B personality disorders often lack empathy. They often seem unable to see things from other people's point of view and unable to feel some echo of what another person is feeling. This lack of empathy could result partly from poor mental flexibility or poor skill in reading other people's emotions. However, the problem could also reflect the fact that their own emotional reactions are not normal. If you would not feel fear or excitement in a given situation, you may find it hard to understand why other people would do so. This tendency to low emotional arousal is probably partly genetic. However, I think that the lack of empathy can also have a social dimension. I suspect that human beings are instinctively more attuned to the whims of high-ranking, dangerous people and far less attuned to the suffering of harmless, low-ranking people—just as you would be more concerned about the intentions of a leopard than the intentions of a sparrow.

A person's genes cannot be changed, but it often is possible to help someone develop greater mental flexibility and greater empathy. Some academic subjects were developed specifically for that purpose. These subjects include the classical liberal arts (including logic and rhetoric) and the humanities (especially history, philosophy, and literature). Yet to study those subjects, you must be able to read well. Unfortunately, the teachers in our public elementary schools have been trained and often forced to use a method of reading instruction that does not work. Instead of teaching children to sound words out from left to right (phonics), our schools have been asking children to memorize whole words as shapes (sight words). As a result, millions of Americans cannot read well enough to understand a newspaper article or enjoy a novel, much less understand a treatise on philosophy.

In the 1960s, members of the Women's Liberation Movement adopted the slogan, "The personal is political." By that, they meant that some problems that seem to be an individual's personal problems are actually the result of systemic problems within society, such as racism and sexism. Many individuals cannot read well and have not learned the basic rules of logic, despite having spent up to 13 years in public school. As a result, they are more likely to have maladaptive thought patterns. When a large enough percentage of the population cannot reason, then democracy breaks down. Democracy literally means rule by the people. Yet the people cannot rule unless they can work out agreements about matters of public concern through processes of public discussions.

It may be useful to view the personality disorders as spectrum disorders. The word *spectrum* came from the Latin word for image or apparition. Scientists used the word *spectrum* to describe the rainbow of colors that is produced when light passes through a prism. In a spectrum, visible light is displayed according to its frequency (red at the low end and violet at the high end). Light is a form of electromagnetic radiation. There are also invisible frequencies of electromagnetic radiation below red (infrared) and above violet (ultraviolet). Thus, the spectrum is a handy metaphor to describe any phenomenon that varies in degree when the differences of degree can seem to be differences of kind. Orange light may seem to be a different kind of thing from blue light. Yet they are both simply electromagnetic radiation and differ from each other only in wavelength. Likewise, the disorders that make up the autism spectrum may seem to be different diseases, but they are viewed as mild to severe forms of the same basic problem.

For a mental disorder, the spectrum can range from normal to severely distressing or completely disabling. For example, arachnophobia, which is the fear of spiders, could range from mild to severe. A person with a mild case might be only momentarily startled by seeing a particularly large spider unexpectedly. But for someone with a severe case of arachnophobia, just the sight of a spider web could trigger a full-blown panic attack. With spectrum disorders, it can be hard to decide where to draw the dividing line between normal and abnormal. How bad does your fear of spiders have to be before you are considered to be abnormal or in need of help? Likewise, how disordered does your personality have to be before you qualify for a diagnosis of personality disorder?

Each of the DSM-5 personality disorders seems to represent the moderate to severe portion of a spectrum that represents a challenge that everyone must face. Cluster A personality disorders represent the challenge of creating a reliable mental model of reality. All of our mental models are imaginary maps or stories that we use to make sense out of what we can see, hear, smell, feel, taste, and remember. Yet as you can learn from studying optical illusions, even a normal perceptual system is prone to making certain kinds of errors. Thus, even a normal person is faced with the challenge of compensating for the errors of their perceptual system and the biases in their thinking. Thus, normal people are at the mild end of a spectrum. The Cluster A personality disorders might represent the middle of the spectrum, while the psychoses such as schizophrenia might represent the severe end.

Most people manage to compensate reasonably well for the minor flaws in their perceptual system. The proper sort of education, especially training in logic, can improve their ability to reason. In contrast, the people in the middle of the spectrum may have a particularly flawed perceptual system and substandard aptitude for reasoning. Because of these problems, they are less able to develop reliable mental models of reality. Yet they can sometimes be talked out of their false beliefs. In contrast, people with a full-blown psychosis have problems in perception and reasoning that are too severe to be overcome through the use of the intellect. For this reason, an educational model might be useful for people on the normal end of this spectrum, while the medical model is appropriate for people at the severe end. For the people in the middle, the appropriate model might be special education: education specifically tailored to meet the needs of someone with a disability.

Cluster B personality disorders represent the challenge of getting along with other people. As social animals, most human beings are naturally prone to two conflicting impulses: the urge to dominate and the desire to connect. Histrionic behavior represents strategies and tactics that low-ranking people can use to win favors from high-ranking people. In contrast, narcissists are struggling ineffectively to be high-ranking people. The diagnosis of histrionic or narcissistic personality disorder is given to people who are using particularly undignified and often ultimately ineffective political strategies. Why are they using bad strategies? Perhaps they have simply failed to learn better strategies. Either they have never been schooled in the social graces or they simply have a lower aptitude for social learning. As a result, they may have poor social skills. Fortunately, their poor skills can be addressed through an educational model or perhaps a special education model. The same lessons might be useful for helping normal people, as well.

Antisocial personality disorder and borderline personality disorder represent a different kind of problem in getting along with others. Sociopaths view other human beings as things, and people with borderline personality disorder see other people as abstractions of good or evil.

Both problems seem to be related to the person's emotional reactivity. Emotional reactivity may be abnormally low in sociopaths and abnormally high in people with borderline personality disorder. People with abnormal emotional reactivity are likely to have severe difficulties in understanding other people's emotions. Thus, poor empathy is also a feature of antisocial and borderline personality disorders.

The underlying problem with emotional reactivity could be partly genetic. Yet not everyone who has a genetic predisposition to abnormal emotional reactivity goes on to develop a severe personality disorder. Also, it may be possible for a severe personality disorder to occur in someone who does not have that kind of genotype. Antisocial and borderline personality disorders seem to result when someone who is genetically predisposed to abnormal emotional reactivity suffers from abuse or neglect in early childhood. These early experiences may cause the brain to develop in ways that create problems in later life.

Although somatic problems (i.e., bad genes or damaged brain tissue) may be part of the cause of a case of antisocial or borderline personality disorder, medicine has little to offer these patients. Their condition does not seem to respond well to any available medication. However, some kinds of psychotherapy, which would represent a special education model, could be useful. However, the most promising approach is based on a public health model, to prevent brain injury and to prevent children from being abused and neglected.

From studying personality disorders, ordinary people can learn some important lessons. The first is that the strategies and tactics that you would use in dealing with someone who is basically sane will not work when you deal with someone with a serious personality disorder. Thus, it is important to be able to recognize these defects in character in other people, so that you can adjust your approach to dealing with them. The second important lesson is that even the severe personality disorders are just exaggerated forms of problems that even normal people may have. So instead of just asking what is wrong with other people, we all ought to think about what might be wrong with ourselves.

Chapter 11

The Seven Basic Emotions

All mental illnesses involve some combination of abnormalities in perception, thought, feelings, and behavior. For the mental illnesses that are classified as personality disorders, the most obvious abnormality is maladaptive behavior. Yet that maladaptive behavior springs from problems in what the person perceives, thinks, and feels. Some sociopaths do not seem to feel the full range of human emotions. Instead, they seem to have low emotional arousal, like a reptile. For that reason, sociopaths are often described as cold-blooded. In contrast, narcissists are quick to feel contempt and lash out in anger. One of the important goals of psychotherapy is to help patients recognize their own emotions and other people's emotions, so that patients can learn to use their conscience as their guide, instead of being a slave to passion.

It is surprisingly hard to come up with a scientific definition of emotion. Some experts define emotion as a state of feeling that leads to changes in physiology or behavior. In the 1960s, psychologists tried to identify the core emotions, which represent the basic programs that guide behavioral responses. Psychologist Paul Ekman was able to identify seven basic emotions, each of which caused a human being to produce a distinctive facial expression. These seven were fear, surprise, happiness, sadness, anger, disgust, and contempt. People all over the world produce the same facial expression for each of these basic emotions. These expressions are produced involuntarily. You do not have to learn how to make them, and they are hard to suppress. Even if you try to keep a straight face, the telltale expression may flicker over your face in a fraction of a second. Ekman calls these fleeting expressions microexpressions. Ekman has also described some other emotions that are important but that do not produce a characteristic facial expression.

Fear is a primal emotion, which means that it arises out of brain structures that are practically the same in lower animals, such as reptiles, as they are in human beings. Animals show signs of fear in response to some threat of physical injury. Human beings can feel fear in response to some threat of physical or psychological injury (i.e., hurt feelings). Fear is part of an overall response that prepares the body to respond to the threat. That response could involve either fighting or running away. For that reason, this response is called the fight-or-flight response. Fear produces a characteristic facial expression in human beings (Figure 1). The eyes open wide, to take in as much information about the environment as possible. The lips stretch horizontally.

Figure 1: Fear
*Notice that her eyes are wide open and her lips
are stretched horizontally.*

Animals may be particularly fearful of something that is unfamiliar or something that has harmed them in the past. As the object of their fear becomes familiar or time has passed since the object caused any harm, an animal may become less fearful of it. This process of becoming less fearful of something through repeated exposure is called habituation.

Unlike other animals, human beings can use language. As a result, human beings can use logic and reason to deal with their fears. As you mature, you may get better at overcoming your fears. Meanwhile, you learn more about the potential dangers in your environment.

Surprise is the fastest emotional response. It is a response to the unexpected. Surprise produces a facial expression that looks a lot like fear because the eyes open wide, to gather as much information as possible (Figure 2). However, the jaw drops a little as the mouth goes slack. The surprise expression lasts for only about a second. It may then be followed by some other expression, such as fear or happiness.

Figure 2: Surprise!
Surprise looks a lot like fear, in that the eyes are wide open.
However, the jaw is slack. Normally, the surprise expression
is fleeting. It is quickly replaced by some other expression,
such as happiness or fear.

Happiness is the feeling that makes you smile. To get people in New Guinea to smile, Ekman asked them to imagine that friends had come to visit. The French anatomist Guillaume-Benjamin-Amand Duchenne de Boulogne noticed that when people produce a fake smile, such as when they are trying to be polite, they contract the zygomaticus major muscle, which people can do voluntarily (Figure 3).

Figure 3: Social Smile
A social smile is produced by contracting
the zygomaticus major muscle.

But when people are expressing true happiness, they also contract the orbicularis oculi muscle around the eyes, which happens involuntarily. Thus, the genuine smile that reaches clear to the eyes is called a Duchenne smile (Figure 4).

Figure 4: True Smile
A true smile of happiness (Duchenne smile) is produced by
contraction of both the zygomaticus major muscle and the
orbicularis oculi muscle. Notice the crinkling around the eyes.

Sadness is the emotional pain that we feel in response to loss (such as grief, sorrow, or disappointment) or disadvantage (helplessness or despair). In a sad facial expression, the corners of the lips are lowered, but the inner corners of the eyebrows are raised (Figure 5).

Figure 5: Sadness
Sadness is what you feel when you have lost something you wanted. In a sad expression, the corners of the mouth turn down, but the inner corners of the eyebrows are often raised.

A person who is feeling sad may be quiet, lethargic, and withdrawn and may cry. *Homo sapiens* is one of the few species that produce tears in response to strong emotion. In fact, our eyes can produce three different kinds of tears. Basal tears are produced just to keep the surface of the eye moist. Reflex tears are watery tears produced when something irritates your eye. Lacrimation means the production of tears for non-emotional reasons, such as eye irritation. Emotional tears are the tears that are produced in response to some strong emotion. They contain hormones such as prolactin and stress hormones. Emotional tears also contain a natural painkiller, called leucine enkephalin. These hormones could help to explain why people often feel better after a good cry.

The tears themselves are also a powerful social signal. Tears can also be a way of expressing shared emotion, such as shared grief. Crying may be an expression of helplessness. Thus, tears serve as a sign of submission. The idea that tears represent a sense of helplessness could also explain why people cry when overcome by joy.

Anger is the emotion that you feel when you are not getting what you want or when someone has violated your boundaries. Anger can have good or bad effects, depending on what you want and how you try to get what you want. Anger is the emotion that leads to the cardinal sin of wrath. The corresponding heavenly virtue is patience.

Expressing anger can be a way to assert yourself socially: to take what is yours and to police your boundaries. Animals often signal dominance by trying to look larger, by staring, and by baring their teeth. The facial expression of anger in human beings involves lowered eyebrows, pressed lips, and narrowed or bulging eyes (Figure 6).

Figure 6: Anger
Anger is what you feel when someone or something is preventing you from getting what you want. In an angry expression, the eyebrows are lowered, and the eyes may be narrow and glaring. The lips are often tight, unless the person is yelling at you.

Disgust is a reaction to contamination. The disgust expression is a way of shutting off the eyes and nose to unpleasant sensory input. The upper lip and cheeks are raised and the nose is wrinkled (Figure 7). The contamination that evokes disgust can be real or symbolic. People feel disgust in response to bad sights, smells, and tastes. They can also feel disgust in response to injustice. Disgust is a powerful emotion that can have good or bad effects. Disgust causes us to shun things, such as cockroaches and rotting flesh, that could spread disease. Disgust can also lead to righteous indignation that inspires the struggle against injustice. Unfortunately, disgust can also fuel racism that leads to genocide. In particular, be wary of anyone who describes the members of some social group as cockroaches or other vermin.

Figure 7: Disgust
Disgust is a reaction to something rotten. The disgust expression is a way to block bad sights and smells and spit out bad tastes.

Contempt is the feeling that corresponds to being in the superior social position. It indicates that someone is somehow failing to meet your standards. As a result, you are looking down on them. The characteristic facial expression of contempt is a lopsided smirk (Figure 8). I think that this expression is related to the raised lip that a dog uses to threaten another dog.

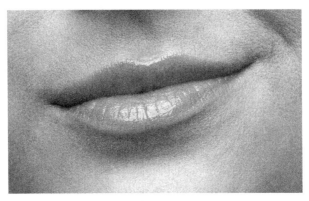

Figure 8: Contempt
*Contempt is the feeling that goes along with being in a superior
social position. This feeling provokes a half-smile. Contempt is the
only one of the basic facial expressions that is not symmetrical.*

I first became interested in the study of facial expressions because I
noticed that a famous political figure always seemed to be smirking.
For that reason, he reminded me of some horrible people whom I knew
personally. I suspected that the smirk was a sign of narcissism. Ekman
has shown that the contempt smirk does indicate that a person is feeling superior to some other person. Since narcissists feel superior to
such a large percentage of the population, they would smirk in practically any social encounter. Of course, not everyone who smirks at you
is a narcissist. It could mean that you have just said or done something
that they think is uncouth. You need to be receptive to this kind of
feedback from other people if you want to get along with them.

Robert Solomon, a philosophy professor at the University of Texas
at Austin, suggested that resentment, anger, and contempt are all part
of a single spectrum of emotional responses. He suggested that contempt is anger directed at one's social inferiors. He viewed ordinary
anger as something that one directs at people whom one accepts as
equals. Resentment is anger directed at the people whom one regards
as socially superior. However, I regard contempt as the emotion that
corresponds with being in a socially superior position. You do not have
to feel anger to feel contempt. In fact, contempt without anger can be a

good thing. Solomon's concept of resentment helped me understand why Eva Mozes Kor, a survivor of Auschwitz, decided to forgive Dr. Josef Mengele.

The documentary *Forgiving Dr. Mengele* tells Kor's story. When Kor's family arrived at the Auschwitz-Birkenau concentration camp, she and her identical twin sister Miriam were promptly taken away from the rest of the family, whom they never saw again. Eva and her twin sister were then taken to Dr. Josef Mengele's laboratory. Mengele would use pairs of twins as test subjects in cruel experiments. When one member of a twin pair died, the other twin would be immediately murdered, usually by an injection directly into the heart. Then, both bodies would be autopsied. Kor and her sister were subjected to dangerous and cruel experiments, but they survived until the Soviet Red Army liberated the camp. However, both of them had serious health problems in adulthood. Miriam died in 1993 of a rare form of cancer. Mengele escaped to Argentina, where he died of natural causes in 1979. Kor eventually settled in Terre Haute, Indiana.

Although Mengele died in obscurity, Kor had the chance to confront one of the SS doctors who had worked at Auschwitz: Hans Münch. However, Münch had refused to participate in the experimentations and the mass murders at the camp, and he had been resourceful in finding ways to keep people alive and to make their lives more bearable. As a result, he was acquitted of war crimes after the war. When Kor interviewed Münch in 1993, she expected to find a monster. Yet he turned out to be a kindly old man who was suffering from depression and nightmares and remorse (remorse is anger directed at oneself). Kor then decided that she would write Münch a letter to express her forgiveness. But then she went further.

In January 1995, she and Münch took part in a ceremony at the site of the camp to mark the 50th anniversary of its liberation. At the ceremony, she read a letter from Münch. His letter was an eyewitness account of what had happened at the camp, and he expressed his sorrow that he had had any connection to it. Münch had joined the Nazi Party and the SS to further his career. Then, he found himself in a horrible nightmare that he could do nothing to stop and that haunted him for the rest of his days. Kor then went further. She declared that she personally forgave everyone who participated in the Holocaust or tried to cover it up. Kor emphasized that she was speaking only for herself, but she felt that it was time for all former Nazis and their collaborators to come forward and testify to the crimes they committed, without fear of prosecution. She concluded, "Here in Auschwitz, I hope in some small way to send the world a message of forgiveness, a message of peace, a message of hope, a message of healing. No more wars... no more experiments without informed consent...no more gas chambers...no more bombs...no more hatred...no more killing...no more Auschwitzes."

Kor's message was in line with the guiding principles of the Truth and Reconciliation process, which was getting underway in South Africa after the end of Apartheid. Yet her statements provoked heated discussion, especially among other Holocaust survivors. Throughout the controversy, Kor kept emphasizing that she was speaking only for herself, and that that forgiveness was something she had to do to promote her own healing.

How could Kor forgive the unforgiveable, and why did she feel the need to do so? The Red Army had liberated Kor physically from Auschwitz in January 1945, but she still had to work at liberating herself mentally. If she had allowed herself to feel resentment, she would have been granting Mengele and the other Nazis the superior social rank that they clearly did not deserve. Even by feeling ordinary anger at them, she would have been accepting them as her social equals. Instead, she needed to demote the Nazis to the bottom of her own imaginary Order of Precedence. She needed to look down upon Mengele and his ilk—to feel contempt.

By the 1990s, Kor no longer had any need for anger at the Nazis. The purpose of anger is to prepare you to struggle against obstacles. After the war ended, Mengele and the other Nazis no longer represented an obstacle. The Nazi regime had fallen. Its leaders had killed themselves or had been hanged at Nuremberg. Although Mengele had avoided capture and trial, he had died in obscurity. Thus, Kor's anger could no longer serve any useful purpose. In particular, it could not bring her family back. So Kor decided to replace her anger with compassion. The combination of contempt and compassion is called forgiveness.

Forgiveness is the nicest possible way to express contempt for another human being. By forgiving someone, you do not lessen the seriousness of his or her offenses. By forgiving them, you do not imply that they should not be held accountable for their wrongdoing. Instead, you are giving up the need for personal vengeance. In civilized societies, the state has the monopoly on violence. Thus, civilized people are supposed to allow the civil authorities to hold criminals to account. When you forgive someone, you discard the ugliness that that person has brought into your life. You may even try to ensure that more ugliness does not ensue. For example, Murder Victims' Families for Human Rights opposes the death penalty, which they view as simply a way of creating more victims. They do not want the offender's family to feel the same pain that they are feeling.

By seeking someone's forgiveness, you deliberately put yourself in the lower social position. In other words, you give up the deadly sin of pride and embrace the heavenly virtue of humility. By forgiving you, the other person takes the moral high ground. He or she gives up the deadly sin of wrath and embraces the heavenly virtue of patience. Yet even if people forgive you for hurting them, they may still be hurting because of what you have done. They have simply decided not to add to their own suffering by nurturing pointless anger. Whether or not you have been forgiven, you still need to work on your own redemption. Redemption is the act of making something better or more acceptable: acceptable to yourself, to other people, or perhaps to the Almighty. Unfortunately, narcissists view themselves as socially superior. As a result, they see no need to work on their redemption story arc.

Forgiveness and redemption can be part of a process called reconciliation. Reconciliation is the act of causing two persons or groups to become friendly again after an argument or disagreement. Of course, some people may not want to become friendly with you, even if they have forgiven you and even if you are working hard at redeeming yourself. The choice is up to them.

The seven basic emotions are hard-wired into the human nervous system. When we feel those emotions, we involuntarily produce the corresponding facial expression. Some people are far better than others at maintaining a neutral facial expression, even when they are feeling strong emotions. Yet even in those cases, the expressions can leak out in microexpressions that last a fraction of a second. Not only do the seven basic emotions cause people to have the corresponding facial expression, but producing that facial expression can actually induce the corresponding emotion.

The famous autistic savant Temple Grandin has explained that autistic people often have to be taught to recognize facial expressions. Their inability to read facial expressions must be profoundly disabling socially. If you cannot read someone else's facial expressions, you would have a hard time telling whether someone likes or dislikes you, and whether people approve or disapprove of something that you are doing. Thus, the ability to read facial expressions can help you navigate your social environment. In extreme cases, it could save your life.

Ann Rule wrote *The Stranger Beside Me*, the definitive biography of serial killer Ted Bundy. She had known Bundy personally, before he became implicated in a string of grisly murders of young women. Rule, who died in 2015, believed that many of Bundy's intended victims survived because they felt fear when they saw his predatory facial expression. They saw his mask of sanity slip, to reveal the predator underneath. Rule noted that many of Bundy's victims bore a striking resemblance to each other. Most of them were pretty young women with long dark hair, parted in the middle. However, many of them had something else in common. They were in the midst of some distracting life event. As a result, they did not carefully study the facial expression of the young man who needed their help with his briefcase because he was on crutches.

The forensic evidence against Bundy in his murder trials in Florida was extremely weak by 21st century standards. Those murders took place before DNA fingerprinting became available. Also, the validity of bite mark evidence, which was used at one of his trials, has been seriously questioned. However, the most compelling evidence in the Bundy case seemed to be Bundy's behavior at trial. He acted as his own defense attorney during the trials, and the emotions that he displayed were often shockingly inappropriate. As a result, Bundy was convicted and sentenced to death. He ultimately died in Florida's electric chair.

I think that the guilty verdicts in the Bundy trials were correct. However, I oppose the use of the death penalty, even for heinous crimes. The death penalty is an expression of wrath, which is one of the seven deadly sins. By allowing our government to carry out a death sentence, we collectively become the sort of person whom we imagine the convict to be. I think that the death penalty was particularly misguided in the Bundy case because so many families were still wondering what had happened to their loved one. Only Bundy could supply those answers, and he could do so only while he was still alive.

Paul Ekman has developed some computerized training programs to help people learn to recognize microexpressions and subtle expressions. I think that such training would be beneficial for ordinary people. It could be particularly useful for everyone except perhaps people with antisocial personality disorder. Sociopaths are predators. They do not need more skill in analyzing their prey. In general, I worry that any attempt to improve a sociopath's social skills could make the sociopath more dangerous.

Learning about facial expressions can help you recognize your own emotions. For example, if you become aware that your face is assuming an expression of contempt or disgust or anger, it can help you become aware of what you are feeling.

Ekman also identified some important emotions that are not predictably associated with a particular facial expression. One of them is shame. Shame is the opposite of contempt. Contempt is the feeling that goes along with being in the superior social position, while shame is the emotion that goes along with being in the inferior social position. This fact explains something important about rape victims. Rape is a crime in which the rapist treats someone else's body as his own property, while murder is a crime in which the murderer turns a person into a thing. Thus, both kinds of offense have similar moral implications. This could explain why rape victims often do not put up much of a fight.

During a sexual assault, the victim may quickly realize that she (or he!) is overmatched physically. Thus, the victim may instinctively act submissively, to minimize the risk of physical injury or death. Rape is a crime of dominance. By definition, it puts the victim in a subordinate social position. By resisting physically, you might cause your attacker to escalate the level of violence being used against you. Thus, it would make sense to submit, to minimize your risk of physical injury or death. The same principle applies in cases of attempted murder. Many people have survived an attempt on their life by playing dead. Once the victim appears to be dead, the would-be murderer often stops the attack. Unfortunately, juries often acquit the defendant in a rape case if the victim did not seem to fight back. Yet they would not acquit someone of attempted murder if the victim played dead.

Rape is a way to humiliate other people, to put some other person in a lower social position. That is why rape victims often feel shame, even though they have done nothing wrong. These feelings of shame are often compounded by a society that blames them for their own victimization. Yet rather than shaming the victim of a crime, we should be shaming the perpetrator. Ideally, the attempt to humiliate other people should backfire, so that the offender never dreams of attempting anything similar again.

Guilt is similar to shame, except that it is private. We feel shame when we are humiliated in front of someone else. We feel guilt when we have failed to meet our own standards of morality. A person can feel shame and guilt at the same time. In contrast, dogs can feel shame but not guilt. When dogs look "guilty," they are actually showing signs of submission, as opposed to guilt or remorse. In other words, your dog feels no guilt. Rather, your dog is just trying to calm you down.

Embarrassment is the emotion that we feel in response to unwanted attention, whether the attention is good or bad. I once organized a book signing for a friend of mine. Many of the people at the event had already read his book and praised it highly. He was so embarrassed by their praise that he looked like he wanted to slide under the table. Human embarrassment seems to be related to the things that monkeys do to appease angry monkeys and promote social ties.

Ekman also identified some good emotions. Amusement is an

emotion that is related to fun. Excitement is the response to challenging new stimuli. Relief is what you feel when something that had aroused strong emotions subsides. Contentment is the feeling that all is right with the world, and that nothing needs to be done. Wonder is the emotion you feel when you are overwhelmed by something incomprehensible. Ecstasy or bliss is the state of self-transcendent rapture, which some people experience through meditation while others experience it through communing with nature or making love with a truly loved one. Ekman uses the Italian word *fiero* to refer to the pride you feel in achieving something. Triumph is the feeling that you get when you win in a competition against someone else. Ekman uses the Yiddish word *naches* to refer to pride in one's children's or students' accomplishments. Elevation is the enjoyable emotion that you feel when you see unexpected acts of kindness or compassion. Gratitude is the appreciation for a gift.

There are also some bad emotions that are nevertheless enjoyable. *Schadenfreude* is a German word for a bad thing: the enjoyment that you feel when you find that your enemy has suffered. Gloating is similar to schadenfreude, except that you are pleased to see that someone has brought suffering upon themselves.

Paul Ekman has worked with Buddhist monks to find practical ways to teach people how to cultivate emotional balance. Buddhists use the term *kleshas*, which is often translated as afflictive emotions, to refer to the mental states that cloud the mind and lead to unwholesome actions. Buddhists have developed mental disciplines of meditation to help overcome those emotions. Many of these disciplines seem to be practical, as opposed to theological, and may thus be acceptable to people of other religious persuasions or no religion at all. Such approaches to dealing with mental problems fall into an educational model. As psychologist Stanton Samenow has explained, such approaches are useful for habilitation, which means to teach someone skills that they never had.

As I explained in Chapter 10, an educational model is appropriate for helping people who are at or near the normal end of a spectrum of mental illness. People who are further toward the abnormal end of the spectrum might need more of a special education model, with the training specifically tailored to help them overcome their handicaps. However, even a special education model might be of little or no use for someone who has serious problems that are due to an underlying brain disorder.

A severe case of narcissism may be classified as a personality disorder, which implies that it is a maladaptive pattern of behavior, but it involves problems with thought and emotion, as well as behavior. Narcissists are people who believe that they deserve an unrealistically high social rank. As a result, the narcissist often feels inappropriate feelings of contempt for other people. Also, the narcissist fails to feel shame when shame would be appropriate. As a result, the narcissist may unwittingly become an object of contempt, as opposed to admiration.

Since other people do not agree with the narcissist's self-assessment, they may not be willing to grant the narcissist the status and privileges that the narcissist thinks are rightfully his or hers. As a result, the narcissist feels that he or she is being wrongfully deprived of his or her due. This sense of deprivation is called narcissistic injury, and it leads to anger called narcissistic rage.

Through expressing narcissistic rage, a narcissist attempts to bully other people into granting the narcissist the superior rank that the narcissist desires. The raging narcissist's goal in lashing out seems to be triumph. The narcissist may not be satisfied until the other person shows submission. Yet since the narcissist, by definition, is trying to occupy a higher social rank than he or she can defend, the narcissist ends up fighting battles that he or she cannot or perhaps should not win. As a result, the narcissist may actually lose social standing instead of rising socially.

There are two possible solutions to the narcissist's problem with social rank. One is to find some way to triumph. The other is to adjust to a realistic lower social rank. To find true happiness, narcissists may need to ask an important question: what do they imagine that they will win if they triumph? Is the feeling of triumph enough to compensate for everything they lose in the struggle? Will their triumphs lead to bliss, satisfaction, and contentment? If those feelings are what you seek, why not try to achieve them directly, rather than through putting other people down? Why seek triumph, when *fiero* is enough?

Chapter 12

Why Does Social Rank Exist?

N arcissism arises out of a conflict over social rank. In the Greek myth, Narcissus loved himself too much and other people not at all. Thus, he put himself above everyone else. Today, the term *narcissist* is commonly used to refer to someone whose self-esteem is much higher than the esteem in which other people hold that person. Because of their inflated self-esteem, narcissists expect others to admire them and to grant them special privileges. Narcissism can be considered a mental illness if someone is suffering or disabled because of an unrealistically high estimation of his or her rank within society. Yet why does social rank even exist? Is it something that can be completely abolished? Yes, but only if you are a turtle.

Turtles have no social life. They have no friends. Their sex life consists of casual chance encounters, rather than any sort of lasting relationships. The female lays her eggs in a nest and then crawls away, leaving her offspring to their own devices. Neither the males nor the females provide any sort of parental care to their offspring. To Chinese people, the turtle's life cycle represents an appalling lack of family values and a shocking lack of culture. For that reason, Chinese people consider it a high insult to refer to someone as a turtle or a son of a turtle. It implies that you are an uneducated sociopath.

If human beings started living like turtles, the human species would rapidly die out. Human babies would quickly die of starvation if someone did not feed them. Likewise, a culture would cease to exist if the current crop of adults failed to pass on their knowledge and moral teachings to the next generation. That is how Europe descended into the Dark Ages after the fall of the Roman Empire.

In a children's book by Dr. Seuss, Yertle the turtle was king of the pond. Yet turtles do not live in kingdoms. They do not have social groupings of any scale. Anthropologists use different words to refer to small- and large-scale human societies. The smallest group would be a nuclear family. In many species, the family group consists of just the mother and her offspring. In a few species of birds and fish, the male lures females to mate with him and leave her eggs in his care. Among mammals, the mother is the one who must nurse the young. In some species, the father also takes part in caring for the young.

The smallest human social group would consist of two persons, such as a mother and child or a married couple. A single-parent family consists of one parent and one or more children. A nuclear family consists of a couple and their children. An extended family includes other members, such as grandparents, aunts, uncles, and cousins. A social unit that consists of several extended families is called a band. A band usually consists of people who are closely related by blood or marriage. Anthropologists believe that for most of human history, most human beings lived in small, scattered bands that lived by foraging (gathering and hunting). In a band society, social relationships are based on personal relationships. Adults can use their superior strength to dominate children, and men can use their strength to dominate women. However, the elderly people would not be able to dominate the younger adults by force. Instead, they are respected because of their knowledge.

The people in band societies have few possessions, and what they have is generally shared. There is no legal system to protect property rights. Instead, decisions are generally made by consensus. Thus, there are no social divisions between rich and poor. However, the young generally look up to the old, who are the repository of knowledge about how to survive in their environment.

The rise of agriculture made it possible for a larger number of people to live within the same amount of space. As a result, many bands could combine into a larger social unit called a tribe. Most of the members of a tribe are related to each other by blood or marriage. However, some of these relationships are distant, and many tribe members do not know each other personally. Sometimes, the tribe may be divided into smaller kinship groups called clans. Political relationships within a tribe are still based largely on kinship ties, and conflicts are still resolved through face-to-face negotiations and reciprocal exchange. Yet the tribe is large enough that there is some formal social stratification. Within a tribe, some members will have greater status than others have. Yet that status is generally granted by general assent. For example, some individuals may be given leadership roles.

As tribes grew larger, some of them became more socially stratified. Thus, they became chiefdoms. In a chiefdom, the leadership roles are monopolized by the legitimate senior members of the high-status families or "houses." Thus, the chieftainship may be an ascribed status, not an achieved status. An ascribed status is something that is thrust upon you, either at birth or later in your life. In contrast, an achieved status is something that you acquire through your own efforts.

When societies grew still larger and more complex, they developed into civilizations. A civilization is a society that has a complex social hierarchy and an organized, institutional government. Many of its people live in cities, and there are important accomplishments in literacy, the arts and sciences, technology, and public administration. The citizens of a great civilization may have less personal freedom than do the barbarians who live in wild places. Yet civilized people get to enjoy many benefits of civilization, including a much lower risk of being killed by another person. Yet for large-scale societies to function, people need to learn many skills that are not instinctual. They have to be taught by masters and learned by students. One of the hallmarks of a great civilization is a reverence for learning and the respect shown to learned men and women.

China has been a great civilization for more than two thousand years. To gain status in most ancient civilizations, you typically had to be born into a wealthy and prominent family. Yet China developed another system, one that eventually spread to the West. If a man wanted to get a job in the Chinese imperial government, he had to pass an examination that only an educated person could pass. Even a man from a humble yet respectable family could pass the Imperial Examination and perhaps get an important government job if he could somehow get a good enough education. As a result, the government was run by a class of scholar-bureaucrats whose family background was respectable but not necessarily aristocratic. Even a high-ranking scholar-bureaucrat could not pass his position down to his own sons. All he could do was to hire tutors to educate his sons, so that they could pass the Imperial Examination on their own.

The idea that high positions within the society should go to people who have proved themselves worthy through their own efforts is called meritocracy. Today, young Americans hope to rise socially through education. This hope is called the American Dream; but for many centuries before it became an American Dream, it was a Chinese dream.

The schools of martial arts that were originally developed in China and Japan also provide a useful educational model that balances meritocracy with the concerns about the dignity of all human beings. For example, when you enter the training facility (dojo) of an Aikido school, you bow to show your respect for the school as a whole. At the beginning of class, you bow to the portrait of the founder, to show your respect for the discipline you wish to learn. Then you bow to your teacher, to show your respect to the people who will teach you the discipline. Yet at the same time, your teacher bows to you, to show respect to you as a human being and as a student. Before every practice move in the class, the partners bow to each other, to show mutual respect. You can rise in rank within the school, but only as you master your lessons. The hierarchy within the school is based on each person's level of achievement.

It would be hard to maintain an unrealistic view of your status within a martial arts class. If you spar with a higher-ranking person in martial arts class, you will almost certainly end up face-down on the mat. But in a battle of wits in everyday life, the losers seldom realize that they have lost, because they lack the ability to judge their own performance. For example, when an ignorant person gets involved in a debate with a scientist, the scientist will usually point out obvious errors of fact and errors of reasoning in the ignorant person's arguments. To a scientist, this is the equivalent of slamming someone face-down onto the mat. Yet the ignorant person does not perceive the scientist's response as an effective put-down. Thus, the ignorant person cannot see that he or she is losing. The ignorant person may then continue arguing until the scientist gives up in disgust and walks away. At that point, the ignorant person will declare victory.

I think that ignorant people such as Internet trolls feel that they are achieving some boost in social status from "winning" in debates like these. But I think that their sense of victory is based partly on general ignorance and partly on poor social skills. Because of ignorance, the ignorant person cannot judge the outcome of a debate accurately. They also do not recognize that they are causing other people to feel contempt, not admiration, for them. As a result, ignorant debaters end up with less prestige and lower social standing than they would have had if they had kept silent. Thus, this kind of ignorant argumentativeness could be considered maladaptive.

In ancient times, there were two basic kinds of society, each of which offered a particular way of life. If you lived in a band or a small tribe, you would enjoy political equality and a great deal of personal freedom. The downside was that your life would be precarious. You had minimal protection against natural or manmade disaster. You could easily die of famine or die as the result of warfare from a neighboring band. In contrast, the people who lived in civilizations had considerable protection from natural or manmade disaster. The king or pharaoh had stores of grain to distribute to the people during times of famine, armies to protect society against foreign invaders, and even some sort of police force to suppress banditry. The downside was that most people lived at the bottom of a highly stratified society and had remarkably little personal freedom. Nor did they have a voice in how decisions that affected the kingdom were made.

From ancient times to the present, many writers from great civilizations have painted a rosy portrait of the lives of "savages" (a term that originally meant people who lived in the forest). During the period of French colonialism in North America, the French Jesuits, in particular, were inspired by the Iroquois, whose society was based on the principles of liberty, equality, and brotherhood. Those ideas later inspired the French Revolution, which eventually spread the ideas of human rights throughout Western Europe. The Founding Fathers of the United States were also impressed by the Iroquois. The Constitution of the United States is based on the Iroquois Constitution. Yet romantic primitivism, which is the idealized portrayal of the band and tribal societies, could be deceptive. As Steven Pinker has pointed out in his book *The Better Angels of Our Nature*, these smaller-scale societies had shockingly high rates of homicide, by modern standards. By suppressing intertribal warfare and interpersonal crime, the civilizations have led to an overall decrease in homicide.

Modern society gives us the opportunity to have the best of both kinds of world. We can have personal freedom and political equality, like a member of a band society, while at the same time enjoying the safety and security and modern conveniences that come from living in a great civilization. Yet modern societies cannot function unless there is some system of social ranking. Although we want everyone to have basic human rights, a society cannot function unless some people, such as judges, are granted special power and prestige. We have achieved a remarkable balance between these two kinds of concern by putting strict limits on the powers of the powerful, and by creating separation of power.

In *Politics*, Aristotle explained that there are three different forms of government: rule by one, rule by several, and rule by many. Aristotle argued that a government of any of these three forms could be good or perverted (Table 2). Aristotle argued that a monarch (a single ruler) can be an exceptional ruler who rules in everyone's interest. However, it would be hard to find such an outstanding leader. Unfortunately, a monarchy can easily degenerate into a tyranny, which is the worst form of government. A government that is run by a few people could be good if those people are the "best people" (*aristoi*), who rule in the interests of the many. Unfortunately, rule by a few can degenerate into oligarchy, if the few who are ruling are not excellent people. In an oligarchy, only the rich have power in government. In contrast, a democracy allows even the poor to have authority in government.

Table 2. Aristotle's Classification of Types of Governments

NUMBER OF RULERS	QUALITY OF GOVERNMENT		
	Good	Bad	Worst
One	Kingship		Tyranny
A Few	Aristocracy	Oligarchy	
Many	Politeia	Mob rule	Demagoguery

Aristotle believed that rule by the many could be good or bad. When it was good, it was the only kind of government that is based on freedom. He argued that the best form of government was *politeia*, which could be translated as polity or as constitutional government. By *politeia*, Aristotle meant that the many were ruling for the good of all. All citizens had a voice in government, but the government itself would have to follow certain laws. Aristotle felt that the multitude could collectively become excellent if individuals pooled their knowledge and restrained each other's baser instincts. Yet Aristotle felt that democracy could go too far, if the poor gained too much power. Aristotle felt that the ideal government would provide some reasonable balance between the interests of the rich and the poor. (Keep in mind that Aristotle also felt that women had no business meddling in politics, and that some people deserved to be slaves.)

Of course, any student of history can tell you that there is really no such thing as rule by one, at least not in any group larger than a small village. Even an autocrat like a Russian tsar or a fascist dictator relied on other people to keep him in power and carry out his wishes. Thus, even rule by one always ends up as rule by a few. Likewise, you never find true examples of rule by many in a group that is larger than a few people. The basic problem with rule by many was captured by a quip, supposedly by Oscar Wilde: "The trouble with socialism is that it would take up too many evenings." There is an easy way to avoid spending too many evenings in political negotiations. The members of a society can choose a few trusted individuals who will then take part in these negotiations on their behalf. But through that process, rule by many turns into rule by a few. Thus, the real question that we must ask is how those few are chosen, and how they are held accountable for their actions. Within a representative democracy, are the people electing the best people and holding them accountable for their behavior? Or are they electing crooks and thieves and turning a blind eye to their misdeeds?

Many people misunderstand this problem. When they think of aristocracy, they think of hereditary aristocracy: people who have inherited the legal right to rule. They think that people with prominent ancestors are somehow magically better than other people. Like the framers of the U.S. Constitution, I think that government should not be a family business. A candidate's family tree should not matter. All that matters is whether that candidate can and will serve the public well.

Aristotle observed that when there is no law but the whims of the majority, a charismatic leader (demagogue) inevitably rises to take control and becomes a tyrant. For that reason, Aristotle promoted the idea of a mixed government, which combines elements of aristocracy and democracy. During the early modern period, European philosophers developed the idea that the government should consist of several independent institutions that limit each other's powers, in a system of checks and balances. For this reason, the United States Constitution established three separate branches of government. The legislature writes the laws and says how money should be raised and spent. The executive branch carries out the laws. If there is any dispute, the judiciary then interprets the laws. The judiciary can overrule laws that violate the Constitution (which, of course, can be amended by the legislature). The legislature can also impeach executives and judges who abuse the public trust. This system of checks and balances makes it possible to have a democracy that does not degenerate into demagoguery and tyranny.

For this kind of constitutional government to serve the interests of the populace, the populace must contain a large enough number of politically engaged rational people. In contrast, if the populace is ignorant and apathetic, then you will end up with a bad form of *rule by a few*. If the richest 1% make all of the political decisions, you have an oligarchy, not a democracy. Today, most people believe that the ability to have reasonable and productive political discussions has been eroding in the United States. I believe that the ugliness and pointlessness of our current political discussions is a predictable result of the flaws in our public education system. The teachers in our public schools have been pressured to stop teaching the fundamental skills (phonics, grammar, etc.) that you need in order to develop higher-order thinking skills and take part in deliberations. As a result, few people know how to have important conversations.

In theory, we have a system in which each adult citizen gets exactly one vote in each election. Yet in reality, many adult citizens (especially poor, black, and brown people) have been disenfranchised because they have been processed through the criminal justice system, often for minor offenses or for offenses that they did not actually commit. Our system also allows wealthy people to buy huge amounts of influence by providing funding for political campaigns. Many of my fellow Americans complain that the government is run by a "shadow government" of wealthy people, who make all the real decisions in society. Yet that can take place only if the vast majority of people allow it to happen. Nothing besides lack of imagination prevents Americans from choosing good people to run in the primary elections of either major party, and then working to support their campaigns in the general election.

In order for a modern democratic society to function, the ordinary people must have an understanding of how its government is supposed to work. They must have some basic grasp of civics, which is the study of the theoretical and practical aspects of citizenship. They must also have a sophisticated understanding of how the world works, so that they can develop workable political strategies that will ultimately enable them to ensure that the government of the people is actually by the people and for the people. Yet for that to happen, we need for a critical mass of the people to think like responsible adults, instead of hoping for a strong leader to guide us.

To survive in an ancient foraging society, children had to look up to the elder members of their family. To thrive in a modern civilization, children must respect their parents and their teachers. For adults to play a productive role in any group activity, including political activity, they must seek out counsel from people who are wise and good. In ancient Athens, Plato wrote about the antidemocratic ideal of the philosopher-king. He suggested that it might be good to use Noble Lies to fool the common people into doing what you want them to do. Meanwhile, the Athenian Assembly gave us a far better model: a large group of citizens making decisions collectively through a process of public discussions.

Even the smallest-scale human society—the parent-child relationship—cannot function unless there is social hierarchy. The larger the scale of a society, the more it comes to depend on various kinds of social hierarchy to function. In order to get the education that they will need for their future, students must respect their teachers. In order for traffic to flow through a city, the drivers of automobiles must obey traffic rules and traffic cops. Many of our art forms depend on a strict hierarchy. Large choirs and orchestras need the leadership of a conductor. Everyone on a movie set must obey the director.

A modern democracy represents the rejection of the model of a philosopher-king who rules by telling lies. Many modern societies have even abolished titles of nobility. Nevertheless, we still have social hierarchies that result from differences in power, property, and prestige. However, in the United States today, we seem to be having problems with the concept of prestige. Too many of us seem to be giving prestige to the wrong sort of people. Today, the most highly paid and highly renowned employee of many of our state universities is not the university president or even the most distinguished scholar but the head coach of the football or basketball program.

I suspect that one of the reasons why sports are so popular is that the rankings represent a true meritocracy. Individual athletes, such as tennis players, and sports teams do not win championships unless they outperform their competition while following rules that apply to everyone. I think that Americans have become disengaged from politics because they do not understand that there are clear rules for winning and losing a debate. People who tell obvious lies and who make ridiculously illogical arguments should be laughed out of the public arena.

In other words, I view our problem with narcissism in the United States as an individual problem and a social problem. On one hand, many individuals have an unrealistic idea of where they rank in society. On the other hand, we have a dysfunctional system of assigning social rank. We grant power, prestige, and property to people who do not deserve them.

Chapter 13

Self-Esteem

~

A mentally healthy person would occupy the happy middle ground between narcissistic personality disorder (overly high self-esteem) and avoidant personality disorder (inappropriately low self-esteem). In other words, a mentally healthy person would have a realistic opinion about where he or she ranks in relation to other people, and how he or she fits into society. When individuals have a poor understanding of their own social rank, they can run into serious personal problems. If a large number of people within society have a poor understanding of how the social ranking system works, then the society is likely to be unjust. For this reason, we must think carefully about self-esteem. In particular, we must think carefully about what we are teaching children about self-esteem.

What is self-esteem? How is it measured? What relationship does it have to other phenomena, such as depression or academic success or good behavior or happiness? If someone has low self-esteem, is that low self-esteem a problem? Should we try to boost the person's self-esteem, or should we help the person solve other kinds of problems and let the self-esteem problem sort itself out? These are all tough questions. I wish I could answer these questions. All I can do is explain how important it is to ask them.

You might expect that a mentally healthy person would be someone with reasonably accurate perceptions and more or less logical thought processes. However, some members of the self-esteem movement want you to hold an unrealistically high opinion of yourself. In other words, they want you to hold biased self-perceptions supported

185

by illogical reasoning. The underlying theory is that if you believe that you are smart, you will become smart. If you believe that you will be successful, you will become successful, and so on. However, this theory is an example of magical thinking. In particular, it is a form of sympathetic magic, which is the idea that like produces like.

In contrast, Aristotle thought that men ought to have accurate opinions of their own abilities and achievements. Aristotle thought that great men should have high self-esteem. The accurate high self-esteem of a great man was called *megalopsychia* (magnanimity, or greatness of soul). It represented the moderate middle ground between vanity and pusillanimity (timidity). In contrast, Aristotle thought that lesser men should have lower self-esteem. The goal was to have your vision of yourself match reality. However, that idea raises the question of how one should decide what is real. What standards should you use in evaluating yourself? Should you rely on other people's opinions of you? Should popular people have high self-esteem and unpopular people have low self-esteem? Or should you use an academic standard? Should the valedictorian in the class have the highest self-esteem? Should other people have lower self-esteem, in accordance with their class rank?

From the dawn of civilization, philosophers have felt that it was bad to have too much self-esteem. Personally, I have serious doubts about self-esteem. By that, I don't mean that my own self-esteem is too low or too high. I mean that I doubt the validity of the concept, as measured by psychologists and applied by many educators. When I try to take the standard tests of self-esteem, most of the questions seem illogical to me. The other questions seem to be about my views about human dignity in general, not about my feelings about myself.

Table 3 shows the Rosenberg Self-Esteem scale, which is a standard measure of self-esteem. For each item, you are supposed to answer strongly agree, agree, disagree, or strongly disagree. Yet for many of these questions, I would either strongly agree or strongly disagree because of my political ideas. My answers would reflect how I feel about humanity in general, not how I feel about myself in particular. I find it impossible to answer some of the other questions because I think they are illogical or meaningless. As a result, I doubt the validity of this test: I doubt that it is really testing what it is intended to test.

Table 3. Rosenberg Self-Esteem Scale. You are supposed to rate each one as strongly agree, agree, disagree, or strongly disagree.

	TEST QUESTION	MY RESPONSE
1	I feel that I am a person of worth, at least on an equal plane with others.	What does *worth* mean? What plane are you talking about, and which others? If you believe in human equality, you will strongly agree with this statement because you consider everyone to be on an equal plane, as far as their basic human rights are concerned, so put me down for strongly agree, even though this test question would tell you nothing about how I feel about myself.
2	I feel that I have a number of good qualities.	Zero is a number, and so is one, and who is to judge what is good? I imagine that everyone must have at least one quality that would be generally regarded as good, so I guess I strongly agree. However, that answer would tell you nothing about how I feel about myself.
3	All in all, I am inclined to feel that I am a failure.	This question commits the cognitive distortion of labeling. Since it is illogical, I strongly disagree. But I would also disagree with the statement, "All in all, I am inclined to feel that I am a success."
4	I am able to do things as well as most other people.	What things? I did not think less of myself when I had a disabling illness than I do now. This question may measure disability rather than low self-esteem, and I don't think that disabled people should feel bad about themselves for being disabled. On the contrary, I would want them to feel a gratifying sense of achievement (fiero) for accomplishments that would seem minor to most people. I cannot answer this question.
5	I feel I do not have much to be proud of.	I think that I have written some useful books, so I strongly disagree. However, that tells you how I feel about my work, not about myself. Also, note that depressed people are prone to the cognitive distortions of minimizing their accomplishments and discounting the positives.
6	I take a positive attitude about myself.	This question is too vague for me to answer.

Table 3. Rosenberg Self-Esteem Scale. Continued...

TEST QUESTION		MY RESPONSE
7	On the whole, I am satisfied with myself.	This question is too vague for me to answer.
8	I wish I could have more respect for myself.	I have never wished that or even thought about wishing that, so I guess I strongly disagree.
9	I certainly feel useless at times.	Like every sane person, I feel helpless when confronted with problems that I cannot solve. If useless means helpless, I guess I strongly agree.
10	At times I think I am no good at all.	Depressed people tend to discount the positive.

For items 1, 2, 4, 6, and 7 add 3 points for strongly agree, 2 points for agree, 1 point for disagree, and 0 points for strongly disagree. For items 3, 5, 8, 9 and 10 add 0 points for strongly agree, 1 point for agree, 2 points for disagree, and 3 points for strongly disagree. The scale ranges from 0-30. Scores between 15 and 25 are within normal range; scores below 15 suggest low self-esteem.

There are several ways to evaluate the validity of a test. One is to establish whether the test is reliable. An unreliable test cannot be valid. If a test yields random results, like having the person flip a coin or toss a pair of dice, then the results of the test cannot tell you anything about that person. There are several criteria for testing reliability. One is repeatability, which means that a person would get the same score if he or she took the test again. Inter-rater reliability means that different psychologists would come up with the same score if they gave the same test to the same person. But even if a test is reliable, it could still be invalid.

There are two basic kinds of criteria for evaluating the validity of a test: content-related validity and criterion-related validity. Content-related validity deals with questions about the content of the test. Content validity includes face validity and construct validity. Face validity deals with the question of whether the test seems to measure what it was intended to measure. Construct validity deals with questions of how the test relates to the underlying theory. Criterion validity relates to how the test relates to other tests that are designed for the same purpose. There are two kinds of criterion validity: concurrent and predictive. In other words, how well do the test results correspond with the results of other tests given at the same time (concurrent validity) and the results of other tests that will be given in the future (predictive validity)?

I have some serious concerns about the face validity and construct validity of self-esteem tests. In the United States, the Rosenberg Self-Esteem Scale seems to correlate well with other measures of happiness or mental health. Of course, some of the questions in the test are about disability and common symptoms of depression. Depressed people tend to take a dim view of practically everything, including themselves. As a result, depressed people generally have low self-esteem scores. So even if low self-esteem scores correlate with depression, it could be because some of the items in the self-esteem tests are actually measuring symptoms of depression. Even if a depressed person has low self-esteem, we do not know whether the low self-esteem caused the depression or the depression caused the low self-esteem. It is possible that each reinforces the other, in a vicious circle.

The Rosenberg Self-Esteem Scale might not be useful for measuring self-esteem in patients who have had cognitive behavioral therapy. The goal of cognitive behavioral therapy is to correct the irrational thought patterns (cognitive distortions) that can lead to depressed mood. Depressed people often make some common errors in thinking about themselves and the world. These cognitive distortions include overgeneralization, labeling, and all-or-nothing thinking. Yet if you don't allow yourself to have those kinds of irrational thoughts, you may be unable to answer many of the items of the Rosenberg Self-Esteem Scale.

Depressed people tend to have low self-esteem, but people who are in the manic phase of bipolar disorder can have extraordinarily high self-esteem. During a manic episode, a person may have delusions of grandeur. These delusions are fantastical beliefs that one is famous, wealthy, and/or enormously powerful. Often, the content of these de-lusions is based on religious, supernatural, or science fiction themes. Delusions are a symptom of psychosis. However, many people who do not qualify for a diagnosis of mental illness have grandiose thoughts that are not quite bizarre enough to be considered delusional. Thus, a high score on a test of self-esteem is not necessarily an indicator of mental health.

I suspect that Quakers and Buddhist monks (who tend to share my views about human dignity) and people who have taken at least an introductory-level course on logic would also have trouble in answer-ing some of the questions on the Rosenberg Self-Esteem Scale. In fact, the self-esteem tests that seem useful in the United States do not seem to be useful in Japan. Studies in Japan consistently show that a large percentage of the respondents have low scores on the standard Ameri-can tests of self-esteem. Yet Japan does not have high rates of the social problems that seem to go along with low self-esteem in the United States. This poor correlation suggests a problem with the validity of the self-esteem tests. At the very least, this poor correlation suggests that the self-esteem tests have problems with generalizability, which is the ability to be used for many different groups in different settings. However, the main problem may be the underlying theory.

The Japanese have a word for self-esteem: *jisonshin*. Yet like the word *pride* in English, it can have negative connotations. *Jisonshin* can imply vanity and vainglory. In Japan, *jisonshin* can imply that the person lacks modesty (*kenson*) and moderateness (*hikaeme*). These concepts corre-spond to the Roman Catholic concepts of humility and temperance. Psychologists are not sure why the self-esteem tests that seem useful in the United States do not seem as useful in Japan. The differences between the Americans and the Japanese who took the tests could re-flect differences in how those individuals think about themselves. However, the differences might just reflect differences in what people in the two countries think is appropriate to say about themselves. The rules for politeness in self-expression are different in Japan than they are in the United States.

Love is a many-splendored thing. So is self-love. The concept of self-esteem has been stretched to cover many different kinds of ideas. So when several different people are talking about self-esteem, each of them could be talking about something completely different. So even if you are skeptical about some of the popular ideas about self-esteem, it would be silly to accept or dismiss every idea or intervention being promoted by people who are somehow allied with the self-esteem movement. To sort out the different definitions of self-esteem, we could start with the story of *The Little Engine That Could*.

Several versions of the story of *The Little Engine That Could* have been told. All of them involve a long train of freight cars that must be pulled over a big mountain. Several large locomotives are asked to pull the train; but for various reasons, each of them refuses. Finally, a small locomotive is asked. She replies, "I think I can! I think I can!" She keeps telling herself "I think I can" as she struggles to drag the train to the top of the mountain. As she descends the other side of the mountain, she rejoices by saying "I thought I could, I thought I could." The story is used to teach children the value of optimism and hard work. It also shows that you can experience joy by doing something difficult to serve others.

Many people who are considered part of the self-esteem movement mainly want to urge people to tell themselves, "I think I can." (This kind of encouragement may be particularly important to people who have been taught to underestimate themselves.) Members of the self-esteem movement also generally want to encourage people to feel that they have permission to succeed in life and to enjoy the fruits of their success. It is a message of not just "yes, you can" but "yes, you may." The best of these programs also provide some sort of direct training in the skills that unsuccessful people seem to lack. So besides teaching someone to believe "I think I can" and "it's okay if I do," they show their students, "and this is how." Practically any training program would meet that description.

Training programs can be judged by three criteria. The first criterion is whether the "yes, you can" message is realistic. Back in the 1970s, some proponents of Transcendental Meditation claimed that if you meditated hard enough, you could fly. Yogic flying meant that you could hover in midair or even fly around the room. In reality, nobody has ever been able to do more than to hop a little while in the lotus position. No meditator's body really left the ground for any longer than that. So the claim that meditation could enable you to levitate was false. Any program that makes false promises would be fraudulent.

The second criterion is whether the "yes, you may" statements are morally acceptable. Is the program teaching people how to be productive, contributing members of society, or is it encouraging them to behave like sociopaths? Is it teaching people how to prosper through voluntary exchanges of value with other people, or is it teaching its students to exploit other people or to run roughshod over them?

The third criterion is whether the "and here's how" portions of the program are effective. Does the training actually teach people the skills that they need for success, or is it a waste of their time or other resources?

A program that satisfies all three criteria might do some good. However, a program that really succeeds in helping you improve your intellectual and social skills will probably cause you to make a lower, more realistic assessment of your skills. The more you learn, the more you realize how little you really know. Thus, a program that is truly effective at raising your skills could lower your self-esteem. Yet even as your self-esteem drops, you might be earning other people's respect. Thus, if you shun the experiences that might damage your self-esteem, you will likely remain an ignorant fool for the rest of your life.

Training programs that raise people's aspirations and then help them fulfil those aspirations can be good. However, the idea that your self-esteem could or should be derived from your self-assessment of skills or achievements raises some practical and ethical concerns. The practical concerns spring from the unreliability of self-assessment. In a formal training program, your achievements would be evaluated by a teacher. But outside of that kind of formal setting, you usually end up grading your own papers. Yet as I explained in Chapter 5, people often give themselves inaccurate grades. The people with the lowest skills tend to rate themselves as above average, while the people with the best skills tend to underrate themselves, relative to other people. This problem is called the Dunning-Kruger effect. The ethical concerns spring from the concept of a human being's worth. When you are hiring someone for a particular job, you want to hire someone who is capable. However, the idea that people should be judged as "worthy" or "unworthy" in some other context makes me uncomfortable. That way lies madness. The German Third Reich had an extermination program for mental patients who were considered *lebensunwertes Lebens* (life unworthy of life).

A training program that teaches you how to recognize your mistakes may make you less arrogant. Thus, it would lower your self-esteem. However, a training program that enables you to accomplish something worthwhile may boost your self-esteem. So should a training program try to raise someone's self-esteem? Should efforts to raise self-esteem be part of the program? Should higher self-esteem be part of the goals of the program? The answer to that question probably depends on the social and political context of the program.

When I was a child, most people assumed that women were simply not as good as men are at science or math. To succeed in those fields, women had to reject the idea this idea of natural inferiority. Even today, women often must struggle to get others to respect their abilities and accomplishments. People of color have faced the same challenges in a racist white society. Anyone who was born at the bottom of any caste- or class-based society would face similar challenges. In that context, it would be entirely appropriate to provide some sort of consciousness-raising to help people believe in their potential. In contrast, people who were born into privilege may need to learn humility.

According to the people in the self-esteem movement, raising children's self-esteem will help them do better in school, along with helping them resist peer pressure to do bad things. But if children are already satisfied with themselves, why would they bother to work at self-improvement? Worse yet, a program that encourages children to believe "I think I can" without showing them "and this is how" could backfire badly. If the program does not teach them how to succeed, they are likely to fail. If the program teaches them to connect success with self-worth, they might take the failure personally, which could then lead to a condition called learned helplessness.

I am particularly concerned about any program that might undermine academic learning. By the mid-20th century, it was obvious that many supposedly progressive approaches to education were actually preventing children from progressing academically. As I explained in my book *Not Trivial: How Studying the Traditional Liberal Arts Can Set You Free*, the so-called progressive approaches to education were actually being promoted by the same wealthy people who were sometimes using deadly force to suppress labor unions. So even though schooling expanded dramatically during this historical period, education was actually being suppressed in many places. More children were spending more time in school, largely because of local taxpayers' willingness to pay high school taxes. However, the curriculum in many schools was watered down so that the children would end up learning surprisingly little. For example, children at John Dewey's Laboratory School at the University of Chicago spent a lot of time doing things like cooking and weaving and sewing, rather than learning to read and write and do arithmetic and studying academic subjects such as geography, history, science, and so on.

In the 1950s, Rudolf Flesch, who was a professor at Columbia University Teachers College, became aware that many American schoolchildren, including his own grandson, were failing to learn to read in school. After looking into the problem, Flesch realized that the cause of the problem was in the way that teachers were being trained. Because of the influence of people like John Dewey, aspiring teachers were being trained to have children memorize whole words as graphic designs ("sight words"), rather than teaching children to sound words out letter by letter (phonics). Experienced teachers were being pressured to stop teaching phonics. Meanwhile, phonics-based reading textbooks were being removed from the schools.

Flesch warned the public about this problem in his 1955 bestseller *Why Johnny Can't Read: And What You Can Do About It*. Yet the problem persisted. As a result, more and more children failed to learn to read. The failure to learn to read derails a child's education. It can also be a terrible blow to the child's self-esteem. You could solve this problem by using an effective method of teaching reading. Instead, teachers have been pressured to waste classroom time on attempts to boost the children's self-esteem artificially.

Phonics is not the only traditional discipline that has been suppressed in public schools. So have arithmetic and grammar. To learn these skills, children must practice. The children must try to solve problems, and you have to tell them whether their answers are right or wrong. However, many educators fear that pointing out a child's mistakes would destroy the child's self-esteem. Yet if children do not develop skills in fundamental disciplines, they will be unable to achieve higher goals. For example, a pianist cannot learn advanced jazz improvisation without first spending many hours practicing scales.

Back in the early 20th century, Dewey claimed that educators should focus on the child's social activities, rather than on academic subjects. He expressed contempt for academic learning, and he was blasé about whether children learned to read in primary school. To people who came of age during the Cold War, Dewey's willingness to sacrifice academic learning to achieve some sort of social goal sounded disturbingly bolshèvist. Yet Dewey was not an agent of the Worldwide Communist Conspiracy. Instead, he spent his career at institutions funded by the world's leading capitalist: John D. Rockefeller, Sr.

In the early 20th century, the Rockefellers' General Education Board was openly contemptuous of the poor whites in rural areas—"neglected rural folk" whom the General Education Board regarded as their "sheep":

> In our dream, we have limitless resources, and the people yield themselves with perfect docility to our molding hand. The present educational conventions fade from our minds; and unhampered by tradition, we work our own good will upon a grateful and responsive rural folk. We shall not try to make these people or any of their children into philosophers or men of learning or of science. We are not to raise up from among them authors, orators, poets, or men of letters. We shall not search for embryo great artists, painters, musicians. Nor will we cherish even the humbler ambition to raise up from among them lawyers, doctors, preachers, statesmen, of whom we now have ample supply.

In short, the Rockefellers' advisors felt that the educational system was already producing enough white-collar workers to meet the needs of the ruling class. Thus, the General Education Board's goal was to improve the efficiency of the rural workforce without raising the people's aspirations for economic and social uplift.

By the late 20th century, the public relations industry had warned rich people to stop comparing working people to sheep, at least in public. Rich people also stopped admitting that they were deliberately designing an educational system that would provide a substandard education to children of the lower classes. During the Vietnam War, the unrest on college campuses raised concerns that working class people's children were getting too much education and were becoming too engaged in politics. Thus, the wealthy people whose philanthropy was shaping education in the United States needed to find politically acceptable excuses for suppressing direct instruction in basic disciplines. In that context, the self-esteem movement provided useful cover for policies that suppressed public education.

Many educators in the United States have been following policies that sacrifice academic learning on the altar of promoting children's self-esteem. As a result, many students have been growing up ignorant and arrogant. Studies have shown that American students tend to have high confidence in their math skills; meanwhile, students in other countries have less confidence but better math skills. Of course, what really matters is whether people are good at math, not whether they *feel* they are good at math. Feeling that you are good at math, when you are actually poor at math, is not a good thing.

Every educational program is based, consciously or unconsciously, on some theory of pedagogy. Pedagogy is the art and science of teaching. Theophrastus wondered how individual Greeks could be so different from each other, even though they had been educated alike. Likewise, modern educators have been grappling with the question of why students in the same classroom can end up with such differences in educational achievement.

Because of a desire to pretend that racial oppression was not a problem in the Land of Opportunity, many people in the United States assumed that academic achievement is mainly the result of differences in students' hereditary traits. To the white Anglo-Saxon Protestants who were dominating academia in the early 20th century, racist ideas provided a comforting explanation for why native-born white students were outperforming black students and many recent immigrants. So was the idea that school performance was a reflection of superior moral values. However, the idea that school performance was a reflection of biological and moral superiority became awkward when large numbers of Jewish and then Asian students started outperforming white Anglo-Saxon Protestant students.

Poor school performance could result from some combination of problems in the child, in the school, or in the child's family. If there is a problem in only one of these three, the other two may be strong enough to compensate. For example, many Asian-American children have been thriving academically in otherwise lackluster public schools. However, their success is due largely to the support they are getting from their families and their ethnic community.

The success of Asian-American students in public schools is largely the result of how U.S. immigration law was written: the laws favor the admission of highly educated, highly skilled immigrants from Asian countries. Many of these immigrants are better educated than the average American. When they settle in ethnic enclaves, they establish institutions, such as tutoring programs, that benefit even the working-class members of their ethnic community. As a result, many Asian-American children have been getting supplemental education that is fueling their success.

This supplemental education is often vital. As I explained in *Not Trivial*, many of the supposedly progressive educational policies promoted by the likes of John Dewey do not actually help children progress. The worst of these was the use of "sight words" instead of phonics for teaching reading. Another was Dewey's idea that children would spontaneously learn academic skills such as arithmetic through doing household crafts such as baking or sewing or some sort of group activity. Another is constructivism: the idea that children should discover practically everything on their own, while the teacher does as little as possible. Yet another was the "Whole Language" fad in language arts education. Whole language was based on the idea that children would spontaneously learn to read and would spontaneously develop high-level skills in the language arts just by being exposed to text, just as they naturally learned to speak by hearing other people talk. Promoters of the Whole Language curriculum told teachers to stop teaching phonics or spelling or grammar and to stop correcting children's mistakes.

The Whole Language approach to teaching language arts has been a disaster, most notably in California, where it was imposed on the public schools in 1987. Not only were teachers not supposed to teach actual skills, such as sounding out words and spelling, but they were discouraged from correcting the children's mistakes. As a result, children could not learn from their mistakes.

In traditional approaches to teaching, the teacher would teach students fundamental skills and then tell the students whether they were doing things well or poorly. Ideally, the lessons would be designed so that the child could learn skills and facts in a reasonable order, so that each lesson builds upon and reinforces what the children have already learned. Thus, the student would progress from success to success. The child's sense of accomplishment (fiero) from each success could then help to encourage the child to apply him- or herself to the next lesson. The goal was to promote a virtuous circle in which success leads to more success. However, many educators thought that correcting a child's mistakes would damage the child's self-esteem. Thus, they feared that correcting a child's mistakes would unleash a vicious circle of low self-esteem, low motivation, and even poorer performance. Yet to believe that, educators had to be completely unaware of a widespread phenomenon called video games.

Video games relentlessly punish the player for making the slightest mistake. However, the players do not seem to mind, perhaps because punishments are based on strictly objective criteria, are relentlessly fair, and are completely impersonal. Rather than refusing to drill children in basic skills, educators could be building those drills into some game that children would actually enjoy playing. By relentlessly pointing out the students' mistakes, the computer enables the students to learn from their mistakes. By keeping track of the students' successes, the computer can help students experience fiero, which is the joy of accomplishment.

Educational policies in the United States have been shaped by a bizarre mixture of B. F. Skinner's behaviorism (which was based on an explicit rejection of the concept of human dignity) and a sincere concern for human rights (which is based on deep concern for human dignity). Behaviorists hoped to shape human behavior by designing systems of rewards and punishments. Yet history has shown us that many of the punishments that have traditionally been used in schools are both cruel and pointless. In response to those revelations, many educators decided to give out nothing but rewards. But then, it seemed cruel to withhold rewards from students who did not earn them, so some educators decided to give rewards to everyone. The result is a scenario similar to the Caucus-Race in *Alice's Adventures in Wonderland,* by Lewis Carroll: "EVERYBODY has won, and all must have prizes." Yet if students are continually being given rewards for nothing, the rewards themselves should not be expected to have any useful effect on behavior.

Traditionally, animal trainers have used some combination of rewards and punishments to influence the behavior of animals. The rewards usually consisted of food, and the punishments often involved the infliction of pain. Because of concerns about animal welfare, many trainers have shifted toward using nothing but rewards. Yet I think that it is fundamentally misguided to use nothing but rewards in the education of human beings. Many trained animals work for food rewards. For the animal, the food reward is the point of the activity. Yet even in kindergarten, children understand that the purpose of school is to learn things, rather than to collect gold stars.

Gold stars and good grades and so on are merely tokens of the teachers' approval. These tokens are merely ways of communicating that the student is progressing in the right direction. Likewise, bad grades and punishments and so on merely signify that the student has gone off course or simply failed to keep up. In other words, rewards are not the end in themselves. Instead, the rewards and the punishment are feedback. Positive feedback means, "Yes, keep doing that." Negative feedback means, "No, stop doing that."

I do not condone cruelty, but I think that people often do need some sort of negative feedback. As Winston Churchill put it, "Criticism may not be agreeable, but it is necessary. It fulfills the same function as pain in the human body. It calls attention to an unhealthy state of things."

Positive and negative feedback are important for regulating social behavior. Social animals express how they feel about the behavior of the other animals in their group. Often, just a threatening look from a high-ranking animal is enough to persuade a low-ranking animal to modify its behavior. Of course, human beings can think and communicate in ways that are simply impossible for any other animals. Not only can we recognize ourselves in a mirror, but most of us can imagine what other people might think of us. Thus, we can alter our behavior in response to what we imagine that other people would think, feel, or do. Thus, most of us are probably playing to an imaginary audience, which represents our imagination of what other people would think and feel, if they knew what we were thinking or doing. This imaginary audience is the basis for our conscience.

If we think that we have disappointed real people, we feel shame. Shame is the emotion that goes along with being in a subordinate social position. But if we disappoint our imaginary audience, we feel guilt. In other words, we feel shame when we disappoint other people. We feel guilt when we disappoint ourselves. When our imaginary audience is applauding, we feel high self-esteem. When the imaginary audience is booing, we feel low self-esteem.

An external audience gives us feedback about what we say and do. Yet some people do not benefit from that feedback. Either they are unaware, or they simply do not care. Some people have such poor skills in reading people that they miss the signals that other people are sending. Other people may be aware of such signals but just don't care—either because they feel that they are being criticized by idiots or because they simply don't care about other people's opinions or feelings. If you are unaware of your external audience's reactions, or if you simply don't care about their reactions, then you will seem to have no shame. Shame is the response that people may want to see when they give you negative feedback.

Our internal audience may have evolved as a way to help us predict how other people are likely to react to what we say and do. However, it also allows us to think about what is good or bad as well as what is right or wrong. At one level, your internal audience can help you predict what other people want you to do. At a higher level, it can help guide you in doing what you feel you ought to do. It helps you figure out how to do what is right, as opposed to what is popular. Thus, it serves as the basis for your conscience.

Your conscience is the product of your own imagination. Your conscience is shaped by what you know and how you feel. It may—or may not—lead you in the right direction. You conscience represents what you imagine that other people should feel about you. If you are religious, you may imagine that your conscience represents how God feels about you. However, people who imagine that they can read God's mind and know God's will can be dangerous. Various religious traditions have developed disciplines to discourage people from making that kind of mistake. Judaism had rabbinical courts that made decisions about matters of religious law. Rabbis who dissented from the rulings of a court could state their dissent and teach accordingly, but they had to obey the rulings of the court. Similarly, the Roman Catholic Church had an elaborate system of canon law. Some Protestant denominations also have some sort of structure of ecclesiastical authority. Of course, some do not. Many individual Protestants are a law unto themselves.

Aristotle felt that a person's self-esteem should be accurate. In other words, the opinions of your imaginary audience should match the opinions of the real people who know you and are qualified to judge you accurately. Yet this is precisely where the problem of narcissism arises. Narcissism results when the person's internal audience is far less critical than real people would be. As a result, the narcissist ends up with unrealistically high self-esteem. In other words, narcissists are people whose self-esteem is higher than the esteem that other people hold for them. If you try to boost someone's self-esteem artificially, you could make this problem worse.

On the other hand, some people have unrealistically low self-esteem because their imaginary audience is overly critical. Sometimes, this problem arises because the individual was abused or neglected in childhood. Thus, their imaginary audience represents the horrible people they encountered in their formative years, rather than representing sane and reasonable people. To solve this problem, the individual must learn to become a better judge of other people, and then adjust their own self-concept in response to the judgments of intelligent and decent people.

I think that the people who are involved in the self-esteem movement are prone to making two kinds of error. One is to mistake an effect for a cause. For example, you may notice that winners tend to have high self-esteem. But does high self-esteem create winners, or does winning produce high self-esteem? Putting a gold medal around someone's neck does not cause that person to win at the Olympics. The other error is to try to alter how people feel, when the real problem is in the domain of thoughts.

There are many reasons why a person's self-esteem could be inaccurate. Simple ignorance can lead to falsely high self-esteem. As Dunning and Kruger demonstrated, people with poor skills tend to overrate themselves because they cannot spot their own mistakes. On the other hand, people who have been oppressed may have an unrealistically low opinion of themselves and their abilities. I think that many people became interested in boosting children's self-esteem because they wanted to undo the damage inflicted by racial and class oppression. I share that goal.

A person could have low self-esteem from accepting the unfair judgments of biased people within his or her society. Back in the 1940s, psychologists Mamie and Kenneth Clark did some studies that showed the damage that racial oppression had inflicted on black children's sense of self. The Clarks got some dolls that were identical except for the color: some resembled a white child, the others a black child. They showed a white doll and a black doll to black children, ages 6 to 9, from segregated schools and asked the following questions, in this order:

Show me the doll that you like best or that you would like to play with.

Show me the doll that is the "nice" doll.

Show me the doll that looks "bad."

Give me the doll that looks like a white child.

Give me the doll that looks like a colored child.

Give me the doll that looks like a Negro child.

Give me the doll that looks like you.

Many black children preferred the white doll, which they thought was the nice doll. They thought that the black doll was the bad one. When asked which doll looks like them, some of the black children picked the white doll. Others either refused to pick a doll or started crying and ran away. The disturbing results of this study helped to persuade the Supreme Court of the United States to outlaw segregation in the public schools. The study also helped to inspire the Black Is Beautiful cultural movement.

Self-esteem is the judgment rendered by the imaginary audience within your own psyche. Ideally, this imaginary audience will help you predict how the real people in your society will respond to what you say and do. Thus, it can help you navigate your social environment. However, if the people in your society are biased for or against you, your imaginary audience may adopt those biases. As a result, the wealthy and powerful may develop an inflated self-concept because of all of the smarmy praise they receive. Thus, they may become vain and foolish. (The oldest surviving Greek comedies made light of the vanity and foolishness of powerful men.) In contrast, people who are at the bottom of an oppressive society may end up with unrealistically low self-esteem because of psychological injury.

The low self-esteem that results from oppression has been a serious problem for many black and Native American children. It has also been a problem for gay children and children with disabilities and children who are unloved for one reason or another. To undo this kind of low self-esteem takes more than affirmations. It takes a form of political awakening that has been called conscientization. The goal is not to promote vanity or vainglory but to help people develop dignity and compassion for themselves and for other people who are in a similar situation. Once people achieve conscientization, they will no longer take part in their own oppression. Instead, they will stand up for themselves and for other people. Thus, this approach to raising self-esteem is a revolutionary act.

Rather than trying to boost self-esteem, I think that we should be trying to help people develop compassion. The word *compassion* came from the Latin for "to suffer with." It means a strong sense of sympathy and sorrow for another person's suffering, along with a desire to relieve that suffering. All of the major religions classify compassion as a virtue. I am not sure that boosting self-esteem improves happiness. However, scientific experiments have shown that systematic training of the mind can boost a person's capacity for empathy and compassionate behavior, and that these changes promote happiness and mental well-being. One of the side effects of becoming more compassionate toward others is that you learn to be compassionate toward yourself. As a result, you will treat yourself as you think someone ought to be treated.

Another form of low self-esteem can result from having false ideas about how people learn and succeed. Many American children have been led to believe that success in school, and particularly in math class, is mainly a result of "brains"—innate ability—as opposed to hard work. Children who think that their success is a reflection of their innate abilities will not bother to put much effort into their schoolwork. As a result, they will get poor grades, which will make them feel stupid. You cannot correct this problem by simply telling children that they are smart, any more than you can give them athletic ability by handing them a trophy. Instead, you have to teach them how to succeed in their schoolwork. It would be cruel to urge the children to think of themselves as smart without teaching them how to succeed in school. Such an approach could backfire badly. It could unleash a vicious circle of failure, lower self-esteem, low effort, and yet more failure.

Some people want children to focus on their strengths, as a way to boost their self-esteem. However, it may be better to teach the child to focus on correcting his or her weaknesses. To help children do that, you must first let children understand that it is okay to have and acknowledge weaknesses. (Humility and self-compassion are useful in this regard.) By correcting weaknesses, you eliminate a potential source of shame (for a sane person) or narcissistic rage (for a narcissist).

Aristotle believed that great men should have high self-esteem and that lesser men should have lower self-esteem. The point was that one's self-assessments should be accurate. If someone seems to have inappropriately low self-esteem, the problem could spring from depression, just as overly high self-esteem can be a feature of mania. If some problem with self-esteem springs from a problem like bipolar disorder or major depression, the self-esteem problem may resolve when the underlying mood problem is managed medically. In cases of avoidant personality disorder, low self-esteem seems to spring from an anxiety problem, combined with poor skill at reading other people. The goal of treatment would be to manage the anxiety and improve social skills. As a result, the self-esteem problem may sort itself out. In other words, the focus ought to be on developing accurate self-assessments and reasonable emotional responses, rather than to cultivate mindless self-worship.

Some psychologists claim that there is such a thing as "healthy narcissism" or that there is a "healthy side of narcissism." Often, they claim that there is a "right degree" of narcissism, by which they mean that a person has reasonable self-confidence. However, I think that the word *narcissism* should be used only to describe an unhealthy form of self-worship: self-esteem that is so unrealistically high that it is causing some sort of problem for the person or for others. The ancient Greeks themselves considered the myth of Narcissus to be a cautionary tale.

Many psychologists today argue that narcissists lack an identity, a sense of self. According to this theory, the narcissist compensates by developing a "false self." This false self is then opposed to the "authentic self," which is supposed to be the core of who you really are. I think that this theory is nonsensical. All concepts of self are mental images. All mental images are only images and thus can never be completely faithful to whatever reality they supposedly depict. Even a reflection in the world's best mirror is a flat, reversed image of the outward appearance of an object from only one point of view. Narcissists do have a sense of identity. Otherwise, they would be unable to recognize their reflection in a mirror. Narcissists simply give themselves better grades than other people think they deserve. That's why the other people judge them as narcissistic.

Both self-esteem and esteem are social judgments, and neither judgment is necessarily fair. When people are depressed, their self-esteem tends to be low because their internal audience is biased against them. When people are suffering from delusions of grandeur, their internal audience is overly worshipful. Likewise, real people can be biased for or against someone. Thus, a mismatch between self-esteem and esteem does not always mean that the self-esteem is inaccurate. It might mean that one is on the right side of history. In 1918, an American trade unionist named Nicholas Klein said the following in an address to the Third Biennial Convention of the Amalgamated Clothing Workers of America:

> And, my friends, in this story you have a history of this entire movement. First they ignore you. Then they ridicule you. And then they attack you and want to burn you. And then they build monuments to you. And that, is what is going to happen to the Amalgamated Clothing Workers of America.

On the other hand, when your internal and external audience disagree, sometimes your external audience is right. According to an old Yiddish proverb, if one person says that you are jackass, ignore him; but if 10 people say that you are a jackass, buy a saddle. In other words, criticism is not always accurate, but it should lead to introspection and perhaps to a downward revision of one's self-concept.

Some of the popular approaches to building self-esteem seem designed to bias your internal audience in your favor, rather than to make it more accurate. One of these approaches is to repeat affirmations, which are basically self-compliments. These self-compliments, if accurate, could be a useful corrective for people whose internal audience is biased against them. However, the last thing that anyone with an uncritical internal audience needs is more self-congratulation. The goal should be to enable the person to develop accurate self-assessments, along with self-compassion, as opposed to developing mindless self-worship.

Unfortunately, people who are predisposed to narcissism may be particularly attracted to interventions that are intended to boost their self-esteem. In general, people with personality disorders tend to prefer the therapeutic approaches that make them worse, not better. I think that this general pattern reflects the fact that personality disorders can often be viewed as a failure of maturation. Perhaps people with these disorders are simply people who are avoiding the kinds of unpleasant experiences that would help them grow up.

I hope that this chapter has inspired you to rethink the concept of self-esteem and the role that self-esteem plays in mental health. We really need to be careful about how we define and measure self-esteem. We also need to be more critical of the studies that relate self-esteem to other concepts, such as depression. In particular, we need to have a clear understanding of the direction of causal relationships. What is the relationship between low self-esteem and other phenomena, such as depression? If low self-esteem really is correlated to some other problem, does the correlation reflect a causal relationship? If it does, which way does the causality run? Does the low self-esteem cause the other problem, or vice versa? Might both of them be the result of some other cause? Should we try to alter self-esteem directly, or should we focus on other problems and allow a self-esteem problem to sort itself out?

I suspect that some of the interventions that have been done in the name of raising self-esteem might be useful, at least for some people. People whose internal audience is biased against them because of a horrific childhood or an unjust society probably do need an ego boost. They probably do need to give themselves permission to strive and to succeed. They might benefit from repeating some true affirmations. Yet I worry that the endless, unearned praise that many children are receiving could warp their character and stunt their moral and intellectual development. The challenge will be to find ways to enable people to develop accurate self-assessments, so that their internal audience can give them better guidance on how to interact with their environment and with other people.

Chapter 14

Logic and Reason

To a narcissist, social life is a continual game of king of the hill. Narcissists want to prove themselves to be the best and the brightest. They love to debate, and they love to imagine that they win those debates. Because of their inflated self-esteem, narcissists are convinced that their ideas are logical and reasonable. Anyone who argues with them must therefore be illogical and unreasonable. Therefore, the narcissist always declares him- or herself to be the victor.

The word *debate* came from a medieval French word meaning fistfight. As Western civilization emerged from the Dark Ages, Europeans increasingly started using their words, as opposed to their fists, to settle disagreements. A debate focuses on a disagreement, either about what is true or about what should be done. Yet there are better ways to settle those disagreements.

To settle a disagreement about what is true, people can engage in a type of discussion called dialectic. As I explained in Chapter 5, dialectic is a process in which individuals pool their knowledge and correct each other's errors in reasoning. There are no winners or losers. Instead, everyone can "win" because everyone gains a deeper understanding of the problem at hand. To settle a disagreement about what should be done, people engage in negotiation. The purpose of a negotiation is to find a mutually acceptable solution to some conflict. In a negotiation, you can't always get what you want; but if you try sometimes, you'll find, you get what you need.

From the narcissist's point of view, both dialectic and negotiation have a serious drawback. Narcissists want to win through the sheer force of their personality, like an aggressive hen struggling to rise within her flock's pecking order. Unfortunately, the narcissist's opponents can prevail in a scientific discussion by speaking the truth. The narcissist's opponents in a negotiation can prevail if the facts and the law are on their side. Thus, to the narcissist, truth and morality and even the law seem to be subversive forces that threaten to destroy the proper social order.

Narcissists have always wanted to feel that they are the smartest person in the room. Now that they have the Internet, they want to feel that they are the smartest person on the planet. As a result, they often engage in battles of wits with people who are far smarter and far better educated than they are. Usually, narcissists imagine that they win these battles. When a sane person walks away from a stupid argument with a stupid person, the stupid person declares victory. Typically, the narcissists lack the intellectual skills to judge the outcome of the contest. In other words, they are not smart enough to realize that they are making themselves look stupid. Thus, they do not realize that their attempt to achieve intellectual dominance has backfired badly.

I became aware of the problem of narcissism in the 1980s, when I started working as a copyeditor, which meant that it was my job to keep people from looking stupid in public. Occasionally, I would encounter people who would rather look stupid in public than allow a trained copyeditor to fix their grammatical mistakes when nobody was looking.

I suspect that narcissists are less prone than normal people to a common fear: the fear of looking stupid in public. If you have no respect for other people's opinions, then you have no fear of looking stupid. If people disagree with you, then they are the stupid ones. You may become angry at their insubordination, but you would not be shamed by their disapproval. In contrast, people who do have respect for others are often held back by their fear of looking stupid in public.

There is an easy way and a hard way to avoid looking stupid in public. The easy way is to keep your mouth shut. Like most other people, smart people tend to imagine that other people are like themselves. This tendency to imagine that other people think and feel as you do is called psychological projection. Because of psychological projection, smart people tend to assume that you are also smart, until you say or do something that convinces them otherwise. The quickest way to make a smart person think that you are stupid is to argue with them. Smart people usually have good reasons for believing what they believe. You would probably be better off listening to what they have to say than trying to persuade them that you know better than they do. Many people are afraid to ask questions, out of fear that asking a question will make them look stupid. However, if you ask honest and reasonable questions and listen to the answers, smart people will like and respect you. In the process, you will gain knowledge and wisdom.

The hard way to avoid looking stupid in public is to get a good education. In particular, you need to develop skills in the basic disciplines of logic and rhetoric. These disciplines were highly valued in the ancient civilizations of Greece and Rome. From the Middle Ages onward, they were central to a classical education, which was an education that was based heavily on the literature of ancient Greece and Rome. The goal of a classical education was to enable a privileged young man to become a functioning member of the ruling class. The disciplines that are taught as part of a classical education are a product of civilization. People are not born with these skills, and they do not learn them through ordinary experience. Instead, these skills are a form of technology that must be taught and learned. These skills are taught and learned because they are necessary for running a civilized society.

If you had lived in the Stone Age, your social life would have involved only a small group of closely related people who had known each other from birth. Disputes within your group would have been resolved through personal negotiations, often involving force or threats of force. If you met a strange man on your territory, you would probably just kill him, if he did not kill you first. However, as societies grew in scale, they had to develop ways to resolve disputes among people who were not close relatives, and who did not necessarily know each other well. During the days of the Athenian democracy, the Athenian citizens had to work out ways for an assembly consisting of thousands of men to come to agreements about matters of public concern. As a result, Athenians worked out and wrote down some of the basic rules for figuring out what is true. The rules were called logic. The Athenians also wrote about the techniques of persuasion. The art of persuasion is called rhetoric.

Logic is the study of arguments. In logic, you take some statements of fact that you know to be true and use them to figure out what else must be true—or at least unlikely to be false. Rhetoric deals with questions that transcend ordinary logic—questions about what is good or bad and what should be done. The most important ancient texts on logic and rhetoric were compiled by the students of Aristotle, who had been the tutor to Alexander the Great. Those texts were then shared widely throughout the empire that Alexander conquered. The Romans later embraced these studies and added some important texts.

Those ancient Greek and Roman texts are still being used to teach people how to think rationally and to express themselves persuasively. In particular, some of those ancient writings found their way into an anthology titled *The Columbian Orator*. This book fell into the hands of a 12-year-old slave boy, who eventually became known as Frederick Douglass. He became an important figure in the abolition movement and in the first wave of the women's movement.

The liberal arts fell into disuse during the Dark Ages that followed the collapse of the Roman Empire. Europeans rediscovered the liberal arts during the High Middle Ages. The liberal arts then laid the intellectual groundwork for the rise of modern science and philosophy. Unfortunately, the disciplines of grammar, logic, and rhetoric have been largely suppressed in the public schools in the United States. As a result, even people who are regarded as mentally healthy are often limited in their ability to draw reasonable conclusions from evidence or to make reasonable arguments in negotiations or political discussions. As a result, many people cannot think logically or express themselves reasonably and persuasively. Thus, people who have never had any training in the liberal arts are likely to have distressing and perhaps disabling problems with thoughts and emotion. These problems would qualify as a mental disorder if they were not so commonplace.

In *Not Trivial: How Studying the Traditional Liberal Arts Can Set You*

Free, I argued that everyone should get a solid grounding in the classical liberal arts (grammar, logic, rhetoric, mathematics, geometry, music, and astronomy). I think that mental health professionals, in particular, should be well trained in grammar, logic, and rhetoric. Without a solid grasp of grammar and logic, how could they decide whether someone has a thought disorder? Without grounding in the study of rhetoric, which deals with the appropriate role of emotion in decision-making, how could they recognize whether someone has a mood disorder or a personality disorder? Mental health professionals also need some familiarity with the basic principles of philosophy, such as ontology (how to name and sort things), epistemology (the nature and limitations of knowledge), and ethics (right and wrong). Mental health professionals need to understand these subjects well enough to teach them to their patients.

To the ancient Greeks, it seemed obvious that basic training in the liberal arts and philosophy would help a man become a better person—a more reliable citizen in peace and war and a better companion. Mental health professionals have already begun incorporating some lessons on logic into some forms of psychotherapy, especially cognitive behavioral therapy for depression and dialectical behavioral therapy for people with borderline personality disorder. My modest proposal is that someone should try providing direct, formal instruction in grammar, logic, and rhetoric to all schoolchildren and to any mentally ill person who is not downright delusional. Those disciplines teach you that there are basic rules for deciding what is true and false, and what is good and bad. Intelligent, mentally healthy people often figure out a few of these rules on their own. Yet anyone would benefit from studying these rules and getting feedback on how well they know how to apply them.

Grammar is the study of how words are altered and combined to form meaningful sentences. As I explained in Chapter 10, people who have never studied grammar can have such poor reading comprehension that they can seem practically schizotypal when confronted with a complicated sentence. Instead of understanding and addressing the sentence's literal meaning, they often free-associate on the more colorful words that are in the sentence. Unfortunately, if people cannot understand and address the literal meaning of what someone else is saying or writing, no real communication can take place.

You need to master the basic principles of grammar before you can begin to study logic. Logic is the study of arguments, and arguments are made of propositions, which are sentences that consist of a subject and a predicate whose main verb is in the indicative mood. Thus, a proposition is a statement of fact, as opposed to a question or a command. Each argument consists of one or more statements that serve as premises, which means that they are reasons for accepting the truth of another statement, called the conclusion.

Classical logic deals with two basic kinds of arguments: deductive and inductive. The purpose of a deductive argument is to show that the conclusion cannot be false if the premises are true. Mathematical proofs are deductive arguments. A deductive argument whose conclusion would definitely be true if the premises are true is called valid. If the premises of a valid argument are true, then the argument is described as sound. If the argument is invalid and/or if at least one of the premises is false, then the argument is unsound.

In contrast, the purpose of an inductive argument is to show that the conclusion is unlikely to be false if the premises are true. The likelihood that the conclusion is true if the premises are true is called the inductive probability. If the inductive probability is high, the argument is described as strong. If the inductive probability is low, the argument is described as weak. If it is strong and the premises are all true, it is called cogent. In a criminal case, the prosecuting attorney generally makes an inductive argument that the defendant is guilty. To win the case, the prosecuting attorney must make a cogent argument. The defense attorney's job is to point out the weaknesses in the argument.

A basic type of deductive argument that was developed in ancient Athens is the syllogism. The syllogism deals with questions of all, some, and none. For example, here is an example of a sound argument in the form of a syllogism: "All men are mortal. Socrates is a man. Therefore, Socrates is mortal." The argument is valid, and the premises are true. As a result, the conclusion has to be true. In contrast, some syllogisms are invalid: "All Greeks are men. Some men are not philosophers.

Therefore, some Greeks are not philosophers." The first premise of that argument is false because some Greeks are women. The second statement is true, and the conclusion is true. However, the argument is invalid. It would be possible for all Greeks to be philosophers even if some men were not philosophers, because some men are not Greek. The syllogism has long been regarded as the cornerstone of the logical thinking that underpins Western science and philosophy. Syllogistic reasoning also helps people become less bigoted because it teaches them to think rationally about the concepts of all, some, and none.

One common form of inductive argument is an argument by analogy. The underlying concept is that if two things have some things in common, they may also have other things in common. For example, two chemical compounds that have a similar molecular structure might have similar chemical properties. The strength of an argument by analogy depends on the strength of the analogy (e.g., the number of important properties that the things that are being compared have in common).

Logic also deals with conditional statements, which are sentences that have an "if" clause (which describes the condition) and a "then" clause (which describes the consequence). Once you are good at analyzing if-then statements, you can begin to study causality, which means cause and effect. To understand cause and effect, you need more than logic. You need to study a branch of philosophy called metaphysics. People who have a poor grasp of cause and effect are likely to make poor choices in life.

Classical logic deals with statements of fact: statements about what is true or false. That kind of information is useful. But if you want to use it to help you make decisions, you need to apply some of the principles that are covered in the study of rhetoric. Rhetoric is the art of persuasion. Aristotle pointed out that there are three means of persuasion: logos, pathos, and ethos. Logos refers to logic and reason. Pathos refers to feelings. Ethos refers to character, such as the reputation of a speaker. We use logos to figure out what is true or false, and what the consequences of each course of action are likely to be. But to pick which course of action would best suit our needs, we need to refer to pathos (feelings) as well as logos. If we need guidance in making these choices, we may seek guidance from someone we trust. Thus, we would rely on ethos. Although rhetoric is generally conceived as the art of persuading other people, it involves the disciplines that help you make good decisions on your own.

In the *Star Wars* movies, the Jedi monks use a magical power called the Force to make suggestions that many individuals cannot resist. However, this technique, called the Jedi mind trick, works only on the weak-minded—people who are suggestible because they do not think for themselves. Through studying the classical liberal arts, you realize how easily your brain can lead you into false conclusions. As a result, you realize that your sense of conviction, your sense that you know the truth or perhaps that God is on your side, is a feeling that is created in your own brain. It is an enjoyable feeling. Some people find it addictive. Yet like other addictions, it can destroy your life.

Grammar, logic, and rhetoric were called the trivium, which literally meant three courses. The word *trivium* gave rise to our word *trivial*. Originally, the word *trivial* was used to mean that something would have been obvious to any educated person. Thus, it did not need to be explained. Today, however, the word *trivial* is used to mean that something is unimportant. Yet the classical trivium is not trivial, in the modern sense of the word *trivial*. The studies of grammar, logic, and rhetoric help us learn the basic skills for mental hygiene. They help us learn to think clearly, to use our emotions to guide decision-making, and to decide whether to trust other people.

Unfortunately, the study of the classical liberal arts would not correct an underlying biological disease of the brain. Thus, even a good classical education could not prevent someone from having delusions during a psychotic episode. However, disciplines of grammar, logic, and rhetoric may be useful as education or special education for people in the mild to moderate range of the personality disorder spectrum.

Democracy can thrive only if the education that is freely provided to everyone helps people develop good skills in reasoning. However, not everyone who has these skills is willing to use them all the time. Sometimes, people choose to think irrationally, for reasons that I explained in the discussions of personality disorders in Chapter 10. For example, people with tendencies toward Cluster A personality disorders enjoy magical thinking. As a result, they will ignore the facts that would dispel the myths they enjoy.

People with narcissistic personality disorder want to be socially dominant. As a result, narcissists have a slippery relationship with logic and reason. They will gladly use logic and reason when doing so serves their purposes of social domination. However, they can become maddeningly irrational when challenged in any way. Narcissists want to be in the one-up position. They want to be the one who knows, and the one who calls the shots. As long as you do not try to get them to change their mind about something, you will get along fine. But if you make any attempt to inform or persuade them, you will be viewed as a challenger, as a threat. This perceived threat is narcissistic injury. The narcissist may react with narcissistic rage. Narcissistic rage is a primitive emotional response. Do not expect the narcissist to think or behave rationally while in its grip. As a result, even an educated person can become shockingly anti-intellectual in this situation. The more you try to reason with them, the more threatened they feel, and the more furious they become. The situation can spiral out of control.

Dependent people also have a slippery relationship with logic. They have an emotional need to submit to a leader. When in the grip of this emotional need, many seemingly intelligent people think irrationally. For example, many deeply religious people do not mind if their religious leaders violate the rules of their religion. This tolerance of misbehavior may seem like hypocrisy, but it is really a form of co-dependency. It means that they have surrendered their moral sense to their authority figure. Thus, they cannot even conceive of the idea that their authority figure has done something wrong. The suggestion that their guru has done something immoral would make no sense to them.

In George Orwell's novel *Nineteen Eighty-Four*, one of the goals of the philosophy of Ingsoc was to train people to avoid having socially unacceptable thoughts:

> *Crimestop* means the faculty of stopping short, as though by instinct, at the threshold of any dangerous thought. It includes the power of not grasping analogies, of failing to perceive logical errors, of misunderstanding the simplest arguments if they are inimical

to Ingsoc, and of being bored or repelled by any train of thought which is capable of leading in a heretical direction. *Crimestop*, in short, means protective stupidity.

Orwell also explained that the people in his fictional Oceania deliberately practiced a kind of thinking called doublethink. Ordinary logic is based on an idea called the law of noncontradiction—i.e., that a proposition cannot be true and false at the same time. For example, a swan either is a bird or is not a bird. It cannot be a bird and not a bird at the same time. Yet in Oceania, people were supposed to cultivate a kind of thought called doublethink:

> To know and not to know, to be conscious of complete truthfulness while telling carefully constructed lies, to hold simultaneously two opinions which cancelled out, knowing them to be contradictory and believing in both of them, to use logic against logic, to repudiate morality while laying claim to it, to believe that democracy was impossible and that the Party was the guardian of democracy, to forget whatever it was necessary to forget, then to draw it back into memory again at the moment when it was needed, and then promptly to forget it again, and above all, to apply the same process to the process itself—that was the ultimate subtlety: consciously to induce unconsciousness, and then, once again, to become unconscious of the act of hypnosis you had just performed. Even to understand the word "doublethink" involved the use of doublethink.

As George Orwell warned us, we have all been trained to ignore politically inconvenient truths. It should therefore come as no surprise that the disciplines of logic and rhetoric and even basic literacy have been suppressed in our public schools. As a result, most of us will have to struggle on our own to learn how to think rationally. If you succeed, you may find that you are out of step with much of the rest of humanity. When that happens, should you fall back into line, or should you set a new rhythm for others to follow?

Chapter 15

Professional Help
and Self-Help

⁓

As I explained in Chapter 10, the American Psychiatric Association has spelled out the diagnostic criteria for a condition that they call narcissistic personality disorder. Unfortunately, psychiatrists have had poor success in treating this condition. Narcissists do not think that they are mentally ill. Also, they are likely to think that they are smarter than any psychotherapist. As a result, they are simply unreceptive to traditional psychotherapy. After all, traditional psychotherapy was developed to help patients who are likely to have low self-esteem, such as patients with major depression. If we want to help people with pathologically high self-esteem, we need to take a broader view of what psychotherapy ought to be and how it might be delivered.

In her Ann Landers advice column, Esther Pauline "Eppie" Lederer often advised people to seek professional help for their mental illnesses. By that, she meant that people should seek help from someone who has been trained and licensed to diagnose and treat mental illnesses. The kind of professional help that you should seek depends on the nature of your problem. If your mental illness is due to a somatic disease that can be treated medically, you would need help from a medical doctor. But if you are just having too many arguments with your spouse, you might seek help from a marriage counselor.

Professional help is expensive. Unfortunately, the cost might not be covered by insurance. For that reason, many people turn to other sources of help. For example, they may go to their pastor for counseling, or they may simply turn to their friends for sympathy and advice. They may also turn to self-help groups and self-help books for guidance.

Even if the cause of your problem is purely medical, the self-help groups can provide valuable information and emotional support. Self-help groups can help you find the kind of medical care that you need, including experimental treatments that have not yet been approved. Self-help groups can also help you find the kinds of social supports that you need. Self-help groups have also played an important role in promoting reforms within the psychiatric and psychology professions.

Many people turn to some sort of religious or spiritual counseling for their mental and emotional problems. Many religious traditions do include valuable practical lessons on how to be at peace with yourself and with other people. In fact, different religious traditions often come up with remarkably similar solutions to the same emotional and moral problems. For example, you can find some version of the Golden Rule (do unto others as you would have them do unto you) in all of the world's great religions. Good advice is good advice, regardless of its source or history. If you dismiss a good idea because you do not like its historical origin, you are making an error in reasoning called the genetic fallacy. On the other hand, nearly all religious institutions have some dark chapters in their history—a fact that makes me hesitate to accept all of their advice at face value.

All religious traditions have an important weakness: they have been passed down from one generation of human beings to another. In each generation, the teachings are reshaped to serve whoever is in power. As a result, wealthy people and powerful people support the theologians who preach messages that serve the wealthy and powerful. In my book *Not Trivial*, I described how Roman Catholic and Protestant theologians have served the needs of the rich and powerful. At first, I was afraid that devout Christians would be upset by what I wrote. However, all of my devout Christian friends took these passages in stride. As my friend Kevin Leland explained, "Christians don't need to be told that there are buyers and sellers in the temple. Jesus himself told us that. It's in the Bible."

In the Middle Ages, the Roman Catholic Church provided ideological support for feudalism. After the Reformation, some Protestant theologians provided ideological support for many aspects of capitalism.

In today's consumerist society, the religious institutions that are thriving are those that do the best job of marketing to consumers. Unfortunately, some preachers might be pandering to people's desire to feel good about themselves, rather than teaching the hard lessons that people need for redemption. As a result, you could end up choosing religious teachings that will make you worse, not better. That is not a new idea. The Bible itself warns people to beware of false prophets.

I become especially wary whenever anyone uses the word *spirituality*. That word has been used to mean so many different things that it ends up meaning nothing in particular. Sometimes, people use the word *spirituality* to refer to imagination or aesthetics or ethics—mental faculties and branches of philosophy that any reasonable person would think are important. However, con men and superstitious people often use the term *spirituality* as cover for promoting magical thinking, which is probably bad for your mental health. In particular, a tendency toward magical thinking can make you an easy mark for con artists who are selling goods and services of no real value.

The psychiatric and psychology professions also have dark chapters in their history. Fortunately, these professions can be reformed through political means, by putting pressure on the professional organizations and by lobbying the state governments that issue and take away licenses.

To become a psychiatrist, psychologist, advanced practice nurse, or licensed clinical social worker, you need an advanced degree from an accredited college or university. The teachers at the colleges and universities do research, which is subjected to peer review before it is published in the scientific literature. This system is designed to ensure that the ideas that are being taught at those colleges and universities are scientifically accurate.

Mental health professionals must pass their state's licensing requirements. They can lose their license if they fail their recertification examinations or fail to meet the ethical standards of their profession. In other words, the professions are regulated to protect the public. In contrast, the unlicensed practitioners and the people who write pop psychology books and provide self-empowerment programs are completely unregulated. For that reason, you should be especially skeptical of the guidance they give you. You should also be cautious about accepting religious teachings. As Plato showed us in the Euthyphro dialogue, even divine commandments can be judged on their own merits. If your holy scriptures never mentioned that it is wrong to enslave other people, they are at best incomplete.

The treatments that mental health professionals use fall into two basic categories: medication and talk therapy. Some members of the antipsychiatry movement have opposed the use of medications to manage any cases of mental illness. Yet as I explained in Chapter 8, some of that opposition was due to an ideologically motivated refusal to accept that any mental illness could be the result of an underlying medical problem. The scientific evidence has shown that some kinds of medical treatments can be helpful in managing some kinds of mental illness.

Medicine is an art that is supposed to be grounded in science. The decision of whether to use a medicine should be based partly on the results of scientific research and partly on the patient's responses, preferences, and circumstances. Yet even if someone's mental illness is clearly due to a brain problem, the person might benefit from some sort of talk therapy. You cannot expect to talk a schizophrenic patient out of having delusions. However, you need to do more than hand them a bottle of pills and turn them out onto the street. People with major mental illnesses need a lot of supportive care, including some sort of talk therapy.

As I explained in Chapter 10, some mental illnesses do result from disease of the brain. Others result from purely psychological causes. Still others result from a combination of physical and psychological causes. Talk therapy may be enough to solve a purely psychological problem. However, people whose illness involves some physical problem in the brain may also benefit from some sort of medication, even if it does nothing but relieve some symptoms. Nevertheless, even patients whose problem is clearly the result of a brain problem, such as brain damage from a stroke or from a blow to the head, may benefit from some sort of talk therapy, to help them learn how to cope with their condition. So whether a case of mental illness is physical or psychological in origin, the patient may benefit from some sort of psychotherapy.

What is the purpose of psychotherapy? To answer that question, think about the definition of the term *mental illness*. A mental illness is a problem that is in the realm of thoughts, feelings, or behavior and that leads to suffering or disability. Thus, you might expect that the goal in treating mental illness would be to relieve the suffering (for the patient and for other people in that patient's life) and to improve the patient's ability to function. To achieve those goals, the psychotherapist may have to teach the patient how to think more clearly, how to regulate his or her emotions, and how to make better decisions, especially about how to interact with other people. To achieve those same goals, the ancient Greeks developed what they called philosophy.

The word *philosophy* means love of wisdom. Philosophy deals with three main concerns: truth, conduct, and governance. The branch of philosophy called epistemology deals with the questions of what you can know, how you can know it, and how confident you can be in your knowledge. Conduct means an individual's behavior, and governance deals with how society should treat the individual. The branch of philosophy called ethics deals with the questions of right and wrong behavior. Thus, good psychotherapy could be viewed as practical lessons in philosophy.

To give their sons the basic skills they would need in the study of philosophy, the ancient Greeks developed the classical liberal arts curriculum. As I explained in Chapter 14, the purpose of the classical liberal arts curriculum was to help students learn to think rationally and to express themselves persuasively. The ancient Athenians, in particular, felt that this kind of education helped one become a better citizen—more dependable during wartime and a more pleasant companion during peacetime. Although some early Christian zealots worked to suppress the works of "pagan" philosophers, the Roman Catholic Church eventually recognized the value of the works of Aristotle. As a result, the classical liberal arts formed the basis of the curriculum of the universities that were founded in Europe during the High Middle Ages. The classical liberal arts give you the basic intellectual framework for studying other things, such as architecture, law, medicine, or theology.

The liberal arts were called the liberal arts because they were considered appropriate for freeborn men, as opposed to slaves. They have always been valued in societies with a democratic or republican political structure, and they have been suppressed in tyrannies and dictatorships. Even in a democracy, these studies tend to be reserved for the children of the privileged. In my book *Not Trivial: How Studying the Traditional Liberal Arts Can Set You Free*, I explain how the classical liberal arts were suppressed in the public schools in the United States. Because of this suppression, many people never learn the basic skills in the verbal and numerical arts. Fortunately, that problem can be solved through adult education.

As I explained in Chapter 6, the classical liberal arts are the time-tested way to help people learn to think more clearly. Thus, it should come as no surprise that some psychotherapists have taught their patients some of the lessons from the classical liberal arts. In particular, rational emotive therapy and cognitive behavior therapy teach some important grammar lessons.

Grammar is the study of how words are altered and combined to form meaningful sentences. One of the key concepts of grammar is the mood of verbs. The mood of a verb is a way of expressing how you feel about the action described in the sentence. The moods of verbs fall into two categories: realis and irrealis. Realis moods are used to express statements of fact. In English, we have only one realis mood, called the indicative. (Other languages have some additional realis moods, to express degrees of certainty.) However, we have several irrealis moods, which are used to express something that is not known to be true in reality. Examples of irrealis moods include the interrogative mood, which is used for asking questions, and the imperative mood, which is used for making commands and requests.

Grammatical modality is tricky in English because we do not clearly mark our verbs for mood. In English, we often use adverbs (such as *perhaps*) or expletive constructions (such as *it is possible that*) to express uncertainty. We often use auxiliary verbs to express the mood of another verb. For example, if I say "I go to the gym twice a week," I am making a statement of fact. On the other hand, if I say, "I *should* go to the gym twice a week," I am expressing my feelings about my going to the gym. If my physical therapist tells me, "Go to the gym twice a week," he is giving me a command. In other words, the study of grammar helps you learn to tell the difference between a fact, an opinion, a desire, and a command.

Should and *must* are such common words that people seldom give them much thought. Yet those small common words can have powerful psychological effects. Psychologist Albert Ellis, the founder of rational emotive therapy, pointed out that many people drive themselves to distraction through the careless use of the words *must* and *should*. He called this problem *muster*bation. Others have called it demand thinking. By using *must* and *should* statements carelessly, people may be making unreasonable demands of themselves, of other people, and of the universe in general. When their unreasonable demands are not met, people become frustrated, angry, and depressed. Through rational emotive therapy and cognitive behavioral therapy, patients are taught to avoid careless use of those modal auxiliary verbs. As a result, they learn to become more reasonable.

The study of logic can also have important psychotherapeutic effects. For example, the purpose of the classical syllogism was to help people grapple with the concepts of all, some, and none. For example, if you know that all men are mortal and that Socrates is a man, then you know that Socrates is mortal. But even if you knew that some Greeks are philosophers, you must not conclude that all Greeks are philosophers. In other words, bigots are people who have poor skills in syllogistic reasoning.

Logic also deals with if-then statements, which are tremendously important in science. One example is the classical *modus tollendo tollens* argument (the way that denies by denying). If you know that if P then Q is true but that Q is false, you know that P is also false. So if you want to know whether P is true, find something that would have to be true if P were true. Then, look to see if that thing is false. For example, many people believe that high-carbohydrate diets cause diabetes. If that were true, then diabetes would be common in populations that eat a high-carbohydrate diet. However, we know that diabetes is rare in populations that eat high-carbohydrate diets. Thus, we know that high-carbohydrate diets *do not* cause diabetes. (If that information comes as a surprise to you, read my book *Thin Diabetes, Fat Diabetes: Prevent Type 1, Cure Type 2*.) It may seem "illogical" to think that eating more carbohydrate would lower your blood sugar. Nevertheless, the more carbohydrate you eat, the more sensitive you become to insulin and the more efficient your body becomes at managing blood sugar.

Aristotelian logic dealt only with statements of fact, which are sentences in which the main verb in the predicate is in the indicative mood. In the 1960s, logicians started to work out the rules of modal logic, which deals with questions such as what *can be true* (but might not be true) and what *cannot be false* (i.e., is necessarily true). However, to deal with questions of what *should* be, you need more than logic. You need to study rhetoric. (Aristotle's students compiled a classic textbook on rhetoric.) Traditionally, rhetoric has been described as the art of persuasion. But through the study of rhetoric, you learn how to use facts as well as feelings for making decisions. You also learn how and when to rely on other people's advice and opinions. These are basic skills that a mentally healthy person is expected to have.

I have just described what the goals of psychotherapy could or should be (irrealis mood), regardless of what those goals are or have been (indicative mood). Unfortunately, psychotherapists are mere mortals, and they can sometimes do more harm than good. There are some dark chapters in the history of psychiatry. In the mid 20th century, tens of thousands of lobotomy procedures were performed in the United States. No one knows how many gay and transgender men and women were given what amounts to physical and psychological torture, in a pointless attempt to "correct" their sexual orientation and gender identity. Not only did these treatments fail to alter the person's sexual orientation, they increased the likelihood that the patient would go on to attempt suicide. The Gay Rights Movement played a crucial role in reforming how psychiatrists regard gay people.

Psychotherapy has the potential to do good as well as the potential to do harm. Likewise, when you study pharmacology, you learn that any substance that is powerful enough to have some effect on the body is likely to produce a mixture of wanted and unwanted effects. Since psychotherapy can have good or bad effects, state governments regulate the practice of psychotherapy, just as they regulate the power to prescribe powerful drugs. Theoretically, a trained mental health professional should be able to figure out what kind of therapy would be good for a particular patient. Unfortunately, people with personality disorders tend to prefer the kinds of therapy that make them worse, not better. This unhealthy attraction to unwholesome influences is one of the reasons why personality disorders tend to persist. A person who is willing to embrace the kinds of lessons that promote their mental and moral development would probably outgrow a personality disorder. A case of arrested development suggests that the person is a bit like Peter Pan, who did not want to grow up.

As I explained in Chapter 10, the American Psychiatric Association groups the personality disorders into three clusters: A, B, and C. People with the Cluster A personality disorders primarily have a problem with developing an accurate understanding of the world and people around them. Their main problem is in their relationship with reality. They are prone to superstition, which means false beliefs about cause and effect. Thus, you can expect that people with a tendency toward a Cluster A personality disorder will seek out the kinds of mystical mumbo-jumbo that would make them even more superstitious than they were before. As a result, they are likely to seek out fortune telling, trance channeling, past life regression, and magical crystals. There is no shortage of alternative providers who are willing to provide these services, typically for a fee. But what people with a tendency toward the Cluster A personality disorders really need is better skill in reality testing.

People with tendencies toward a Cluster A personality disorder are likely to be attracted to pop psychology and New Age therapies that seem more like magic than science. Magic is the use of rituals, symbols, actions, gestures, and language for the purpose of exploiting supernatural forces. However, supernatural forces are the forces that, by definition, are outside of the laws of nature. In other words, they supposedly do not follow the rules that describe how the universe actually works. Magic does not work. If it did, magic would be taught at trade schools and polytechnic universities, such as the Massachusetts Institute of Technology. To believe in magic, you have to turn your back on science.

One ever-popular form of magic is the incantation. An incantation is a spell that is cast by using words. However, the proponents of New Age pop psychology have a new name for this age-old practice: affirmation. Comedian Al Franken (who later became a U.S. Senator) poked good-natured fun at affirmations through his *Saturday Night Live* character Stuart Smalley. Smalley hosted a fictional television program called *Daily Affirmation, with Stuart Smalley*. In every episode, the viewers are informed that Smalley is not a licensed professional but has taken part in several 12-step programs. At the end of each episode, Smalley would affirm, "I'm good enough, I'm smart enough, and doggone it, people like me!"

To affirm something is to say that it is true. However, *saying* that something is true almost never *makes* it true. One exception would be if you are officiating at a wedding and declare the couple to be married. When the officiant pronounces that the couple is married, they are. Another would be if you are the King or Queen and knight someone. In other words, some kinds of official pronouncements can change someone's legal status. But mere words cannot change someone's physical or biological properties. Nevertheless, many people feel that if you wish hard enough, your wishes will magically come true. In other words, some people believe that if you keep telling yourself, "I am strong," you will become strong. According to New Age thinking, when you make affirmations, you generate vibrations that then go out to affect the universe. That is a half-truth. Yes, when I speak, my vocal cords vibrate, which causes sound waves to propagate through the air. Unfortunately, the vibrations that I make when I speak can have surprisingly little practical effect. The sound waves that I generate when I try to reason with certain people seem to have no useful effect at all.

To believe that affirmations would have a magical effect on the universe, you would have to have a severely distorted view of how the universe actually works. It would be silly to imagine that you could become smart simply by chanting, "I am smart." Nevertheless, some kinds of affirmations might actually be useful because they represent a form of self-talk—an attempt to influence the virtual audience in your own imagination. This kind of self-talk could affect your emotions and thus help to support the right kind of behavior.

Affirmations can even be a useful part of a meditative practice. Meditation is a general term for practices that help you develop awareness of your own thoughts and emotions. The word *meditation* came from a Latin word meaning to think, contemplate, devise, or ponder. Thus, it is perfectly reasonable to imagine that some kinds of meditative practice can help you become more thoughtful and insightful and more aware of how your own thoughts and emotions may be hampering you. In theory, affirmations could be a way of correcting bad thought patterns. By affirming things that are actually true, you practice thinking correct thoughts.

If you are going to practice affirmations, you should probably try to limit your affirmations to statements that are actually true. A lie is still a lie, no matter how many times you repeat it. You may wish to utter statements about what you want to be true. However, such statements are not affirmations. They are wishes. So one important goal of psychotherapy and meditative practice would be to improve your skill at figuring out the difference between what is true and what you want.

People with Cluster B disorders are dramatic and erratic. Their most obvious problems are in their relationships with other people. When they do seek out therapy, they often do so for the wrong reasons. For example, histrionic people love attention, so they would enjoy anything that would make them the focus of attention. Since the psychotherapist is an audience, histrionic people are likely to remain in therapy for years. This explains why so many show business people remain in therapy for so many years without making any noticeable progress. The therapy is an end in itself, rather than an attempt to learn how to complete their coming-of-age story arc.

Narcissists are far less likely than histrionic people to seek out psychotherapy. To engage in psychotherapy, the narcissist would have to subordinate himself or herself to the therapist. By definition, narcissists are socially ambitious people who love to feel superior to others. Thus, they are likely to be attracted to the kind of program that boosts their ego and offers them an easy (but potentially expensive) way to get power and prestige. They love programs that teach them an impressive new vocabulary that makes them feel smarter than the people around them. Of course, if the program offers something of real value, the individual may learn something of value—something that would convey power and prestige and thus legitimately boost the person's social standing. As a result, the gap between their inflated self-regard and their actual social standing might get narrower. Unfortunately, people who are intellectually lazy would be attracted to programs that provide lots of show but no substance. As they progress through the levels of such a program, their self-esteem may rise still more. Meanwhile, the gulf between their self-concept and their actual level of achievement widens. As a result, they become even more narcissistic than they were to begin with.

To someone with Cluster A tendencies, an affirmation may be a form of magic. But to a narcissist, affirmations are the psalms that they sing in self-worship. Since narcissists already have an unrealistically high opinion of themselves, they should not be encouraged to affirm how marvelous they are. Affirmations are like crack for a narcissist. Since narcissists lack the ability to judge themselves accurately, they are not in a good position to evaluate whether the statements that they are affirming are actually true. Nor can they rely on the people around them to make those judgments, because narcissists tend to surround themselves with sycophants. Narcissists generally do not want what they desperately need: an accurate view of themselves.

Narcissism is clearly a public health problem. We may even be in the midst of an epidemic of it. Unfortunately, the traditional approaches to psychotherapy are unlikely to be useful against narcissism. Narcissus is unlikely to realize that he is to blame for the problems in his life (assuming that he even realizes that there are problems in his life!), and he is unlikely to seek out therapy for a character flaw that he does not realize that he has. By seeking therapy, he would be putting himself in a one-down position relative to the therapist. Narcissists are horrified by the very idea. In contrast, Echo is likely to seek therapy, and it might do her a world of good—unless she seeks out the kind of therapy that would reinforce her emotional dependency. Psychotherapy was designed for people like Echo. So was Al-Anon. Alcoholics might go to Alcoholics Anonymous, but usually only after they have made such a mess of their lives that even they can no longer deny that they have a problem.

Narcissists clearly need some sort of help. The challenge is to figure out how to offer help in a form that they find appealing. One way is to frame the help as a way to achieve something positive, as opposed to correcting something that is negative. When I worked at an advertising agency, I was taught that Baby Boomers do not like to be reminded that they are aging. If you want to sell a product to treat an age-related disease, you have to describe the product as a means of health promotion, rather than treatment of disease. For example, you would not talk about arthritis, you would talk about joint health. Narcissists want to feel superior to other people. Thus, they might be attracted to a program that is billed as a way to maximize human potential, rather than a program that offers to repair their defective personality. For that reason, you might succeed in persuading them to try some sort of training program that would enable them to outshine other people. Then, you give them the lessons that they would need in order to achieve magnanimity, or greatness of soul. There would be no shame in signing up for a program like that. In fact, this sort of program would be good for anyone, even someone who is mentally healthy to start with.

Since narcissists do not want to subordinate themselves to a teacher, and they do not want to take corrections from any other human being, you need to computerize the lessons and the scoring as much as possible. The computer can point out their mistakes. It can then tell them how they rank, in relation to the general population. Since this potentially unwelcome information would come from a machine and in private, it would be much easier for the narcissist to tolerate. Eventually, the narcissists may take pleasure in seeing their scores improve, along with their standing relative to other people. Yet as their training starts to enable them to spot their own mistakes, their bloated self-esteem might deflate.

After the student learns some basic skills in reasoning, the training could go on to teach some basic skills in how to recognize other people's emotional reactions. One of the reasons why fools tend to remain foolish is that educated people are often too polite to correct them. People who are not only foolish but arrogant can become aggressive when challenged in even the mildest possible way. As a result, wise people rarely try to engage with them. But once individuals start to become aware of their intellectual limitations, they may benefit from some training in how to read other people. If an educated person cringed when you said something, you probably said something stupid or horrible.

Schooling is based on a model in which the student is subordinate to the teacher because the teacher knows things that the student needs to learn. During the 20th century, members of the so-called Progressive Movement in education rebelled against this model. The members of the Progressive Movement wanted the teachers to be "facilitators" and "co-learners" who did as little real teaching as possible. Meanwhile, children were expected to figure things out for themselves while following their own interests. This approach was called constructivism. Unfortunately, this approach does a terrible job at teaching children what they need to know in order to become civilized adults. I am afraid that this passive approach to education might be increasing the prevalence of personality disorders because it is failing to teach young people the lessons that could help them accomplish their coming-of-age and redemptive story arcs.

Training in the classical liberal arts and philosophy and the humanities could help a narcissist become less obnoxious. That kind of training may help people improve their reasoning skills and interpersonal skills. Yet as they develop these skills, they learn how to spot their own mistakes. As a result, their self-esteem might decline. Yet since inflated self-esteem is the core problem in narcissism, this decline in self-esteem can be a good thing.

There is a particular kind of affirmation that could serve as a remedy to narcissism. That is to have the person fill in the blanks in this sentence:

I am glad that _____ knows more than I do about _____ because _____.

For example, you may say, "I am glad that Hans knows more than I do about social media because I could certainly use his advice on how to boost traffic at my Web site." Of course, people with narcissistic tendencies will have trouble filling in those blanks. They resent taking a back seat to anyone. The beauty of this exercise is that it forces them to think about how they can benefit personally from someone else's superior knowledge and skills.

A similar technique could help you get over envy and jealousy. Envy is when you want something that someone else has, and jealousy is when you hate them for having it. Narcissists have an extraordinary sense of entitlement. They want to be regarded as the smartest, the most beautiful, the wealthiest, and so on. Thus, they can easily become jealous of anyone who could outshine them in any way. As a result, they cannot enjoy other people's good qualities or feel happy about other people's good fortune.

The traditional way to cure envy and jealousy is to pray for nice things to happen to other people. Then, when one of those nice things happens, you feel that your wish was fulfilled. Even atheists could include a similar technique in their meditative practice. Just picture making something nice happen to other people. The goal is not to make nice things happen by magic. Rather, the goal would be to make yourself happier by helping you develop compassion.

I think that narcissistic people are narcissistic because they have poor reasoning skills and poor interpersonal skills. I expect that the narcissist and everyone around the narcissist would benefit if the narcissist's skills in these domains improved. However, it might be dangerous to give that kind of training to a sociopath. Sociopaths love to manipulate people. As a result, they will enjoy the kinds of therapy that would enable them to manipulate other people even better. In particular, they may enjoy therapy that teaches them how to read other people's emotions better. However, such training could make them more dangerous to other people. Sociopaths in prison may also enjoy manipulating the prison psychologists. For example, they may tell heart-breaking tales of about their horrible childhoods. Some of these tales may actually be true, but the sociopath's goal in telling these stories is not to heal psychologically. The goal is to tug at someone else's heartstrings. People who pity the sociopath are easy for the sociopath to manipulate.

Sociopaths do not need you to throw them a pity party. They have no pity for others. Because of their low emotional arousal, they probably do not even feel much pity for themselves. What they really need is to be held accountable for their behavior. That is why 12-step programs put such an emphasis on accountability. Unfortunately, people with sociopathic tendencies (including many alcoholics and addicts) are not interested in accountability because they do not care about their responsibilities to other people. That is probably the main reason why so many alcoholics refuse to engage with Alcoholics Anonymous until even they realize that they have made a complete mess of their lives. After they have hit bottom several dozen times, they may start to look around for some new strategy.

People with borderline personality disorder may seem to enjoy therapy, at least at first. Initially, they may have an almost worshipful attitude toward the therapist. Then, suddenly, that attitude can turn 180 degrees, at which point they decide that the therapist is a horrible person. People with borderline personality disorder want to have close relationships with other people. They fear abandonment, yet their dramatic and often obnoxious behavior tends to drive people away. People with borderline personality disorder are likely to follow exactly the same pattern in their relationship with their therapist. For that reason, the traditional approach to psychotherapy does not work well with these patients. As I explained in Chapter 10, dialectical behavioral therapy is an effective form of therapy for borderline personality disorder. DBT involves group training that takes place in a classroom setting, along with individual therapy to teach the client how to apply the lessons learned in class.

People with Cluster C disorders have problems related to fear and anxiety. To manage these problems, they try to avoid or control aspects of their environment, including other people. People with avoidant personality disorder withdraw from the things they fear. As a result, they never learn to get over their fears. For the therapist, the main challenge in these cases is gaining the patient's trust. In some ways, avoidant personality disorder is the opposite of narcissistic personality disorder. Narcissists rush in where people with avoidant personality disorder fear to tread. Narcissists overestimate themselves, and people with avoidant personality disorder tend to underestimate themselves. Perhaps it would be good for an avoidant person to repeat some encouraging affirmations—as long as the statements that they are affirming are true.

If Narcissus had narcissistic personality disorder, Echo probably had dependent personality disorder. People with this problem are likely to become clingy and dependent on the therapist. An incompetent or unethical therapist could end up fostering their dependence rather than teaching them self-reliance. Perhaps the key to managing these cases is to provide approval only if the patient does things by and for him- or herself.

People with obsessive-compulsive personality disorder love to follow and enforce rules. By following these rules, they gain a sense of control and security. They are terrified by uncertainty and unpredictability. Thus, they would be attracted to inflexible, rule-based systems, especially if those systems would enable them to feel superior to others. People with obsessive-compulsive personality disorder can become dangerous if they acquire too much political power. They view themselves as the righteous guardians of decency, and they do not hesitate to punish the unworthy. Their saving grace is that they would cheerfully study grammar and learn the rules of logic. So they might willingly participate in the same kind of computerized training in the liberal arts that would be good for narcissists. At first, this kind of training might make the persnickety person more persnickety about other people's grammar. But as they learn how to apply the rules of logic and the principles of rhetoric, they are likely to become more flexible in their thinking.

People with obsessive-compulsive personality disorder like to follow rules. Unfortunately, they tend to follow a small set of simple rules, even when those rules are inappropriate. They may even feel that they are entitled to enforce the rules, sometimes by violence. For this reason, people with a severe case of obsessive-compulsive personality disorder can be dangerous.

People with obsessive-compulsive personality disorder need to learn how and when to bend or break the usual rules. Like narcissists, people with obsessive-compulsive personality disorder need clear feedback about whether their answers are right or wrong, and computerized training is probably the best way to provide a lot of this feedback.

This concept of feedback is key. Psychotherapy is simply a formalized way for an educated person to provide feedback about matters of philosophy and interpersonal relationships to someone who needs it. For someone whose brain is reasonably healthy, psychotherapy should be like schooling. It can teach them the lessons that would enable them to achieve greatness. Psychotherapy may also help someone learn to compensate for the distortions of perception and thought that occur even in a healthy person. Either way, psychotherapy could help people learn the lessons they need in order to complete their coming-of-age and redemption story arcs. To achieve those goals, psychotherapy should promote the development of consciousness and conscience—to develop and fine-tune the virtual audience that presumably exists in the individual's imagination.

Psychotherapy should give you feedback, but it should also teach you how to recognize and handle feedback. Some people are not good at noticing feedback. Sometimes, they are unaware of nonverbal messages. For example, many autistic people have to be taught the meaning of different facial expressions. I became aware of this problem because of a conflict at work. I once had to report to my boss about a dispute that was aired at a meeting. I explained that one of the executives was furious with one of our vendors. My boss asked, "What did he say?" I answered, "He didn't say anything." My boss then gave me a puzzled expression and said, "But then how do you know that he was angry?" I said, "I was sitting right across the table from him." From the baffled expression on my boss's face, I realized that my boss had no idea that human faces express anger. Eventually, I realized that my boss also could not perceive sarcasm, either. If you said, "Oh gee, that's really great," meaning that something was terrible, my boss would think that you meant that it really was great. From that point on, I made a point of saying exactly what I meant, and documenting everything in writing, so that there would be no miscommunication.

People with personality disorders tend to be bad at judging feedback. Either they miss messages that were being sent, or they imagine messages that were never intended. For example, paranoid people are likely to imagine nonexistent insults and threats. Likewise, narcissistic people are also quick to take offense over imaginary slights. Since narcissists are trying to defend an unrealistically high social rank, they can become offended at anyone who seems (to the narcissist at any rate) to pose a challenge to their dominance. You can offend a narcissist just by being pretty, thin, smart, capable, or popular in their presence. The narcissist wants to be the best in many or all of those domains. If the narcissist cannot bully you into submission, the narcissist may try to drive you out of the group. If the narcissist is your boss or even a co-worker, your job may be in jeopardy. In other words, you can get into trouble at work just for doing exactly what you were hired to do, or even just for being good looking.

Psychotherapy should also help you learn to judge the feedback that you get. To evaluate feedback, you need to understand that each human being has a scope of expertise. That scope of expertise can involve facts and feelings (opinions are feelings tied to matters of fact). You can err in either direction when deciding whether something is within somebody's scope of expertise. Lately, many people have been turning their backs on the world's foremost authorities on infectious disease. Instead, they prefer to take medical advice from uneducated celebrities. In other words, they think that the real experts' scope of expertise is narrow or nonexistent, while granting a broad scope of expertise to people with no scientific credentials.

Of course, even a completely uneducated person is an expert on one important subject: how he or she is feeling. A newborn baby does not know any facts, but it is an expert on how it is feeling. When newborn babies are hungry or uncomfortable or lonely, they cry. When people are angry with you, their anger is real, even if you think that they should not be angry. In other words, other people really do feel what they feel, even if you think that they should not feel that way.

There are moral and practical reasons for recognizing and respecting other people's feelings. The moral reasons spring from the Golden

Rule, which holds that you should treat others the way you would want to be treated. The practical reasons spring from the fact that people who have been wronged sometimes fight back. Sometimes, they nurse grudges for years before they get an opportunity to take revenge.

Hens think only of their immediate needs in the present. A hen does not worry about the feelings of the hens beneath her in the pecking order. Likewise, many people seem to be blind to the feelings of the people beneath them in the social pecking order. Since a powerless person's anger does not matter, at least in the short run, that anger might as well not exist. Of course, human beings are not chickens, and the tiny victory you win today could be your undoing in the end. If you ignore other people's anger, they are likely to feel resentment. Eventually, some of them may seek revenge. During the days of slavery, slave owners treated their slaves with appalling cruelty. As a result, the slave owners also lived with the constant fear that their household servants would someday poison their food or murder them in their beds. Yet after emancipation, few former slaves sought vengeance. The vast majority simply wanted to get on with their lives.

Slavery has been around since prehistoric times. Yet today, slavery is illegal everywhere. It persists only in areas where crime and political corruption allow it to continue. This change in attitude about the most basic of human rights was the result of an intellectual movement that resulted from the invention of the printing press. Advances in science, along with widespread literacy, undermined the power of the monarchies and the Church. Meanwhile, French Jesuit priests were bringing back stories about the Iroquois in North America, who had no kings and no prisons. Instead, the Iroquois had a constitutional government and a political philosophy based on liberty, equality, and brotherhood. These developments led to a philosophical movement called the Enlightenment, which advocated democracy, individual liberty, freedom of expression, and eradication of religious authority.

Philosophers of the Enlightenment understood that in order to be a good person, you must have good skills in figuring out the truth and you must have compassion for other human beings. As the French philosopher Voltaire put it, "Those who can make you believe absurdities can make you commit atrocities." Thus, the goals of good psychotherapy would be similar to the goals of the Enlightenment: to enable people to figure out the truth for themselves, and to teach them how to be responsible members of a peaceful and prosperous democratic society.

Ideally, human relationships would be based on reciprocity, which means give and take. Reciprocal social relations are based on a sense of fairness. Sociopaths have no sense of fairness. You give, and they take. Narcissists also have problems with the concept of fairness. Because of their sense of entitlement, they think that their "fair" share should be huge. In contrast, some people with dependent personality disorder are willing to give, but they often give to people who have no interest in giving back.

Dog trainer Cesar Millan emphasizes the importance of establishing rules, boundaries, and limitations in your relationship with a dog. You should also be able to establish and enforce reasonable rules, boundaries, and limitations in your relationships with other human beings. Unfortunately, people with tendencies toward dependent personality disorder have poor skills at establishing and enforcing rules, boundaries, and limitations. In contrast, people with tendencies toward the Cluster B personality disorders have little interest in or even awareness of the rules, boundaries, and limitations that a reasonable person would set. That is why co-dependent relationships are bad for both parties.

Besides teaching you how to recognize and understand other people's emotions, psychotherapy may teach you the right way to respond to other people's feelings. The branch of philosophy that deals with right and wrong—and good and bad behavior—is called ethics. Alcoholics Anonymous and other 12-step programs place a strong emphasis on ethics. These programs encourage people to make an inventory of how they have harmed other people, and to make direct amends to those people, unless doing so would harm someone. This training in ethics may be necessary to reduce the suffering that mentally ill people experience or cause.

Good psychotherapy would help you improve your ability to judge feedback. Bad psychotherapy, like bad religious training, would undermine your ability to judge feedback. The usual goal of such bad psychotherapy is to enslave you mentally. It is bad enough when people try to make you too frightened to stand up for yourself. What is worse is when they make it impossible for you to think for yourself. Yet that was the stated goal of the educational reforms that took place in Prussia after its humiliating defeat by Napoleon. As Johann Gottlieb Fichte explained, "If you want to influence him at all, you must do more than merely talk to him; you must fashion him, and fashion him in such a way that he simply cannot will otherwise than you wish him to will." In other words, Fichte was aiming at mind control, not persuasion.

Psychotherapy poses the same kinds of risks that are inherent in any type of schooling: the risk that you will be indoctrinated instead of educated. George Orwell provided a chilling depiction of mind control in his novel *Nineteen Eighty-Four*. Early in the story, the protagonist Winston Smith writes in his diary, "Freedom is the freedom to say two plus two equals four. If that is granted all else will follow." Yet in Orwell's dystopian view of the future, that freedom was not granted. After Smith is arrested for thoughtcrime, he is taken to the Ministry of Love, where he is tortured by O'Brien, who is a member of the Inner Party. O'Brien explains that Smith is insane, and that to become sane, Smith must believe—not just say but really believe—that two plus two equals three, or five, or any other number that the Party chooses. O'Brien explains that the Party's goal is power, and that "power is tearing human minds apart and putting them back together in new shapes of your own choosing."

Whenever you educate people, you bring about some reshaping of their mind. So what is the difference between education and mind control? Education empowers, whereas mind control disempowers. Many "progressive" educators, such as John Dewey, were uncomfortable with the idea of teaching people some unquestionable facts and truths. In contrast, the ancient Greeks understood that you must learn some basic academic skills in order to develop independence of mind. You develop many of these skills through academic exercises that have clear right and wrong answers. For example, two plus two always make four—never five or three.

These basic academic skills are like the basic skills that musicians learn. Progressive educators may take a dim view of "drills in skills," which they view as mind-numbing. Yet musicians must practice their scales and etudes if they want to master their instrument. The great jazz clarinetist Benny Goodman practiced his scales every day, to the end of his life. Jazz musicians need to learn theory and technique and then practice scales and riffs until they become second nature. Once musicians master those basic skills, they can then play anything that they can imagine. Likewise, education should give people the basic understanding of how the mind and society work, so that individuals will have a reasonable chance of achieving their dreams and will be able to fulfill their responsibilities to their family and their community. Psychotherapy could serve as remedial education for people who did not learn those lessons through their formal education.

To get along with other people, you do need to pay attention to what they think and how they feel. You do want to be kind and considerate, and to avoid hurting people's feelings needlessly. However, that does not mean that you should ignore your own feelings and judgments. Some advice and some opinions are best ignored. Throughout history, the people whom we regard today as heroes stood up for what they thought was right, even when many other people thought they were wrong. To be a hero, you must have the wisdom to figure out the right thing to do and the courage to do it despite fierce opposition. You do need to have the courage of your own convictions. But if you ignore feedback from wise people, you could end up as a tragic figure or perhaps a clown.

Chapter 16

Leaders, Followers, and Team Players

Some people have a natural desire to lead. They want to be large and in charge. They want other people to look up to them and follow their advice. In contrast, many other people have a natural desire to follow. They want some large and in-charge person to tell them what to do. This leader-follower relationship can end well or badly. When a magnanimous person inspires other people to do the right thing, good things happen. When a narcissistic or sociopathic person hoodwinks dependent people into doing bad things, or even into doing good things for the wrong reasons, bad things happen. To avoid becoming tangled up in bad things, you must think carefully about whom you follow and what orders you will obey. You must work to put good people in positions of power, and then you must put limits on their power. You must hold them accountable for their actions. Of course, once you start engaging in this kind of give and take, you are no longer a mere follower. You have become a team player.

Leader-follower dynamics can occur on a small scale, even between just two persons. The parent-child relationship has to be a leader-follower relationship, at least when the child is young. Those roles may be reversed as the parents enter their "second childhood." In contrast, a co-dependency is a leader-follower relationship that is occurring between two people who should be treating each other as equals.

Leader-follower relationships can also occur within a larger group, such as within a church. They can also occur on a national scale. For example, Mohandas K. Gandhi led the nonviolent movement that persuaded the British Empire to "quit India"—to grant independence to

India. For that reason, Gandhi was called Mahatma, which means great soul. In contrast, Josef Stalin used a reign of terror to maintain his rule over the Soviet Union. Stalin's apologists claimed that Stalin's ends justified his brutal means. In contrast, Gandhi argued that evil means never lead to good ends. He argued that a country could gain its independence through violence or nonviolence. However, a country created through violence would be far different from a country created through nonviolence.

Of course, Buddhist philosophy teaches us that a good thing can emerge from a bad thing, just as a lotus blossom emerges from the mud. Nevertheless, I think that Gandhi's advice to shun violence is sound, especially for anyone who needs to enlist the support of volunteers. Gandhi wanted the Indian people to stand up for justice. His campaign for Indian independence succeeded because millions of Indians did what he asked them to do. Millions followed him because they respected his moral authority. If Gandhi had urged people to do bad things, he would not have commanded such respect and would not have inspired such cooperation.

In any group activity, you will end up playing one of three roles: leader, follower, or team player. In early childhood, we are all trained to be followers. As you grow up, you are expected to learn how to play on a team. As a member of a team, you do not just play follow the leader. Instead, the members of the team must cooperate with each other. You might even get to have some say in what the team does, or how it does it. Thus, as a member of a team, you may get to exercise a little bit of leadership. As you mature, you may get opportunities to exercise more leadership. As a leader, you have to give directions to other people. But to be a good leader, you have to do some following. You need to get feedback from your followers, and you need to respond appropriately to that feedback. Thus, a good leader is not just a leader but a team player.

Even in the follower role, you have responsibilities that go beyond simple obedience. You must choose your leaders wisely. You must think carefully about whether to do what they say. You must set limits on their power. You must also hold them accountable for their behavior.

In other words, you must lead from below. That is the theory behind representative democracy. In a representative democracy, the political "leaders" are actually supposed to be the servants of the populace. The populace is supposed to be the leader. Of course, the populace cannot rule directly. Instead, the populace must choose a few individuals to act on their behalf. In other words, the populace must choose champions. Their champions will then do the work of governing.

In a democracy, the decisions are made through a process of public conversations. As I mentioned in Chapter 5 and explained at length in *Not Trivial*, there are two main types of important conversations: dialectic and negotiation. Scientific discussions are dialectical. In dialectic, people pool their knowledge and correct each other's errors in reasoning, in order to search for truth. The purpose of dialectic may be to figure out what possible courses of action are available, and what the likely outcomes of each one might be. In contrast, a negotiation is an attempt to find a solution to a conflict. Ideally, people would first engage in dialectic, to figure out what their options are. Then, they would engage in negotiations, to find the best option that is acceptable to everyone. For these conversations to be productive, the participants must have the skills in logic and rhetoric that I described in Chapter 14. They must also know the relevant facts. Note that Aristotle's students compiled writings on logic and rhetoric that have remained influential to the present day.

People who never got a classical education are poorly equipped for dialectic or even for negotiation. Yet even if you have had a classical education, you may be unwilling to use that knowledge appropriately in dialectic or negotiation. As I explained in Chapter 10, people who have tendencies toward the Cluster A personality disorders enjoy magical thinking. They want to embrace mystical ideas, even if those ideas are clearly untrue. Likewise, people with tendencies toward dependent personality disorder may be more concerned about what is politically correct than what is really correct. Narcissists embrace nonsensical ideas that enhance their feelings of entitlement, which is why they are often racist. Narcissists also tend to reject obvious truths that come from a lower-ranking person. That is why narcissists often seem to be shallow or anti-intellectual. They simply refuse to engage appropriately in intellectual battles that they might lose. In contrast, dependent people will reject obvious truths that make their chosen leader look bad. I will explain this problem more in Chapter 17.

Education and knowledge have always been viewed as the property of the upper classes, who have traditionally been viewed as natural leaders within society. As I explained in Chapter 3, members of the Brahmin varna in India served as priests, teachers, and protectors of learning. Eventually, this varna became formalized as a set of hereditary jatis or castes, into which a person had to be born. However, the printing press, free public education, and now the Internet have made it increasingly easy for people of any social background to gain knowledge. Also, the ruling and military elite are no longer selected from the members of the titled aristocracy (similar to the Kshatriya varna). Instead, the rise of democracy means that the people become the ruler, while the elected officials are supposedly public servants, rather than rulers. Social reformers have even found ways for ordinary working people to use economic power effectively. Thus, economic power is no longer held only by the rich (the Vaishya varna). Thus, the working class (the equivalent of the Shudra varna together with the outcastes) can exercise its traditional power in numbers. Working people can exert power through organizations, such as labor unions, and through broad-based political movements.

Are you a leader, a follower, or a team player? The answer to that question may vary from one situation to the next. For example, Rosa Parks worked as a seamstress in a department store, which is a follower position. Yet she became a leader in the Montgomery Bus Boycott. The boycott ultimately succeeded in getting the city to desegregate the buses because the boycott organizers persuaded a huge proportion of the black population of Montgomery to work as a team. The boycotters refused to ride the buses until the buses were desegregated. Meanwhile, the boycott organizers persuaded the owners of private cars to set up an alternative transportation system. Even so, many boycotters ended up walking long distances. The boycott lasted 381 days. The boycott did not bring about the immediate end to segregation on the buses.

However, it conveyed a powerful message to the American people. It kept the issue alive while lawsuits were working their way through the court system. More importantly, it helped to persuade many people all over the country that racial segregation should have no place in a society based on equality.

The Montgomery Bus Boycott shows how a nonviolent political campaign can succeed if it harnesses the power of numbers. The secret to harnessing the power of numbers is coordination. If only a single person refused to ride the bus, nothing would have happened. But once a large number of people started refusing to ride the buses, the bus company started to feel the sting. During the boycott, the decision of whether one should ride the bus took on a moral and political dimension. After the boycott was over, it was okay for everyone to resume riding the bus.

The Montgomery Bus Boycott was organized by a group called the Montgomery Improvement Association, whose leaders included Ralph Abernathy, E. D. Nixon, and Martin Luther King, Jr. These leaders of the local civil rights movement had been waiting for the right person to be arrested for violating the segregation rules on the buses. In other words, they needed a hero or heroine with whom the audience would sympathize. Thus, the right actor had to be cast in that role. Parks was a good candidate because she was employed and married and thus "above reproach." The leaders of the boycott could not force their followers to do anything. Instead, they used persuasion and inspiration. As a result, a huge number of people chose to take part. Many of the leaders of the Montgomery Bus Boycott became famous. In particular, we now celebrate Martin Luther King Jr's birthday as a national holiday. However, the success of the boycott was due not just to their leadership but to the teamwork of the movement as a whole.

Musicians understand the concept that an individual may play different roles in different situations. Sometimes, they are soloists, sometimes they are members of an ensemble, and sometimes they get to conduct. Many of the things that musicians do are solitary, which means that you do them by yourself. To be a good musician, you have to spend a lot of time practicing by yourself. Composers also usually work in solitude. Yet those solitary activities are generally a way to prepare for a social activity—performing for an audience. Practicing by yourself may be a solitary activity; but performing, even if you are alone on the stage with your instrument (or your voice), is a social activity.

If you are playing entirely by yourself, you have complete freedom of expression—except that you cannot harmonize. For that, you need to play with other musicians. As soon as you start playing with other musicians, you need to coordinate your activities with theirs, which limits your freedom. You need to keep in time and in tune with the rest of the ensemble. (*Ensemble* comes from the French word meaning together.) The smallest ensemble is a duet, which means two musicians. One special kind of duet involves a soloist (typically a singer) and an accompanist. The singer is the leader, and the accompanist follows. For example, if the singer goes off-key, a great accompanist will transpose on the spot to stay in tune. (I have actually heard a professional piano player do that.) However, some other kinds of duets and small ensembles have no official leader. But the larger the group, the harder it is to keep everyone together. Thus, the larger the ensemble, the more need there is for formal leadership.

To make a positive contribution to a group effort, you need to understand what your role is and how you can play it effectively. From childhood, most of us have been trained to be followers. In school, students are mainly followers. To learn the material that they are expected to learn, students must do what the teacher tells them to do. They must listen to the lectures and do the assigned readings and other homework. If you resist doing those things, you cheat yourself out of an education. Some progressive educators try to downplay the teacher's leadership role by depicting teachers as "facilitators" or "co-learners." Yet the classroom cannot function unless the teacher exercises good leadership.

Leaders can be judged in several domains. One is their ability to get people to follow orders. Yertle the turtle was able to persuade the other turtles to stack themselves up. Yet the turtle stack did not serve a good purpose. The stack was harmful to the turtles in the stack, and it was ultimately bad even for Yertle. But up until the point at which the turtle stack tipped over, Yertle might have been rated as a highly effective leader, simply because the other turtles did as he asked. In contrast, good leaders must do more than get their underlings to follow orders. A good leader gets people to work together to achieve good things. A great leader inspires people to work together to achieve great things.

Businessmen and –women are usually judged by financial results, such as revenues or profits. However, nonprofit organizations and governments must be judged by other criteria. For example, if an area is hit by a major natural disaster, no sane person would mind if the government and the relief agencies spent more than had been budgeted. Instead, the government and the relief agencies may be judged on how many lives they save. Public institutions such as governments and charities are judged by how well they serve the public. Many Americans believe that we need to elect businessmen (and maybe businesswomen) to public office, so that they can get the government to run as efficiently as their businesses do. Yet this theory seldom works in practice. Businesses have simpler goals than governments have and thus are far easier to run.

To be a good leader, you need many of the same skills as a good parent, a good teacher, a good athletic coach, and a good orchestra conductor. Like a parent, you may need to teach people right from wrong. Like a teacher, you may need to teach technical and social skills. Like a coach, you may need to provide guidance and encouragement. Like an orchestra conductor, you may need to help a group of people to work in harmony. The overall goal is to get the team to accomplish far more than the individual members could achieve on their own.

Many people balk at the idea that leaders are like parents. They do not like the idea of adult followers being treated like children. Ideally, adults should never have to be treated like children. Yet leaders often have to remind their followers to fulfill their adult responsibilities. A good leader would provide whatever guidance the followers need, regardless of the followers' chronological age. Ideally, the leader's influence should help to propel the followers along their coming-of-age story arc, so that they do not need to be reminded to behave like responsible adults.

One myth that has been popular among businesspeople is the idea that a good manager can manage anything. But what would have happened if someone had asked Vince Lombardi, the legendary coach of the Green Bay Packers, to conduct the Green Bay Symphony Orchestra? Or asked Leonard Bernstein, the legendary conductor of the New York Philharmonic, to coach the New York Jets? Likewise, someone who is good at managing salespeople might be terrible at managing scientists or engineers, and vice versa. Some leadership roles require a special kind of knowledge and training. Yet a leader does not necessarily have to know how to do the jobs of everyone on his or her staff. Likewise, an orchestra conductor does not have to know how to play all of the instruments in the orchestra. He or she just needs to know how to get the musicians to play together well.

Followers are judged mainly on their obedience. Often, obedience is the secret to success. As an old choir director of mine put it, "There are three secrets to succeeding in the music business: show up, show up on time, and keep your mouth shut." For actors, the rules are simple: show up, know your lines, and hit your marks. In other words, the people who are running the show want the show to run smoothly. They want you to do exactly what you are supposed to do, exactly when you are supposed to do it, because time is money. The fewer problems you create for them, the more work they are likely to give you. In the movie *Tootsie,* Dustin Hoffman plays the role of a brilliant actor who could not find work because he had a well-earned reputation for being difficult to work with. Many people complain about the role of personal relationships in success in show business and other industries. They say, "It's not what you know, it's who[m] you know." By this, they discount the importance of building a reputation for professionalism. Many producers and directors like to hire the same actors over and over because they know what to expect from them.

Many famous movie stars have a well-earned reputation for emotional instability. Partly because of their emotional intensity, they can deliver some electrifying performances. However, the quality of their performances can be uneven. Fortunately, thanks to the miracle of film and now video recording, their most electrifying performances can be recorded and then spliced together. Meanwhile, their misfires end up on the cutting room floor. In contrast, stage actors have to make the same routine performance compelling, day after day, evenings and matinees, for the run of the show. Few people have the star power of someone like Marilyn Monroe. The rest of us need the self-discipline and professionalism of the stage actor if we want to succeed at anything.

Of course, obedience is not always a good thing. In the war crimes trials that were held at Nuremberg after World War II, many of the accused claimed that they had just been following orders. Today, even people in the military are supposedly expected to follow only the lawful orders.

The rules for being a good team player are similar to the rules for being a good follower. You need to do what people want and expect you to do, when they want and expect you to do it. For example, an orchestra musician must play exactly the right notes at exactly the right time. The goal is to contribute to a harmonious whole, as opposed to standing out, at least until it is time for your solo. However, there is one important difference between being a mere follower and being a team player. Followers play follow-the-leader. Team players follow each other and even provide some guidance to each other. There is a give and take among team players. The members of the team even give useful feedback to the leader.

Over the years, I have seen good teamwork and bad teamwork. The recipe for good teamwork is simple. The team members need to have mutual respect and clear communication. Each member of the team must do his or her bit, and must do it correctly and at the right time. However, the team also needs to have the right kind of leadership and authority structure. Good teams are generally meritocracies: the leadership roles are given to people who deserve them. Bad teams usually fail in one or more of those domains. Some team members do not show proper respect to others. The team members may fail to communicate with each other, and they fail to do what they are expected to do. Often, the least capable person is the one running the show. The authority structure is not based on merit, or the high-ranking people ignore valuable input from the low-ranking people. Often, the group resembles a baboon troop, in which social rankings are based on irrelevancies like age, gender, political connections, and aggressiveness. A friend of mine got to see this problem first-hand.

Early in her career, this friend worked on a team that had to produce a report. Since she is a good writer, she volunteered to collect everyone else's input and write the final report. To her surprise, the project became a horrible ordeal. Some of her coworkers were simply uncooperative. A few even became angry when she edited what they wrote. After the ordeal was over, she asked a sociologist friend for advice on how to avoid similar problems in the future. Her friend said, "Were you the youngest person on the team?" Yes, she was. "Were you the best-educated person on the team?" Yes. "Were you the only woman on the team?" No. There was one other woman. "Did she open her mouth?" No. The sociologist concluded that the project was doomed from the start. The problem was primate biology. The older males instinctively felt that they should outrank a young female. Rather than feeling respect for the most educated person on the team, they felt contempt and resentment for an uppity young female. What this team needed was a high-ranking person to discipline the grumpy older males and get them to behave.

The poorly educated older males on the team instinctively felt that they should outrank a young female, regardless of her academic qualifications. You could consider them to be narcissistic. They were trying to occupy a higher social rank than they could reasonably defend. Unfortunately, they were thinking like monkeys, not like philosophers. Their idea of rank was based on primal instinct, when the situation called for a social rank based on higher considerations, such as knowledge and ability. Yet to follow something other than primal instinct, you need emotional maturity.

When you manage a team, you need to deal with this kind of conflict over rank. You could minimize these conflicts by selecting team members who respect each other and who can listen to reason. Nevertheless, you will also have to set up some sort of authority structure that is based on merit. The more childish the team members are, the more important the authority structure is. When people are thinking with their monkey-brain, they are immune to reason. However, they can clearly understand threats from a higher-ranking monkey.

Larger organizations tend to need a more rigid authority structure, especially if many of the people involved are young or irresponsible. Smaller organizations and organizations whose members are more emotionally mature and more professional can have a more flexible authority structure. As a result, these smaller organizations can be nimble and respond better to changing circumstances.

Teams work more smoothly if the authority structure is based on merit, which means that the people who are best suited for leadership are in the leadership roles. You can undermine the effectiveness of your organization by putting unqualified or immature people in management positions. If you want to spot the managers that are most likely to be dysfunctional, compare the organizational chart to the resumes. You may find that some managers are less qualified than the people who report to them. Sometimes, this pattern is a result of favoritism, such as nepotism.

The word *nepotism* means favoritism granted to relatives. The term originally arose in the Middle Ages, when Catholic popes and bishops would give special favors to their nephews. In other words, many people are given a job because of their personal or family connections, not because of their personal merit. Favoritism and nepotism can be toxic to an organization because the favored ones are not held to the same standards as everyone else. They are allowed to fail and misbehave, and they cannot be disciplined.

If promotions are based on favoritism rather than merit, the authority structure often becomes dysfunctional. This kind of dysfunctional authority structure is practically a recipe for workplace bullying. Unqualified managers are trying to occupy a higher social position than they deserve. Thus, you can expect them to show signs of narcissism. Unqualified managers often feel threatened by the capable people who report to them. To neutralize that perceived threat, these managers may try to drive the good workers out of the company, or at least undermine the workers' ability to achieve anything. The easiest way to spot these dysfunctional managers is to read the performance reviews that they write. Many of these reviews are like a tale told by an idiot —full of sound and fury but signifying nothing.

In many settings, leaders have the power to give orders to their

followers. The leaders may think that they want their followers to follow orders to the letter. However, a good team player sometimes has to
disobey direct orders. I saw a perfect model of this kind of loyal dis-
obedience when I worked in Morristown, New Jersey, home of The
Seeing Eye, which trains dogs to guide blind people. To be a good
guide, a dog must know how and when to disobey orders. For example,
the dog will not follow an order to cross the street until it is safe to
cross. A good leader would give the team members enough latitude, or
freedom of action, to make the right decision.

Few leaders have as much faith in their followers as blind people
have in their dogs. Thus, many leaders try to monitor and control their
subordinates' work too closely. This problem is called micromanagement. Leaders with narcissistic tendencies are particularly prone to
micromanagement. Sometimes, they do it strategically, so that they
can take credit for all successes while shifting blame for all failures. As
a result, they often fail to give their followers enough latitude to make
good decisions. The traditional way for workers to resist micromanagement is called a strike of zeal (in French, *grève du zèle*). In Canada, it
is also called working to rule. During a strike of zeal, workers follow
their instructions to the letter. They do exactly as they are told, neither
more nor less. The point is to show how foolish it is for management
to treat workers as if they were machines that are incapable of independent judgment.

In a business setting, managers often have the power to hire and
fire employees. In every one of the United States except Montana, all
employees are considered to be at-will employees, unless their contract
says otherwise. An at-will employee can be fired for any reason or for
no reason. Fortunately, there are some exceptions to this rule. For example, the Civil Rights Act of 1964 makes it illegal for your employer to
fire you for refusing to have sex with your boss. Also, most states allow
a public policy exception. In those states, employees cannot be fired for
complying with federal or state law.

If you work for a business, you can be fired for misbehavior. But if
you are in the military, you could be imprisoned or even put to death if
you do not do as you are told. Members of the military and sailors on

merchant vessels must obey the orders of the people above them in the chain of command. The lower-ranking people often grumble about this. If the sailors or soldiers rise up in rebellion, the uprising is called a mutiny. The most famous mutiny in history was the mutiny on the British Royal Naval vessel HMS *Bounty*, which was supposed to carry breadfruit trees from Tahiti to the West Indies to provide food for the slaves on the sugar plantations. Ten of the mutineers were eventually brought back to England to face court martial, and three of them were hanged. However, some of the mutineers and their Tahitian wives settled on Pitcairn Island, a remote island whose position had been incorrectly charted by earlier explorers. By the time someone from the Royal Navy discovered the mutineers' refuge, all but one of the mutineers had died.

If you work for a badly run company, you may decide to quit your job before you are laid off or the company collapses altogether. If you decide to try to keep your job, you may have to cultivate the difficult art of "managing up." One television character who mastered this art was Corporal Walter Eugene "Radar" O'Reilly on *M*A*S*H*. He was the capable administrator who kept everything running for his unfocused and indecisive commanding officer, Lieutenant Colonel Henry Braymore Blake. This relationship worked because Colonel Blake did not care about maintaining military discipline. Radar had much less latitude under the new commanding officer, Colonel Sherman Tecumseh Potter, a career military officer who was nearing retirement.

Managing up is dangerous if your boss is a narcissist. Like a Seeing-Eye dog, you might try to prevent your boss from walking into danger. Unfortunately, a narcissistic boss could react to this perceived slight with narcissistic rage. So you are probably best off if you show no loyalty to the company that put the fool in charge of you. Just get out while you still have your dignity.

If you live in a society with a government that is badly run, you may decide to leave, or you may decide to get involved in a movement for political reform. The First Amendment to the U.S. Constitution gives Americans the right "peaceably to assemble, and to petition the government for a redress of grievances." Unfortunately, few Americans have a clear idea of how to do that.

Most Americans are clueless about how their government runs. As a result, they have no idea of how to make it run better. I did not know how serious this problem is until a friend of mine ran for Congress. An astonishing number of the potential voters I talked to had no idea that a Congressperson is a member of the House of Representatives in Washington, DC. Only a tiny minority of the people I talked to had any idea who their current Congressman was. Most of them had no idea what his voting record was really like. For example, they thought that he had a good record on veterans' issues and the environment, when his voting record on those issues was actually dismal. Nevertheless, they admired him because he came from a rich and famous family. The astonishing thing was that these were college-educated white people in a wealthy suburb. They could not use lack of schooling as an excuse.

Since then, whenever I go to a supermarket, I ask the person behind me in the checkout line to tell me who the people on the covers of the gossip magazines are. Nearly everyone can give me details about the life stories of even minor celebrities, such as stars of some idiotic television show that I had never even heard of. Then I ask them who their Congressperson and U.S. Senators are, and they give me a blank stare. These people are clearly able to remember facts about people. They simply do not know facts that matter about the people who have power over them. This epidemic of political ignorance did not happen by accident. It is the result of deliberate educational policy.

Our modern model of public schooling was created at the dawn of the Industrial Revolution. The goal was to prepare the children of the working class for life as a factory worker. As a result, there was a great deal of emphasis on regimentation and obedience. Students were taught to show up on time and do exactly as they were told. The goal was to teach the students just enough to make them useful, without teaching them enough to make them dangerous to the social order. Parents may have sent their children to school in hopes that education would lead to social uplift. Local governments were raising ever-larger amounts of money to pour into the public schools. Meanwhile, the captains of industry were hiring professors of education to figure out ways to water down the curriculum. The challenge was to make the public think that this elite attack on public education was somehow a beneficial reform.

The big industrialists wanted the public schools to prepare most workers to do nothing but take orders on the factory floor. The goal was to teach children to read well enough to fill orders, but not well enough to read the Communist Manifesto or even the Holy Bible. Like the Communist Manifesto, the biblical book of Exodus teaches potentially subversive lessons about workers' rights. To suppress literacy, wealthy people hired professors of education to promote a method of reading instruction that does not work. Instead of teaching students how to sound out any word they encounter, the schools taught children to memorize a small list of words as graphic designs, without regard to the sounds expressed by the letters. Because of this "sight word" method of teaching reading, tens of millions of Americans remain functionally illiterate, even though they have spent up to 13 years in public school. The fact that the sight word method continues to be used is a sign of how badly public education has been degraded by this assault by the wealthy and powerful.

Many of the professors at teachers' colleges have come up with bad teaching methods. The educational foundations supported by wealthy philanthropists selectively promote these bad methods. The methods are then built into the textbooks and other materials that publishing companies sell to local school boards. Consequently, the teachers in our public schools have been trained and often forced to use teaching methods that are guaranteed to fail. As a result, millions of Americans have failed to learn basic skills like reading, writing, and arithmetic. Of course, the parents often notice if their children are not learning to read, write, or figure. But the parents are told that the problem is in the child's brain. The child is given a diagnosis of a learning disability, such as dyslexia or dysgraphia or dyscalculia. These are medical-sounding terms, but they simply mean that the child has not yet learned to read, write, or do arithmetic. Often, the child simply needs to be taught the skills that he or she lacks. Yet many of the professors at teachers' colleges are horrified by the idea of teaching skills directly.

One of the big fads in education today is the concept of "learning differences." Yes, some children really do have disabilities that interfere with learning. Helen Keller, for example, became blind and deaf in early childhood. As a result, she had to be taught to use the manual alphabet, to read Braille, and to read lips. Yet it was obvious even to a casual observer that there was something wrong with young Helen. Today, however, many of the children who are being labeled as disabled seem perfectly normal, except that they are not learning much in school. I suspect that many of these children are not truly disabled. They are simply being miseducated.

Teachers should be finding ways to help children develop the basic skills that they need. However, many teachers, especially special education teachers, have been trained to teach children how to work around their weaknesses. Instead of helping children learn to read well enough to do their assigned readings, the teachers may allow the student to listen to an audio recording of a text. I have nothing against audiobooks. I like to listen to them while I do household chores. I think that audiobooks are a godsend for people with poor eyesight. I suppose that audiobooks could even help children develop better skills in listening. But audiobooks should never be used to hide or compensate for the fact that a student has not yet been taught to read. Do not blame teachers for these problems within our educational system. They did not create these problems, and they are the only people who can solve them.

Because of the use of the sight-word method, millions of Americans cannot read well enough to read a newspaper article or a blog post. An even larger number are astoundingly ignorant about the things that should be taught in school. Millions of Americans do not know important facts about history or science. Nor can they appreciate great works of literature. More importantly, only a tiny percentage of the population have any idea of how the government works. Many people complain that we do not have a labor party in the United States. But we lack a labor party because most of the working class has grown up ignorant about political science. That kind of knowledge is reserved for the wealthy and for the people who serve them.

Here in the Land of the Free, we have serious political problems. We supposedly have a government "of the people, by the people, and for the people," yet surveys tell us that most Americans in the early 21st century feel that the country is going in the wrong direction. Some of my friends feel that this problem is due to flaws in how political campaigns are funded. The problems with campaign finance are real and serious. However, the main underlying causes of our political problems are educational and moral, not financial. Most Americans know so little about the world that they do not know what their political options are. Nor have they been successful in picking and supporting the champions who will stand up for them. Instead, they pick confidence artists who betray them, or they disengage totally from political life. Yet as Plato warned us, "the price that good men pay for indifference to public affairs is to be ruled by bad men."

A political champion must be strong, brave, and selfless but also wise. To serve the people, the champion must follow strategies and use tactics that will actually work. Thus, the champion must actually know things. But we in the United States tend to heap scorn on people who know things. If you actually know the technical details of how society runs, and how it ought to run, you are likely to be called a policy wonk. Back in the 1950s, such people were called eggheads. Now, they are called nerds.

As I explained in *Not Trivial*, children who actually care about the things that they are supposed to be learning in school are likely to be unpopular. The main reason is that they are not giving their full attention to the struggle for popularity. In other words, they are already more mature than an adult with histrionic personality disorder. Another reason for the smart kids' unpopularity is that many teachers and administrators allow bullies to torment them. By tolerating the bullying of smart kids, educators teach the lesson that it is foolish and dangerous to take your schoolwork seriously. Thus, they allow the bullies to undermine the educational mission of the school. Yet another reason for the unpopularity of bright people is the nerd trope that is so popular in Hollywood. (A trope is a common or overused theme or device.)

The entertainment industry is like flypaper for intellectually shallow histrionic and narcissistic people. Their cluster B personality disorders give them a competitive edge in a business based on looks and drama. Unfortunately, people with cluster B personality disorders have a pathological desire to outcompete wise people for favorable attention. As a result, they do not like smart people. For that reason, the smart characters in movies and television shows are stereotypically depicted as badly groomed, socially awkward, unsexy, and boring. (In contrast, Joss Whedon, who is a Shakespeare buff, created smart characters who turn out to be sexy and cool, and cool and sexy characters who turn out to be smart.)

Of course, the nerd stereotype has an underlying grain of truth. The good students would rather spend several hours a day studying for their AP exams than spend those hours preening in front of a mirror. Also, the kids who are good students can take part in productive conversations about subjects that matter. Thus, they would seem boring to a shallow histrionic person and threatening to a narcissist. Unfortunately, we are allowing the histrionic and narcissistic people in Hollywood to bias us against smart and educated people.

The people who do well in the popularity game in junior high school may imagine that they are the ones with the superior social skills. Not everyone agrees. Autistic savant Temple Grandin dismisses them as "social yakity yaks." Grandin has taught us that the people who have the most to offer society are the people who are serious about something besides their appearance and their popularity.

Most Americans have never learned how to tell a hero from a villain. (Those are lessons that they should have learned in English class and history class in high school.) As a result, they elect confidence artists instead of champions. A few people know how to spot a champion, but most of them do not know enough about the political system to get that person elected in the primary elections. As a result, the choices in the general election tend to be so disappointing that many people do not even bother to vote.

Perhaps I am a foolish optimist, but I feel that the Internet has given us the opportunity to solve these problems. The Internet enables us to provide education to the people who were short-changed in school. It also enables us to teach the lessons in political science that ordinary people desperately need to learn. We just have to start using the Internet for spreading something other than cat videos.

Chapter 17

Drama, Drama, Drama

~

Narcissistic personality disorder is a psychiatric diagnosis. Thus, it is technically a medical diagnosis. Like other medical diagnoses, narcissistic personality disorder is a label that can be recorded in a patient's medical records. But unlike regular medical diagnoses, such as diabetes or Alzheimer's disease, narcissistic personality disorder does not mean that something that has gone wrong with the patient's body, or even with the patient's brain. Instead, the diagnosis of narcissistic personality disorder implies that the patient has a set of unreasonable attitudes and expectations that create conflict in his or her relationships with other people. These conflicts provoke the narcissist to act in dramatic ways.

Narcissistic personality disorder is one of the Cluster B or dramatic personality disorders. The people who qualify for a Cluster B personality disorder often cause pointless drama. Sociopaths often create tragedies, but narcissists usually create farce.

The BBC mockumentary (fake documentary) *The Office* focuses on the farce created by a narcissist. The setting of *The Office* is the sales office of a company that sells office paper in Slough, which is a real town halfway between London and Reading, England. To a British audience, this setting is funny. The English word *slough* (which rhymes with plow) means a muddy place. In John Bunyan's allegory *The Pilgrim's Progress*, the Slough of Despond is a sump that collects the scum and filth produced by sin. In this low and filthy place, the sinner awakens to the fact that he is lost. Sadly, the real town of Slough was used as a dump for war surplus materials between the wars. Then, it became a major factory town right before World War II. The poet Sir John Betjeman was so disturbed by the changes to the town that he wrote a famous poem, which began, "Come, friendly bombs, and fall on Slough!/ It isn't fit for humans now,/ There isn't grass to graze a cow./ Swarm over, Death!" In a guide to English churches, he described one church as "dangerously near Slough" and another as "beyond the tentacles of Slough."

The Office focuses on two main characters, each of whom is childish in his own way: general manager David Brent and salesman Tim Carpenter. David Brent wants so badly to be liked and admired that he irritates people and makes a fool of himself. He makes inappropriate jokes and other inappropriate remarks. He is also prone to jealousy and one-upmanship. In contrast, Tim Carpenter is intelligent and likeable. But like David Brent, Tim resists taking on adult responsibilities. Thus, Tim is feckless, which means incompetent and ineffectual or not fit to assume responsibilities. Tim has done nothing to pursue his dream of studying psychology. At age 30, he is still living at home with his parents. He even fails to win the hand of the receptionist, Dawn Tinsley, whom he loves. Instead of choosing the kind and thoughtful but feckless Tim, Dawn chooses a surly but decisive man who has no respect for her artistic talent.

Tim Carpenter could use his energy and ingenuity to crawl up out of his Slough of Despond. Instead, he uses them to play clever but cruel pranks on Gareth Keenan, a dull-witted and neurotic man whose desk is next to Tim's. (David Brent refuses to discipline Tim because he thinks the pranks are funny.) Like David Brent, Gareth Keenan is narcissistic. But instead of imagining himself to be a great entertainer, Gareth imagines himself to be a great warrior because of his service in the Territorial Army. Tim Carpenter and Gareth Keenan each represent half of mentally healthy adult. Tim represents intelligence without self-discipline or ambition, while Gareth represents self-discipline and ambition without intelligence. At the end of the series, Tim even turns down the offer to serve as David Brent's replacement. As a result, Gareth Keenan replaces David Brent as the manager of the office. Thus, Tim has no one to blame but himself for his predicament.

The Office is an example of cringe comedy, a comedy genre in which the humor is derived from social awkwardness. The focal character is typically an egotistical person who annoys and offends people by breaking social rules in a clumsy way. The mockumentary format allows individual characters to address the television audience directly in interview segments. The supposedly unscripted scenes allow the audience to watch how the characters interact. In the interview segments, David Brent explains that he views himself as a philosopher and an entertainer as well as an inspiring leader. Yet the scenes show that most of the other characters think that he is an annoying fool.

David Brent has two key problems. One is that he does not understand the nature of leadership. As I explained in Chapter 16, good leaders are like good parents. To be a good leader, you have to be a responsible adult who gets other people to behave like adults. Instead, Brent is still playing the role of class clown: a powerless child who is trying to gain attention through irreverent and disruptive behavior. Brent has failed to grow up because he is blind to feedback from other people. He does not notice the horrified facial expressions of the people around him. In the first episode, he even makes a show of throwing away a fax message without reading it. The message was an agenda for a meeting with someone from the head office. As a result, Brent is unprepared for the meeting.

As a narcissist, David Brent has an unhealthy desire to be the most highly admired person in any given situation. In one episode, two of the minor characters (David Brent's boss Neil and Tim's girlfriend Rachel) do an impressive, well-rehearsed dance routine from *Saturday Night Fever* as part of a charity event. As Neil and Rachel dance, you can see expressions of joy and delight on most of the other characters' faces. The exceptions are Dawn, who is jealous of Rachel, and David Brent, who is clearly jealous of Neil and remarks that Neil's dancing is "gay." After the dance ends, David Brent refuses to put money in the charity bucket, telling Neil that he has actually raised more money already. Then, Brent brags about his own dancing. Rachel then tells Brent to "show us your moves." Brent then makes a fool of himself by doing his own awkward impromptu dance. As he is dancing, you can see the other characters reacting with dismay or horror. When he finishes, a few people clap politely.

To appreciate cringe comedy, you have to know the social rules that the focal character is breaking. You also need to be able to see and understand the looks of horror and dismay on the faces of the other characters. Many people dislike cringe comedy, which they find more horrifying than funny. In many ways, cringe comedy is like slapstick, which is a style of comedy in which actors engage in physical activities that would be painful in real life. In slapstick comedy, the humor comes from the sense of relief, when you realize that the actor was not really injured. Similarly, the humor from cringe comedy comes from the relief that you were not the fool that made those gaffes, and the relief that the person who made them did not suffer as a result.

The Office teaches us many important lessons. One is that the comedy that you see on stage or on television is the work of professionals. Do not try the same stunts yourself, especially not at work. David Brent is played by Ricky Gervais, the gifted comedian who created the show. As a professional comedian, Ricky Gervais is continually testing new material in front of audiences. Professional comedians refine their act by keeping and expanding on the bits that work and discarding the bits that fall flat. Through this kind of interaction with audiences, comedians learn the boundaries of what an audience will accept.

Professional comedians often say horrible and shocking things, but in a way that delights their audience. Professional comedians learn how dark they can go (black comedy deals with serious, disturbing themes such as death) and how blue they can go (by using obscene language or talking frankly about sex). A comedian who goes close to the edge of what the audience cannot bear is called edgy. In contrast, David Brent's attempts at humor usually fall flat, and he usually goes completely over the edge. Unfortunately, David Brent usually seems to be completely unaware of the disapproval that the other characters are expressing, usually nonverbally. His narcissism persists because he cannot perceive or learn from feedback from other characters. Brent is not an evil person. He is often well meaning. His main problem is childishness. He is a naughty boy who never learned where the boundaries of acceptable behavior are.

To help someone like David Brent, you must teach him the interpersonal skills that he does not know that he lacks. Fortunately, Brent fancies himself to be a philosopher. He might actually be receptive to the kind of management training that would help him become a better person and a better manager. His main problems are a lack of ability to read people and a lack of self-restraint.

Although *The Office* was a fake documentary, it might actually be useful for helping people overcome narcissism. As you watch the series, take note of what David Brent does, and how other people react to him. Study the horrified looks on the other characters' faces. Then, as you go about your business, watch the facial expressions of the people you encounter. If people give you those same facial expressions in real life, then you probably need to refine your act.

If you want to be popular, you need to study how other people react to you. You need to keep the bits that work and discard the bits that fall flat. In short, you need to refine your act. However, you could take this process too far. If your ultimate goal is popularity, you will probably end up like someone with histrionic personality disorder: an intellectually shallow people-pleaser with no moral compass. To maintain your own dignity, you must accept that you cannot please all of the people all of the time.

Unfortunately, not all narcissists are irritating but harmless buffoons like David Brent. In real life, some narcissists do appalling things to assert themselves socially. The worst cases can lead to tragedy. The narcissistic desire to go out in a blaze of glory is the underlying motivation behind many mass shootings. People with narcissistic personality disorders want to cast themselves in the role of hero. If they cannot get other people to accept them in that role, they may try to play the role of an antihero, as in a gangster film, or the role of a supervillain. Narcissists assign other kinds of roles to other people. Most people are just extras. If you are unlucky, you may find yourself playing the role of victim. If you oppose the narcissist in any way, you will be cast in the role of antagonist. To avoid that fate, you may need to develop the ability to spot Cluster B personality disorders from a distance. If you can spot the danger early on, you may be able to write yourself out of the script before the curtain rises.

Psychotherapist Ross Rosenberg teaches a particularly useful way to disengage from a narcissist. He calls it the "observe, don't absorb" technique. If you know that a bottle contains poison, you might look at the bottle or maybe even handle it, but you would not drink from it. Likewise, you may observe that a narcissist is misbehaving, but you do not need to drink the poison that the narcissist is trying to serve you. Rosenberg encourages people to use visualizations to help them disengage. For example, he suggests that you visualize yourself wearing a suit made of Teflon, so that insults slide off you. Or you might imagine how Mr. Spock from *Star Trek* would respond to the situation—attentive and analytical yet emotionally detached.

Often, the best strategy is to put social or even physical distance between you and a toxic person. This disengagement can be emotional or social. For example, you may simply stop granting some people the power to hurt your feelings. They may still hurl insults, but you stop taking it personally. If someone still poses a threat to your well-being, you could shun that person, which means that you refuse to interact with that person socially. Fortunately, the law may be on your side. If someone's behavior is truly threatening, you may be able to get a restraining order, which forbids the person from approaching you. Of course, you should not shun someone for petty reasons. Shunning is something that mean girls do, just to be mean.

In ancient Athens, men who were considered a threat to the state could be ostracized, which meant that they were expelled from Athens for 10 years. (*Ostraca* were the bits of broken pottery that were used as ballots.) If the Athenian Assembly voted to ostracize a man, he had to leave the city within 10 days, or he would be killed. However, he got to keep his citizenship and his property. At the end of his 10-year sentence, he could return to the city without stigma. Of course, the Assembly had the power to shorten the sentence. Likewise, even if you have shunned someone, you may choose to reconcile, especially if that person tries to redeem him- or herself.

The dramas that people with Cluster B personality disorders create tend to follow only a few basic plots. But then, nearly all works of fiction feature one of several basic plots. Scholars and critics quibble about exactly how many there are. Some say seven, while others say 21. In particular, people with Cluster B personality disorders like to reenact the plot of the 1944 movie *Gaslight*.

In *Gaslight*, an evil husband isolates his wife from other people and does various things to convince her that she is losing her mind. Thus, the term *gaslighting* is used to describe a form of psychological abuse in which a person is given distorted information, in the hopes of making that person doubt his or her own memory, perceptions, and sanity. In *Gaslight*, the villain was a jewel thief who was pulling those tricks deliberately, to distract attention from his attempt to find a stash of stolen jewels. In contrast, some people with personality disorders might use gaslighting tactics unwittingly. Their own perceptions and thought processes are distorted, and they may simply want other people to see things their way. If they succeed in infecting another person with their madness, the result is called a *folie à deux* or shared psychosis. Sanity is not contagious. You cannot cause someone to be mentally healthy by being sane and reasonable in his or her presence. Unfortunately, some kinds of madness do seem to spread from person to person.

As I explained in Chapter 8, all mental illnesses involve some sort of problem with thoughts, feelings, or behavior. As I explained in Chapter 10, the personality disorders are mental illnesses whose most prominent feature is misbehavior. Yet a person with a personality disorder can also have less-obvious problems with thoughts or feelings. Narcissism can be viewed as a situation in which people are following their primal drive for dominance but without using the strategies and tactics that would enable them to achieve a high rank within a civilized society. As a result, they struggle to occupy a social rank that they cannot realistically defend. If they were baboons, the question of social rank would be worked out through some sort of physical struggle whose outcome is hard to misjudge. Unfortunately, narcissists often get involved in intellectual struggles that they cannot win and whose outcome they cannot even judge. As a result, they often mistakenly think that they have triumphed. Thus, they give themselves continuous positive feedback for bad behavior. That is why the problem persists.

The strategies and tactics that you would use for getting along with a sane and reasonable person will not work when you are dealing with a narcissist. That is because those strategies and tactics were designed to promote good relationships among civilized human beings who respect each other. To develop and follow those strategies and tactics, you need to have high-level thinking skills and the emotional maturity to engage in give and take. Unfortunately, narcissists' poor interpersonal skills often reflect poor skills in observation and reasoning. Furthermore, narcissists tend to be selfish. Instead of engaging in give and take, they expect you to give, so that they can take. By giving, you signal your submission. By taking, they signal their superiority. The narcissist wants to push you down into a subordinate position. They want to "win," and the only way they can "win" is to make you lose. In other words, they want to play king of the hill while you play follow the leader. Narcissists love win-lose games. They may not even realize that win-win games exist. Thus, no good can come from trying to reason your way out of a conflict with a narcissist.

When you reason with someone, you use language as a means of persuasion. Only human beings can do that. Aristotle pointed out that plants and animals (including human beings) all have a nutritive life, which means that we all grow and develop and reproduce physically. Animals (including human beings) also have an instinctual life. Animals can move around under their own power, and they can engage in behaviors. For example, honeybees instinctively know how to build honeycombs. In addition to having a nutritive and instinctual life, human beings have the ability to make plans and discuss them with other people. As a result, we can imagine and create things that have never existed before. Because of this ability, Aristotle considered human beings to be the rational animal. Although Aristotle felt that all human beings have the ability to reason, they would need lessons in logic and philosophy before they could reason well.

We expect small children to be childish. They know little about the world, and they have not yet developed the ability to control their emotions. Nor have they learned the basic rules for how to find truth and resolve conflicts. In short, they do not know any better. When an adult throws tantrums like a toddler, the cause of the problem could be medical or educational. The person might be suffering from some sort of medical problem, such as bipolar disorder, that leads to a loss of emotional control. Or the person could simply have failed to learn how to think and behave like a civilized adult. Of course, the unreasonableness can be all for show. Some people use bluster when they are negotiating from a position of weakness. According to an old legal adage, "If you have the facts on your side, pound the facts. If you have the law on your side, pound the law. If you have neither on your side, pound the table." Of course, people who do not know the facts or understand the law have no choice but to pound the table.

Logic and reason are highly valued in societies where political power is broadly distributed. However, they tend to be disregarded or suppressed in societies where power is held by a rigid social hierarchy that does not want to give the poor and downtrodden or even the merchant class any opportunity to seek justice. The reason is simple. The powerful do not want the powerless to be able to use truth and the rule of law to serve their own interests. That is why wealthy conservatives want to make it harder for poor people to win lawsuits against large corporations. This campaign is called tort reform; but for most of us, it really means that the law will never be on our side.

Pointing out the facts and the law may be useful ways to resolve a conflict with a reasonable person. But when you are in a conflict with a narcissist, those tactics usually backfire. By trying to reason with the narcissist, you are taking the intellectual and moral high ground. Thus, you put them in the one-down position, which causes narcissistic injury and can trigger narcissistic rage. You may imagine that you are providing information that the narcissist needs in order to make a good decision. But the narcissist does not care about making good decisions. To the narcissist, the more important goal is to get you to show submission and worshipful admiration. Narcissists would rather make a stupendously bad decision than allow someone to question their judgment. This principle is important for business executives to understand. A sociopathic employee may embezzle from the company, but a narcissist may be willing to sacrifice the company on the altar of his or her own ego. You can usually spot embezzlement at an early stage if you have good accounting controls. In contrast, the damage that a narcissist inflicts, such as the loss of your most productive employees, can be harder to measure.

Often, the stakes in a particular conflict are so low that a reasonable person will let the raging narcissist "win." But that strategy can backfire because the victory provides positive reinforcement for bad behavior. By giving in to the narcissist's tantrums, you are providing positive feedback. Thus, you are training the narcissist to throw tantrums. The narcissist may be angling for admiration, but they are usually just inspiring contempt. Contempt is the feeling that corresponds to being in a superior social position. When you see an adult throw a tantrum like a two-year-old, it is perfectly appropriate for you to feel contempt for that person. Narcissists persist in their self-defeating behavior because they have poor social skills. They do not realize that they are making a bad impression. Even if they did have this realization, they may not know any better way to achieve their goals.

Even if you could win in a contest against a narcissist, the victory may be costly. The first *Star Wars* movie made light of this problem. The Wookie Chewbacca became angry when the robot R2D2 made a clever move in a chess-like game. Han Solo told R2D2, "Let him have it. It's not wise to upset a Wookiee." The android C-3PO chimes in, "But sir, nobody worries about upsetting a droid." Han Solo responds, "That's 'cause droids don't pull people's arms out of their sockets when they lose. Wookiees are known to do that." C-3PO says, "I see your point, sir. I suggest a new strategy, R2: let the Wookiee win."

If you cannot stand the idea of letting the Wookiee win some tiny victory, then maybe you are a bit narcissistic yourself! Once you finally break free from a co-dependent relationship with a narcissist, you may feel an urge to put that person in his or her proper place, which is far beneath you in the social hierarchy. In other words, you may crave triumph, combined with schadenfreude, as a form of revenge. Triumph is the emotion that you feel when you win in a competition against someone else. Schadenfreude is a feeling of delight that results from watching other people suffer. To gloat is to feel gratification that someone else is being given a well-earned punishment. Although triumph and schadenfreude can feel good, they are dangerous emotions. They can come only from win-lose games, never from win-win games. Wookiees win because they are willing to break the ordinary rules of civility that make good social relationships possible. To win against a Wookiee, you would have to out-Wookiee the Wookiee. You would have to become more narcissistic than the narcissist.

Unfortunately, you may not even realize that you are playing with a Wookiee, or even that a game is being played. Narcissists, like many people with serious personality disorders, often wear a mask of sanity. Because of their self-confidence, they can even seem bright and charming. But then, you may say or do something that causes that mask of sanity to slip and reveal their major mental illness. Unfortunately, you cannot cure or control that person's mental illness, and you might end up catching it. The stress of dealing with someone with severe character flaws can deform your own character. You may end up doing regrettable things in self-defense, and you may even be tempted to do some nasty things in revenge. The only way to "win" a game like this is not to play.

For someone with narcissism, anything that poses a challenge to their grasp on their social rank can cause that mask to slip. For example, you may need to tell the narcissist something that he or she does not yet know, or you may need to point out some error in the narcissist's reasoning. Thus, you would pose a threat to the narcissist's self-concept as "the smartest person in the room." Or you may need to ask the narcissist to stop misbehaving. Thus, you would pose a threat to the narcissist's self-concept as "the paragon of virtue." Perhaps you need to get the narcissist's cooperation in the plan to solve some problem that affects them as well as you. Thus, you pose a threat to the narcissist's self-concept as "the leader." You may be trying to share important information and solve important problems. However, the narcissist may feel that you are challenging him or her to a duel, and the narcissist will fight to win.

Narcissists have a fundamental misunderstanding of the economics of knowledge. If I find a $20 bill lying on the ground, I could give it to you. At that point, you will have the $20 and I will not. The $20 bill will have changed hands, but the total amount of money in the society is unchanged. In contrast, if I find a piece of information and share it with you, then both of us will have that piece of information. Now, the total wealth of knowledge in the society, as measured in person-facts, has increased. However, a narcissist may not want to accept the knowledge you want to share because the narcissist already "owns" the truth.

This reluctance to learn from other people reveals one of the reasons why narcissists fail to achieve the high social rank that they desire. If someone has knowledge that you lack, that person is in a one-up position relative to you. But if you pick that person's brain and learn everything that he or she knows, then you pull yourself up to his or her level. Unfortunately, narcissists cannot pull themselves up to someone else's level because narcissists view themselves as already superior. Thus, if you try to tell a narcissist something, even something that the narcissist needs to know, you might as well be talking to a brick wall. Because of this resistance to learning from other people, narcissists learn slowly, even if they have a high IQ. Thus, they tend to fall further and further behind other people, while still maintaining their self-concept of being the smartest person in the room.

Anyone can unwittingly do things that cause trouble or annoyance for other people. If you ask a sane person to stop doing something that is causing problems for you, the sane person will probably honor your request and will probably throw in an apology, as well. That is how civilized people behave. By making such a request to someone, you imply that you think that that person is civilized, which is actually a compliment. However, a narcissist will probably interpret such a request as a personal insult. To the narcissist, any request may seem like an attempt to assert social dominance because all commands and requests are supposed to flow from the top down. The highest-ranking person is supposed to be the one who makes and enforces the rules, which apply only to the underlings. Asking the narcissist to change his or her behavior is worse than talking to a wall. It is like poking a hornet's nest with a stick.

What if you need other people's cooperation to solve some problem that affects all of you? For example, you might write a computer program that would automate some task that was wasting everyone's time at work. A sociopathic coworker might steal your idea and take credit for it. In that situation, you would at least get the satisfaction of having solved the problem. In contrast, if you are working with or for a narcissist, that narcissist may do everything in his or her power to thwart your plan. By succeeding at something, you threaten to outshine the narcissist. Often, the narcissistic boss is too stupid to realize that he or she could legitimately take credit for your accomplishments. No matter how good of a business case you make for your plan, the narcissist will not be persuaded. You might as well be talking to a brick wall.

The narcissists and sociopaths who stalk the workplace have always caused misery for their coworkers, who represent a captive audience. But in the 21st century, psychologists and sociologists have started to study the harm that narcissists and sociopaths do to the companies that employ them. Because of scandals in the business world, such as the collapse of Enron, sociologists have been paying a lot of attention to the dangerous sociopathic tendencies of many of the top executives of large corporations. Sociopaths can be dangerous because they are relentlessly self-serving. As a result, they may bite the hand that feeds them. Nevertheless, I would rather work for a sociopath than for a narcissist. A sociopath would work you like a rented mule and then take credit for everything you do, but a narcissist may make it impossible for you to do your job because the narcissist is afraid that you will outshine them. A sociopath will never respect your humanity, but a narcissist will try to destroy your self-respect.

Narcissists love to play mind games, and they play to win. The *Postcards to a Narcissist* blog (https://postcardstoanarcissist.wordpress.com/games-narcissists-play/) put together a list of games that narcissists love to play. Here is an abridged version:

> **Death by a thousand cuts**—This game involves shredding your soul, your ego, your accomplishments, and any of your beliefs that do not agree with theirs. The goal is to depict you as completely unworthy, an utter failure. The narcissist can score extra points by taking credit for anything good that has ever happened to you. The narcissist gets double extra points for putting all blame for everything bad onto other players.

The pity party—The longest (dullest and worst) party EVER for the victims.

Twenty-one—In this popular game, you are not allowed to reach 21, ever. Even if you are 50 years old, you will still be treated like a child (a stupid child, a bad child, a silly child, etc.). You do not get to have face cards, and if YOU get an ace, it is only worth 1 point.

The king/queen game—No one can know the rules of this game except the king or queen, who can make up the rules as he or she goes along, without telling the other players. Thus, the king/queen always wins (even when you play fairly by that day's rules). You can be penalized for breaking the rules, even if king/queen chooses not to tell you the rules.

Spite and malice (cat and mouse)—This is a kind of competitive patience (solitaire) game for two players. It is also known as cat and mouse. The cards are arranged from low to high with the kings being wild. Suits (normal order of things and / or common societal rules) are irrelevant in the game. The game ends when someone wins by playing the last card of their payoff pile. The game can also end if the players run out of cards, in which case the result is a draw. This is a perfect game for a narcissist because (1) it is actually a form of solitaire and (2) it requires "one-upmanship" and pulling out "better" cards to use to beat the other player. It involves a "payoff"—for the narcissist, that usually means hurting you somehow. They keep track of real or imaginary things you do, have done, or might do. This is their "pile" and they nurture it, obsess over it, and dump it on you whenever possible.

Liar's poker—All people with narcissistic personality disorder play this game superbly. They are consummate liars.

Crazy eights—When you try to hold the narcissist accountable for his or her appalling behavior, the narcissist will tell you that you are crazy—you have a very vivid imagination, you don't know what you're talking about, they have no idea what you're talking about, or you're simply making things up to hurt them or cause problems. This infuriating tactic is also called gaslighting.

Keep away—This is the only game you should ever play with a narcissist. They hate it. Narcissists never admit that they are playing games, so it is up to you to stop playing.

Chapter 18

Don't Feed the Narcissists!

When I mentioned that I was writing a book about narcissism, several of my friends said that it is badly needed. But then, they pointed out that narcissists would not bother to read the book because narcissists do not think that they have any problem that needs to be fixed. I agree wholeheartedly. People who are like Narcissus will probably not read this book. If they do read it, they will not realize that they are the sort of people I am talking about. But I did not write it for them. I wrote it for thoughtful parents and teachers who do not want children to grow up to be narcissists. I also wrote it for codependent people—people like Echo, as well as for people who are like the other turtles in Yertle's pond. In particular, I wrote this book for the decent people who are being bullied at work, simply for being good at their jobs. Those antiheroes desperately need to find ways to preserve their sanity and their dignity in a dystopia.

I want to encourage good people to find the strength of character to be heroes. In other words, I want to encourage people to take part in nonviolent campaigns for justice, and to refuse to cooperate with anything evil. According to Dr. Seuss, Yertle the turtle convinced the other turtles in his pond to stack themselves one on top of another, so that he could sit atop them all. As the stack grew higher, the turtles on the bottom suffered more and more. Yet no stack would ever be high enough to suit Yertle, and the stack that he was sitting on eventually tipped over. When I was a child, I thought that Yertle the turtle was the villain of the story. I thought that Mac, the turtle at the bottom of

Yertle's stack, was a hero because he spoke out for the common turtle. Yet as I grew older, I started to see that Mac and the other turtles were really antiheroes. They were causing their own problems by pledging allegiance to the wrong sort of person and lending their support to a bad project. They made a deliberate choice to serve a bad leader, and they did nothing to save themselves or each other.

I eventually realized that Theodore Seuss Geisel must have written *Yertle the Turtle* as a cautionary tale about fascism. Mussolini and Hitler were able to rise to power only because a large enough number of ordinary people were willing to obey them. Yes, Mussolini eventually came to a bad end. So did Hitler—but not before countless innocent people suffered and died. Thus, the story gives us two kinds of warning. The first is *don't be a narcissist*. The second is *don't feed the narcissists*: it's not good for you or for them or for anybody else.

Narcissism is a foreground-background problem. It is easy to focus on the narcissist in the foreground. However, the narcissist is only part of the picture. We must also look at the people in the background. How did Yertle come to believe that he was the king of all he could see? Where did he get the idea to order the other turtles to sacrifice themselves to his greater glory? Why did the other turtles follow his stupid orders? Yertle's plan to rise higher than the moon was doomed to failure. However, the plan ultimately failed because a turtle stack is physically unstable, not because the other turtles in the pond took any action to save themselves. No turtle Gandhi arose to tell the rest of the turtles that they did not need to cooperate with Yertle.

Of course, real turtles don't have kings. They don't have leaders of any kind, or even any friends. Turtles have no social ties even to their mates and parents and siblings, and they never even recognize their own offspring. Thus, real turtles never have to deal with social relationships. In contrast, a human being always has to deal with social relationships, unless he or she lives alone on a desert island. Social relationships virtually always involve some sort of negotiation for power, property, and/or prestige. By confronting narcissism, you recognize that those negotiations are taking place. You deal with the question of how the individual can fit into his or her society, as it currently exists.

You must also address the question of how the society ought to be structured—how power, property, and prestige should be distributed.

Do you want to enjoy the freedoms that are available within a democracy, or do you want to be ruled by an oligarchy or a tyrant? By the end of World War II, many people throughout the world had come to recognize the horrors of fascism. As a result, the United Nations passed a Universal Declaration of Human Rights. The first clause of that document reads, "Whereas recognition of the inherent dignity and of the equal and inalienable rights of all members of the human family is the foundation of freedom, justice and peace in the world...."

If you run a large company, you have practical as well as moral reasons for thinking about narcissism. Do you want the rank-and-file workers to be led by honest and capable people, or are you willing to sacrifice your business on the altar of the ego of some narcissistic middle managers?

We do need for all members of the human family to have equal and inalienable rights. However, we also do need to have some social rank. Children need to look to their parents and teachers for guidance. Whenever there is any sort of group activity, even adults need leadership. Even in a democracy, the people choose public servants to make some decisions on their behalf. The question is whether the leadership positions are being given to the right sort of people, and whether those powerful people are being held accountable for how they use that power.

Many Christians are reluctant to judge other people because Christ reportedly said in the Sermon on the Mount: "Judge not, lest you be judged." Yet when you look at that commandment in its broader context, you realize that it means that you should judge other people by the same criteria that will be used to judge you. In other words, you should not be a hypocrite. I think that we desperately need to judge other people, and especially to judge the people who are in a position of public trust.

When we judge public figures, we end up in a conflict between our instincts and our reason. Hens lack the ability to understand the concept of right and wrong. Thus, they never question the dominant hen's right to use her power to serve her own needs. Thus, hens instinctively accept that might makes right, and that they should submit to bigger hens. In contrast, monkeys have a primitive sense of fairness. They can become angry if they feel they are being short-changed. Because of the uniquely human gift of language, human beings can develop highly sophisticated concepts of right and wrong. Yet it is very easy for human beings to act like birdbrains, and to assume that might makes right. Many people willingly submit to the powerful, even if the powerful are doing something that even a monkey would think is wrong. As a result, it is all too easy for people to submit to a strong leader, which is how demagogues become tyrants. This principle also explains many of the bad things that happen within a badly run religious organization.

In a troop of monkeys, the highest-ranking males have the most opportunities for mating. Similarly, many human beings seem to take it for granted that powerful men should be allowed take their pleasure with whomever they want. As a result, when people are thinking with their monkey-brain, they ignore their leaders' criminal sexual offenses. True believers can react that way even if they belong to a religious organization that commands everyone to be chaste. By now, everyone is aware of the pandemic of sexual abuse by Roman Catholic priests. However, the problem is not uniquely Catholic or even Christian. As the novelist Arthur Koestler explained in *The Lotus and the Robot,* "Guru are worshiped in a manner barely distinguishable from divine worship. It is therefore unimaginable to question the [guru's] character or to disobey his whims. ... He represents the will of God and God himself."

In a dictatorship, the dictator makes the rules and the people are expected to submit. But in a democracy, the people make the rules. The government officials who are expected to enforce those rules are the servants of the people, not their masters. When we judge government officials or other political leaders, we must decide whether they are really serving the people. If the leaders fail in that respect, we need to hold them accountable for their actions. Most importantly, we need to persuade the turtles that are holding the tyrant up to leave the stack. But before a turtle can see the need to leave the stack, it must overcome its protective stupidity.

A diagnosis of narcissism is a social judgment. If you feel that someone is a narcissist, you feel that he or she is trying to occupy a higher social position than you think he or she deserves. Before we make any political contributions or cast a vote in any election, we must ask ourselves whether the person we are supporting really deserves to occupy the office in question. Is that person technically and morally capable of serving the public? During the 1960 Presidential campaign in the United States, a campaign poster showed an unflattering picture of Richard M. Nixon and asked, "Would you buy a used car from this man?" That is a good question to ask about any politician. We should also ask it about any public figure.

We should also be cautious about accepting someone as a public intellectual. A public intellectual is a scientist or scholar who reaches out to the public to help promote scientific understanding and the betterment of society. Unfortunately, the people who are being promoted in the commercial media as public intellectuals are not necessarily great scientists or distinguished scholars. In fact, many people are turning to uneducated celebrities instead of to respected scientists and scholars for help in understanding the world. Like the turtles in Yertle's pond, we are allowing the wrong sort of people to rise to great heights.

Many people are worried that there is an epidemic of narcissism in the United States today. As always, many people want unearned admiration and privileges. But because of the overemphasis on self-esteem over the past few decades, along with the rise of social media, narcissism is probably becoming more common. It is certainly becoming more obvious.

Narcissism is a character flaw. If a character flaw is particularly severe and persistent and is causing suffering and disability, it can be considered a form of mental illness called a personality disorder. Although personality disorders can cause a great deal of suffering, the person with the personality disorder might not be the one who is feeling the pain. Often, he or she is inflicting the pain on other people. For many people with personality disorders, their own suffering seems to consist mainly of appetites that can never be satisfied, typically because of their inability to connect with other people as equals. Thus, the person who seeks therapy *because* of a personality disorder is generally not the person *with* the personality disorder. The people who seek healing are usually the ones who have been injured psychologically or even physically by someone with a personality disorder.

Narcissism is not a demon that can be cast out in an exorcism ritual. Nor is it an infection that can be cured with an antibiotic. Nor is it a tumor that can be cut out with a scalpel. Rather, it simply represents poor progress in the age-old struggle against the cardinal sin of pride. This struggle may be particularly hard for someone whose brain is defective or simply slow to mature. Yet this struggle is something that every human being must undertake. Thus, an understanding of narcissism can help anyone who wishes to become wise and good.

Aristotle was fascinated by a concept that he called the golden mean, which represents the desirable middle ground between two bad extremes. The Chinese philosopher Confucius wrote about a similar concept, called the Doctrine of the Mean. Likewise, Buddhists talk about the Middle Path. In theory, a mentally healthy person would occupy the desirable middle ground between narcissistic personality disorder and dependent personality disorder. A mentally healthy person would have neither unrealistically high nor unrealistically low self-esteem. A mentally healthy person would be wise and reasonable and would play a productive role in individual and social activities, rather than playing self-destructive games of king of the hill or follow the leader.

An understanding of narcissism can also help decent people recognize the dangers posed by the narcissists and sociopaths in their personal life or their working life and in the political arena. The people who would benefit most from an understanding of narcissism are the people who are currently being victimized by a narcissist. To escape from that victimization, they need to gain or perhaps regain a sense of what is true and what is good and what is possible. They need to learn how to defend their own dignity.

You cannot reasonably expect to have a healthy relationship with a mentally unhealthy person. Nor can you fix someone else's broken personality. Love cannot cure narcissism, just as love cannot cure alcoholism. Instead, your co-dependency may make the problem worse. People who have become emotionally involved with narcissists may have to learn the four C's that are taught by 12-step programs for relatives of alcoholics and addicts: "I didn't cause it, I cannot control it, I cannot cure it, but I don't have to contribute to it." You did not cause another person's narcissism. You cannot control their narcissism or cure it. Nor do you have to continue to provide narcissistic supply. In other words, you do not have to continue to feed the narcissist. Feeding the narcissist is bad for the narcissist, but it is mainly bad for you. It is bad for your own mental health to continue making sacrifices on the altar of a mentally ill person's inflated ego.

Psychotherapy probably can help co-dependent people overcome their co-dependency. However, I doubt that conventional psychotherapy would be effective in cases of narcissism. The therapist-patient relationship is a teacher-student relationship. To benefit from psychotherapy, you have to accept that the therapist knows something valuable that you do not know. Unfortunately, narcissists are typically unwilling to do that. Narcissism stems from a pathological need to feel intellectually and morally superior to others. As a result, narcissists would resist putting themselves in the subordinate role of patient or student. They do not want to hear criticism, nor do they want advice on how to correct their character flaws. Narcissists may enjoy the programs that offer them the opportunity to triumph over other people, but such programs may make their narcissism worse, not better. To help narcissists, we must find ways to make narcissists enjoy learning the intellectual and social skills that they lack.

People with personality disorders may be aware of problems in their social life. However, they seldom understand that many of their problems result from their own emotional immaturity. They may realize that their emotional lives are a wasteland. They may even be trying to fill in that vast emptiness with money, intoxicating drugs, sexual conquests, or a series of tiny victories in petty disputes. Unfortunately, they lack the ability to understand and solve this problem. If they had been able to recognize that the barrenness of their emotional lives was due to their own personality flaws and misbehavior, they would have set out on a coming-of-age or redemptive story arc years ago.

Are personality disorders due to a defect in the brain? The severe cases probably are. Many serial killers have a history of head injury in childhood. However, people on the mild end of the personality disorder spectrum probably have a perfectly normal brain. They have simply failed to grow up. Perhaps they simply missed or shunned some important lessons on how to think rationally and behave properly. They may even be avoiding the kinds of thoughts, activities, and experiences that would help them grow up. Instead, they tend to embrace therapeutic approaches that make their problem worse, not better. Remember Albert Bernstein's warning:

> People who throw tantrums like two-year-olds hardly need to be encouraged to get their feelings out into the open or, God forbid, get in touch with their inner child.

The Beatles once sang, "I get by with a little help from my friends." Mentally healthy people take social cues from their friends. With a little help from their friends, they learn how to improve their behavior. In contrast, co-dependent people take their cues from people who are not their friends. As a result, they get a distorted view of themselves and end up learning self-defeating behavior. Likewise, narcissists tend to make themselves worse by surrounding themselves with worshipful, co-dependent people. Do not be one of those co-dependent people. You did not cause someone else's narcissism. You cannot control it. You cannot cure it. But neither should you contribute to it.

According to Greek myth, Narcissus developed a fatal attraction to his own reflection. Although he loved to gaze at his own reflection, he could not form a meaningful connection with another human being. Likewise, the people whom we consider narcissistic today are in love with their own mental image of themselves. They cannot see themselves accurately. Yet everyone faces the same kind of problem in self-assessment. The great Scottish poet Robert Burns made light of this problem in his poem *To a Louse, On Seeing One on a Lady's Bonnet at Church*. In the poem, the narrator notices that a louse is wandering around on the bonnet of a lady at church. The narrator muses on the fact that a louse regards every human being as equal—as a source of food. In the final stanza, he laments,

> O wad some Pow'r the giftie gie us
> To see oursels as others see us
> It wad frae monie a blunder free us
> An' foolish notion
> What airs in dress an' gait wad lea'e us
> An' ev'n Devotion

In other words, if someone would give us the gift of seeing ourselves as others see us, we would stop making fools of ourselves.

About the Author

Laurie Endicott Thomas has worked as an editor in various aspects of medical publishing for more than 25 years. She is the author of *Not Trivial: How Studying the Traditional Liberal Arts Can Set You Free* (www. nottrivialbook.com), which explains what has gone wrong in public education in the United States. She is also the author of *Thin Diabetes, Fat Diabetes: Prevent Type 1 and Cure Type 2* (www.thindiabetes.com) and *No More Measles! The Truth About Vaccines and Your Health* (www. nomeasles.com). She says that her political agenda is simple: "I'm against violence, ignorance, pestilence, and dangling participles—not necessarily in that order." Follow her on Twitter: @LaurieEThomas.

Printed in Great Britain
by Amazon

24560664R00165